Qt5 C++ GUI Programming Cookbook

Use Qt5 to design and build a graphical user interface that is functional, appealing, and user-friendly for your software application

Lee Zhi Eng

BIRMINGHAM - MUMBAI

Qt5 C++ GUI Programming Cookbook

First published: July 2016

Production reference: 1220716

Published by Packt Publishing Ltd.
Livery Place
35 Livery Street
Birmingham B3 2PB, UK.

ISBN 978-1-78328-027-8

www.packtpub.com

Credits

Author
Lee Zhi Eng

Reviewer
Symeon Huang

Commissioning Editor
Kartikey Pandey

Acquisition Editor
Indrajit Das

Content Development Editor
Priyanka Mehta

Technical Editors
Dhiraj Chandanshive
Ravikiran Pise

Copy Editor
Safis Editing

Project Coordinator
Izzat Contractor

Proofreader
Safis Editing

Indexer
Rekha Nair

Production Coordinator
Aparna Bhagat

Cover Work
Aparna Bhagat

About the Author

Lee Zhi Eng is a 3D artist-turned-programmer who worked in the video game industry as a game artist, game programmer, and a game programming lecturer. Later, he decided to take a break from games and ventured into software engineering by co-founding his current company, *Reonyx Tech*. Since then, he has been involved in multiple projects that are different from what he used to do, including geolocation and near-real-time navigation systems, Big Data analytics, and augmented reality. You can find out more about him at `http://www.zhieng.com`, or you can find out about his company at `http://www.reonyx.com`.

About the Reviewer

Symeon Huang is an experienced C++ GUI software developer and the author of *Qt 5 Blueprints, Packt Publishing*. He has finished his master's degree in high performance computing and has been working as a software engineer in industry.

I'd like to thank Packt Publishing for giving me the opportunity to review this book. As a reviewer, I've also learnt from this book and I'm sure this book will be of great use to all readers.

www.PacktPub.com

eBooks, discount offers, and more

Did you know that Packt offers eBook versions of every book published, with PDF and ePub files available? You can upgrade to the eBook version at www.PacktPub.com and as a print book customer, you are entitled to a discount on the eBook copy. Get in touch with us at customercare@packtpub.com for more details.

At www.PacktPub.com, you can also read a collection of free technical articles, sign up for a range of free newsletters and receive exclusive discounts and offers on Packt books and eBooks.

https://www2.packtpub.com/books/subscription/packtlib

Do you need instant solutions to your IT questions? PacktLib is Packt's online digital book library. Here, you can search, access, and read Packt's entire library of books.

Why Subscribe?

► Fully searchable across every book published by Packt

► Copy and paste, print, and bookmark content

► On demand and accessible via a web browser

Table of Contents

Preface

The continuous growth of the computer software market leads to a very competitive and challenging era. Not only does your software need to be functional and easy to use, it must also look appealing and professional to the users. In order to gain an upper hand and a competitive advantage over other software products in the market, the look and feel of your product is of utmost importance and should be taken care of early in the production stage. In this book, we will teach you how to create a functional, appealing, and user friendly software using the Qt5 development platform.

What this book covers

Chapter 1, Look and Feel Customization, shows how to design your program's user interface using both the Qt Designer as well as the Qt Quick Designer.

Chapter 2, States and Animations, explains how to animate your user interface widgets by empowering the state machine framework and the animation framework.

Chapter 3, QPainter and 2D Graphics, covers how to draw vector shapes and bitmap images on screen using Qt's built-in classes.

Chapter 4, OpenGL Implementation, demonstrates how to render 3D graphics in your program by integrating OpenGL in your Qt project.

Chapter 5, Building a Touch Screen Application with Qt5, explains how to create a program that works on a touch screen device.

Chapter 6, XML Parsing Made Easy, shows how to process data in the XML format and use it together with the Google Geocoding API to create a simple address finder.

Chapter 7, Conversion Library, covers how to convert between different variable types, image formats, and video formats using Qt's built-in classes as well as third-party programs.

Chapter 8, Accessing Databases, explains how to connect your program to an SQL database using Qt.

Chapter 9, Developing a Web Application Using Qt Web Engine, covers how to use the web rendering engine provided by Qt and develop programs that empower the web technology.

What you need for this book

The following are the prerequisites for this book:

1. Qt5 (for all chapters)
2. FFmpeg (for *Chapter 7, Conversion Library*)
3. XAMPP (for *Chapter 8, Accessing Databases*)

Who this book is for

This book intended for those who want to develop software using Qt5. If you want to improve the visual quality and content presentation of your software application, this book will suit you best.

Sections

In this book, you will find several headings that appear frequently (Getting ready, How to do it, How it works, There's more, and See also).

To give clear instructions on how to complete a recipe, we use these sections as follows:

Getting ready

This section tells you what to expect in the recipe, and describes how to set up any software or any preliminary settings required for the recipe.

How to do it...

This section contains the steps required to follow the recipe.

How it works...

This section usually consists of a detailed explanation of what happened in the previous section.

There's more...

This section consists of additional information about the recipe in order to make the reader more knowledgeable about the recipe.

See also

This section provides helpful links to other useful information for the recipe.

Conventions

In this book, you will find a number of text styles that distinguish between different kinds of information. Here are some examples of these styles and an explanation of their meaning.

Code words in text, database table names, folder names, filenames, file extensions, pathnames, dummy URLs, user input, and Twitter handles are shown as follows: "In the `mylabel.cpp` source file, define a function called `SetMyObject()` to save the object pointer."

A block of code is set as follows:

```
QSpinBox::down-button
{
   image: url(:/images/spindown.png);
   subcontrol-origin: padding;
   subcontrol-position: right bottom;
}
```

When we wish to draw your attention to a particular part of a code block, the relevant lines or items are set in bold:

```
QSpinBox::down-button
{
   image: url(:/images/spindown.png);
   subcontrol-origin: padding;
   subcontrol-position: right bottom;
}
```

New terms and **important words** are shown in bold. Words that you see on the screen, for example, in menus or dialog boxes, appear in the text like this: "Go to the **Imports** tab in the **Library** window and add a Qt Quick module called **QtQuick.Controls** to your project."

Warnings or important notes appear in a box like this.

Tips and tricks appear like this.

Reader feedback

Feedback from our readers is always welcome. Let us know what you think about this book—what you liked or disliked. Reader feedback is important for us as it helps us develop titles that you will really get the most out of.

To send us general feedback, simply e-mail feedback@packtpub.com, and mention the book's title in the subject of your message.

If there is a topic that you have expertise in and you are interested in either writing or contributing to a book, see our author guide at www.packtpub.com/authors.

Customer support

Now that you are the proud owner of a Packt book, we have a number of things to help you to get the most from your purchase.

Downloading the example code

You can download the example code files for this book from your account at http://www.packtpub.com. If you purchased this book elsewhere, you can visit http://www.packtpub.com/support and register to have the files e-mailed directly to you.

You can download the code files by following these steps:

1. Log in or register to our website using your e-mail address and password.
2. Hover the mouse pointer on the **SUPPORT** tab at the top.
3. Click on **Code Downloads & Errata**.
4. Enter the name of the book in the **Search** box.
5. Select the book for which you're looking to download the code files.
6. Choose from the drop-down menu where you purchased this book from.
7. Click on **Code Download**.

You can also download the code files by clicking on the **Code Files** button on the book's webpage at the Packt Publishing website. This page can be accessed by entering the book's name in the **Search** box. Please note that you need to be logged in to your Packt account.

Once the file is downloaded, please make sure that you unzip or extract the folder using the latest version of:

- ▶ WinRAR / 7-Zip for Windows
- ▶ Zipeg / iZip / UnRarX for Mac
- ▶ 7-Zip / PeaZip for Linux

The code bundle for the book is also hosted on GitHub at `https://github.com/PacktPublishing/Qt5-C++-GUI-Programming-Cookbook`. We also have other code bundles from our rich catalog of books and videos available at `https://github.com/PacktPublishing/`. Check them out!

Downloading the color images of this book

We also provide you with a PDF file that has color images of the screenshots/diagrams used in this book. The color images will help you better understand the changes in the output. You can download this file from `http://www.packtpub.com/sites/default/files/downloads/Qt5C++GUIProgrammingCookbook_ColorImages.pdf`.

Errata

Although we have taken every care to ensure the accuracy of our content, mistakes do happen. If you find a mistake in one of our books—maybe a mistake in the text or the code—we would be grateful if you could report this to us. By doing so, you can save other readers from frustration and help us improve subsequent versions of this book. If you find any errata, please report them by visiting `http://www.packtpub.com/submit-errata`, selecting your book, clicking on the **Errata Submission Form** link, and entering the details of your errata. Once your errata are verified, your submission will be accepted and the errata will be uploaded to our website or added to any list of existing errata under the Errata section of that title.

To view the previously submitted errata, go to `https://www.packtpub.com/books/content/support` and enter the name of the book in the search field. The required information will appear under the **Errata** section.

Piracy

Piracy of copyrighted material on the Internet is an ongoing problem across all media. At Packt, we take the protection of our copyright and licenses very seriously. If you come across any illegal copies of our works in any form on the Internet, please provide us with the location address or website name immediately so that we can pursue a remedy.

Please contact us at `copyright@packtpub.com` with a link to the suspected pirated material.

We appreciate your help in protecting our authors and our ability to bring you valuable content.

Questions

If you have a problem with any aspect of this book, you can contact us at `questions@packtpub.com`, and we will do our best to address the problem.

1
Look and Feel Customization

In this chapter we will cover the following recipes:

- ▶ Using style sheets with Qt Designer
- ▶ Basic style sheet customization
- ▶ Creating a login screen using style sheets
- ▶ Using resources in style sheets
- ▶ Customizing properties and sub-controls
- ▶ Styling in QML
- ▶ Exposing QML object pointer to C++

Introduction

Qt allows us to easily design our program's user interface through a method that most people are familiar with. Qt not only provides us with a powerful user interface toolkit called Qt Designer, which enables us to design our user interface without writing a single line of code, but it also allows advanced users to customize their user interface components through a simple scripting language called Qt Style Sheets.

Use style sheets with Qt Designer

In this example, we will learn how to change the look and feel of our program and make it look more professional by using style sheets and resources. Qt allows you to decorate your **Graphical User Interfaces** (**GUIs**) using a style sheet language called Qt Style Sheets, which is very similar to **Cascading Style Sheets** (**CSS**) used by web designers to decorate their websites.

How to do it...

1. The first thing we need to do is open up Qt Creator and create a new project. If this is the first time you have used Qt Creator, you can either click the big button that says **New Project** with a **+** sign, or simply go to **File | New File or New Project**.

2. Then, select **Application** under the **Project** window and select **Qt Widgets Application**.

3. After that, click the **Choose** button at the bottom. A window will then pop out and ask you to insert the project name and its location.

4. Once you're done with that, click **Next** several times and click the **Finish** button to create the project. We will just stick to all the default settings for now. Once the project has been created, the first thing you will see is the panel with tons of big icons on the left side of the window that is called the **Mode Selector** panel; we will discuss this more later in the *How it works...* section.

5. Then, you will also see all your source files listed on the **Side Bar** panel which is located right next to the **Mode Selector** panel. This is where you can select which file you want to edit, which, in this case, is `mainwindow.ui` because we are about to start designing the program's UI!

6. Double-click `mainwindow.ui` and you will see an entirely different interface appearing out of nowhere. Qt Creator actually helped you to switch from the script editor to the UI editor (Qt Designer) because it detected the `.ui` extension on the file you're trying to open.

7. You will also notice that the highlighted button on the **Mode Selector** panel has changed from the **Edit** button to the **Design** button. You can switch back to the script editor or change to any other tools by clicking one of the buttons located in the upper half of the **Mode Selector** panel.

8. Let's go back to the Qt Designer and look at the `mainwindow.ui` file. This is basically the main window of our program (as the filename implies) and it's empty by default, without any widget on it. You can try to compile and run the program by pressing the **Run** button (green arrow button) at the bottom of the **Mode Selector** panel, and you will see an empty window popping up once the compilation is complete:

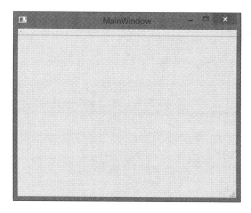

9. Now, let's add a push button to our program's UI by clicking on the `Push Button` item in the widget box (under the **Buttons** category) and dragging it to your main window in the form editor. Then, keep the push button selected, and now you will see all the properties of this button inside the property editor on the right side of your window. Scroll down to somewhere around the middle and look for a property called **styleSheet**. This is where you apply styles to your widget, which may or may not inherit to its children or grandchildren recursively depending on how you set your style sheet. Alternatively, you can also right-click on any widget in your UI at the form editor and select **Change Style Sheet** from the pop-up menu.

10. You can click on the input field of the **styleSheet** property to directly write the style sheet code, or click on the **...** button besides the input field to open up the **Edit Style Sheet** window which has a bigger space for writing longer style sheet code. At the top of the window you can find several buttons, such as **Add Resource**, **Add Gradient**, **Add Color**, and **Add Font**, that can help you to kick-start your coding if you can't remember the properties' names.

    Let's try to do some simple styling with the **Edit Style Sheet** window.

11. Click **Add Color** and choose color.

12. Pick a random color from the color picker window, let's say, a pure red color. Then click **OK**.

13. Now, you will see a line of code has been added to the text field on the **Edit Style Sheet** window, which in my case is as follows:

    ```
    color: rgb(255, 0, 0);
    ```

14. Click the **OK** button and now you will see the text on your push button has changed to a red color.

How it works...

Let's take a bit of time to get ourselves familiar with Qt Designer's interface before we start learning how to design our own UI:

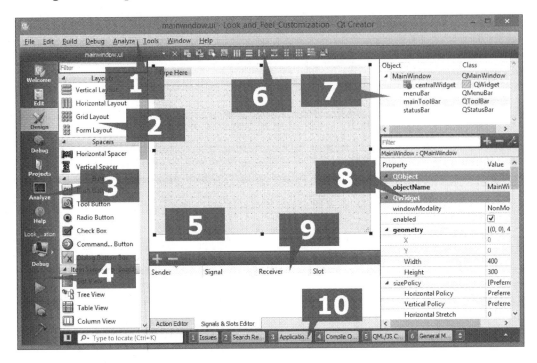

1. **Menu bar:** The menu bar houses application-specific menus that provide easy access to essential functions such as create new projects, save files, undo, redo, copy, paste, and so on. It also allows you to access development tools that come with Qt Creator, such as the compiler, debugger, profiler, and so on.

2. **Widget box:** This is where you can find all the different types of widget provided by Qt Designer. You can add a widget to your program's UI by clicking one of the widgets from the widget box and dragging it to the form editor.

3. **Mode selector:** The mode selector is a side panel that places shortcut buttons for easy access to different tools. You can quickly switch between the script editor and form editor by clicking the **Edit** or **Design** buttons on the mode selector panel which is very useful for multitasking. You can also easily navigate to the debugger and profiler tools in the same speed and manner.

4. **Build shortcuts:** The build shortcuts are located at the bottom of the mode selector panel. You can build, run, and debug your project easily by pressing the shortcut buttons here.

5. **Form editor:** Form editor is where you edit your program's UI. You can add different widgets to your program by selecting a widget from the widget box and dragging it to the form editor.

6. **Form toolbar:** From here, you can quickly select a different form to edit, click the drop-down box located above the widget box and select the file you want to open with Qt Designer. Beside the drop-down box are buttons for switching between different modes for the form editor and also buttons for changing the layout of your UI.

7. **Object inspector:** The object inspector lists all the widgets within your current `.ui` file. All the widgets are arranged according to its parent-child relationship in the hierarchy. You can select a widget from the object inspector to display its properties in the property editor.

8. **Property editor:** Property editor will display all the properties of the widget you selected either from the object inspector window or the form editor window.

9. **Action Editor and Signals & Slots Editor:** This window contains two editors, **Action Editor** and the **Signals & Slots Editor**, which can be accessed from the tabs below the window. The action editor is where you create actions that can be added to a menu bar or toolbar in your program's UI.

10. **Output panes:** Output panes consist of several different windows that display information and output messages related to script compilation and debugging. You can switch between different output panes by pressing the buttons that carry a number before them, such as **1-Issues**, **2-Search Results**, **3-Application Output**, and so on.

There's more...

In the previous section, we discussed how to apply style sheets to Qt widgets through C++ coding. Although that method works really well, most of the time the person who is in charge of designing the program's UI is not the programmer, but a UI designer who specializes in designing user-friendly UI. In this case, it's better to let the UI designer design the program's layout and style sheet with a different tool and not mess around with the code.

Qt provides an all-in-one editor called Qt Creator. Qt Creator consists of several different tools, such as script editor, compiler, debugger, profiler, and UI editor. The UI editor, which is also called Qt Designer, is the perfect tool for designers to design their program's UI without writing any code. This is because Qt Designer adopted the What-You-See-Is-What-You-Get approach by providing accurate visual representation of the final result, which means whatever you design with Qt Designer will turn out exactly the same when the program is compiled and run.

The similarities between Qt Style Sheets and CSS are as follows:

- **CSS**: `h1 { color: red; background-color: white;}`
- **Qt Style Sheets**: `QLineEdit { color: red; background-color: white;}`
- As you can see, both of them contain a selector and a declaration block. Each declaration contains a property and a value, separated by a colon.
- In Qt, a style sheet can be applied to a single widget by calling `QObject::setStyleSheet()` function in C++ code, for example:

  `myPushButton->setStyleSheet("color : blue");`

- The preceding code will turn the text of a button with the variable name `myPushButton` to a `blue` color. You can also achieve the same result by writing the declaration in the style sheet property field in Qt Designer. We will discuss more about Qt Designer in the next section.
- Qt Style Sheets also supports all the different types of selectors defined in CSS2 standard, including Universal selector, Type selector, Class selector, ID selector, and so on, which allows us to apply styling to a very specific individual or group of widgets. For instance, if we want to change the background color of a specific line edit widget with the object name `usernameEdit`, we can do this by using an ID selector to refer to it:

  `QLineEdit#usernameEdit { background-color: blue }`

 To learn about all the selectors available in CSS2 (which are also supported by Qt Style Sheets), please refer to this document: `http://www.w3.org/TR/REC-CSS2/selector.html`.

Basic style sheet customization

In the previous example, you learned how to apply a style sheet to a widget with Qt Designer. Let's go crazy and push things further by creating a few other types of widgets and change their style properties to something bizarre for the sake of learning. This time, however, we will not apply the style to every single widget one by one, but we will learn to apply the style sheet to the main window and let it inherit down the hierarchy to all the other widgets so that the style sheet is easier to manage and maintain in long run.

How to do it...

1. First of all, let's remove the style sheet from the push button by selecting it and clicking the small arrow button besides the `styleSheet` property. This button will revert the property to the default value, which in this case is the empty style sheet.

2. Then, add a few more widgets to the UI by dragging them one by one from the widget box to the form editor. I've added a line edit, combo box, horizontal slider, radio button, and a check box.

3. For the sake of simplicity, delete the menu bar, main toolbar, and the status bar from your UI by selecting them from the object inspector, right click, and choose **Remove**. Now your UI should look similar to this:

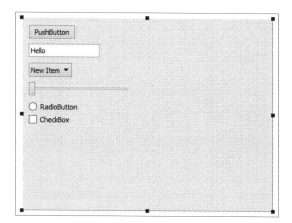

4. Select the main window either from the form editor or the object inspector, then right click and choose **Change Stylesheet** to open up the **Edit Style Sheet**.

    Insert the following style sheet:

    ```
    border: 2px solid gray;
    border-radius: 10px;
    padding: 0 8px;
    background: yellow;
    ```

5. Now what you will see is a completely bizarre-looking UI with everything covered in yellow with a thick border. This is because the preceding style sheet does not have a selector, which means the style will apply to the children widgets of the main window all the way down the hierarchy. To change that, let's try something different:

    ```
    QPushButton
    {
        border: 2px solid gray;
        border-radius: 10px;
        padding: 0 8px;
        background: yellow;
    }
    ```

6. This time, only the push button will get the style described in the preceding code, and all other widgets will return to the default styling. You can try to add a few more push buttons to your UI and they will all look the same:

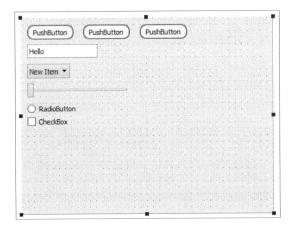

7. This happens because we specifically tell the selector to apply the style to all the widgets with the class called `QPushButton`. We can also apply the style to just one of the push buttons by mentioning its name in the style sheet, like so:

```
QPushButton#pushButton_3
{
    border: 2px solid gray;
    border-radius: 10px;
    padding: 0 8px;
    background: yellow;
}
```

8. Once you understand this method, we can add the following code to the style sheet :

```
QPushButton
{
    color: red;
    border: 0px;
    padding: 0 8px;
    background: white;
}

QPushButton#pushButton_2
{
    border: 1px solid red;
    border-radius: 10px;
}
```

```
QPushButton#pushButton_3
{
    border: 2px solid gray;
    border-radius: 10px;
    padding: 0 8px;
    background: yellow;
}
```

9. What it does is basically change the style of all the push buttons as well as some properties of a specific button named `pushButton_2`. We keep the style sheet of `pushButton_3` as it is. Now the buttons will look like this:

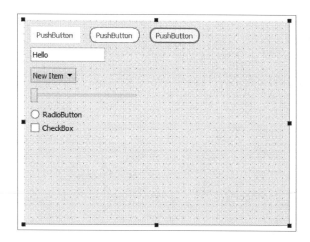

10. The first set of style sheet will change all widgets of `QPushButton` type to a white rectangular button with no border and red text. Then the second set of style sheet changes only the border of a specific `QPushButton` widget called `pushButton_2`. Notice that the background color and text color of `pushButton_2` remain white and red respectively because we didn't override them in the second set of style sheet, hence it will return to the style described in the first set of style sheet since it's applicable to all `QPushButton` widgets. Do notice that the text of the third button has also changed to red because we didn't describe the color property in the third set of style sheet.

11. After that, create another set of style using the universal selector, like so:

```
*
{
    background: qradialgradient(cx: 0.3, cy: -0.4, fx: 0.3,
        fy: -0.4, radius: 1.35, stop: 0 #fff, stop: 1 #888);
    color: rgb(255, 255, 255);
    border: 1px solid #ffffff;
}
```

12. The universal selector will affect all the widgets regardless of their type. Therefore, the preceding style sheet will apply a nice gradient color to all the widgets' background as well as setting their text as white and giving them a one-pixel solid outline which is also in white. Instead of writing the name of the color (that is, white), we can also use the `rgb` function (`rgb(255, 255, 255)`) or hex code (`#ffffff`) to describe the color value.

13. Just as before, the preceding style sheet will not affect the push buttons because we have already given them their own styles which will override the general style described in the universal selector. Just remember that in Qt, the style that is more specific will ultimately be used when there is more than one style having influence on a widget. This is how the UI will look now:

How it works...

If you are ever involved in web development using HTML and CSS, Qt's style sheet works exactly the same way as CSS. Style sheets provide the definitions for describing the presentation of the widgets – what the colors are for each element in the widget group, how thick the border should be, and so on and so forth.

If you specify the name of the widget to the style sheet, it will change the style of a particular push button widget with the name you provide. None of the other widgets will be affected and will remain as the default style.

To change the name of a widget, select the widget either from the form editor or the object inspector and change the property called `objectName` in the property window. If you have used the ID selector previously to change the style of the widget, changing its object name will break the style sheet and lose the style. To fix this problem, simply change the object name in the style sheet as well.

Creating a login screen using style sheets

Next, we will learn how to put all the knowledge we learned in the previous example together and create a fake graphical login screen for an imaginary operating system. Style sheets are not the only thing you need to master in order to design a good UI. You will also need to learn how to arrange the widgets neatly using the layout system in Qt Designer.

How to do it...

1. The first thing we need to do is design the layout of the graphical login screen before we start doing anything. Planning is very important in order to produce good software. The following is a sample layout design I made to show you how I imagine the login screen will look. Just a simple line drawing like this is sufficient as long as it conveys the message clearly:

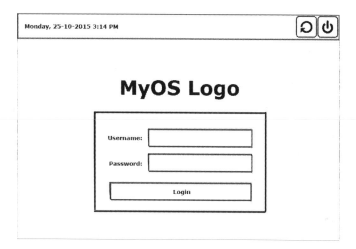

2. Now that we know exactly how the login screen should look, let's go back to Qt Designer again.

3. We will be placing the widgets at the top panel first, then the logo and the login form below it.

4. Select the main window and change its width and height from 400 and 300 to 800 and 600 respectively because we'll need a bigger space in which to place all the widgets in a moment.

5. Click and drag a label under the **Display Widgets** category from the widget box to the form editor.

6. Change the `objectName` property of the label to `currentDateTime` and change its `Text` property to the current date and time just for display purposes, such as `Monday, 25-10-2015 3:14 PM`.

7. Click and drag a push button under the **Buttons** category to the form editor. Repeat this process one more time because we have two buttons on the top panel. Rename the two buttons `restartButton` and `shutdownButton` respectively.

8. Next, select the main window and click the small icon button on the form toolbar that says **Lay Out Vertically** when you mouse-over it. Now you will see the widgets are being automatically arranged on the main window, but it's not exactly what we want yet.

9. Click and drag a horizontal layout widget under the **Layouts** category to the main window.

10. Click and drag the two push buttons and the text label into the horizontal layout. Now you will see the three widgets being arranged in a horizontal row, but vertically they are located in the middle of the screen. The horizontal arrangement is almost correct, but the vertical position is totally off.

11. Click and drag a vertical spacer from the **Spacers** category and place it below the horizontal layout we created previously (below the red rectangular outline). Now you will see all the widgets are being pushed to the top by the spacer.

12. Now, place a horizontal spacer between the text label and the two buttons to keep them apart. This will make the text label always stick to the left and the buttons align to the right.

13. Set both the `Horizontal Policy` and `Vertical Policy` properties of the two buttons to `Fixed` and set the `minimumSize` property to `55x55`. Then, set the `text` property of the buttons to empty as we will be using icons instead of text. We will learn how to place an icon in the button widgets in the following section.

14. Now your UI should look similar to this:

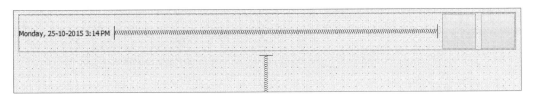

Next, we will be adding the logo by using the following steps:

1. Add a horizontal layout between the top panel and the vertical spacer to serve as a container for the logo.

2. After adding the horizontal layout, you will find the layout is way too thin in height to be able to add any widgets to it. This is because the layout is empty and it's being pushed by the vertical spacer below it into zero height. To solve this problem, we can set its vertical margin (either `layoutTopMargin` or `layoutBottomMargin`) to be temporarily bigger until a widget is added to the layout.

3. Next, add a label to the horizontal layout that you just created and rename it `logo`. We will learn more about how to insert an image into the label to use it as a logo in the next section. For now, just empty out the `text` property and set both its `Horizontal Policy` and `Vertical Policy` properties to `Fixed`. Then, set the `minimumSize` property to `150x150`.

4. Set the vertical margin of the layout back to zero if you haven't done so.

5. The logo now looks invisible, so we will just place a temporary style sheet to make it visible until we add an image to it in the next section. The style sheet is really simple:

   ```
   border: 1px solid;
   ```

6. Now your UI should look similar to this:

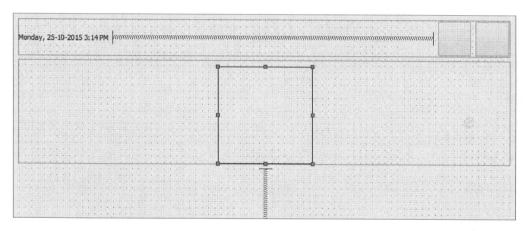

Now let's create the login form by using the following steps:

1. Add a horizontal layout between the logo's layout and the vertical spacer. Just as we did previously, set the `layoutTopMargin` property to a bigger number (that is, 100) so that you can add a widget to it more easily.

2. After that, add a vertical layout inside the horizontal layout you just created. This layout will be used as a container for the login form. Set its `layoutTopMargin` to a number lower than that of the horizontal layout (that is, 20) so that we can place widgets in it.

3. Next, right click the vertical layout you just created and choose **Morph into -> QWidget**. The vertical layout is now being converted into an empty widget. This step is essential because we will be adjusting the width and height of the container for the login form. A layout widget does not contain any properties for width and height, but only margins, due to the fact that a layout will expand toward the empty space surrounding it, which does make sense, considering that it does not have any size properties. After you have converted the layout to a `QWidget` object, it will automatically inherit all the properties from the widget class, and so we are now able to adjust its size to suit our needs.

4. Rename the QWidget object, which we just converted from the layout, to loginForm and change both its Horizontal Policy and Vertical Policy properties to Fixed. Then, set the minimumSize to 350x200.

5. Since we already placed the loginForm widget inside the horizontal layout, we can now set its layoutTopMargin property back to zero.

6. Add the same style sheet as the logo to the loginForm widget to make it visible temporarily, except this time we need to add an ID selector in front so that it will only apply the style to loginForm and not its children widgets:

```
#loginForm { border: 1px solid; }
```

7. Now your UI should look something like this:

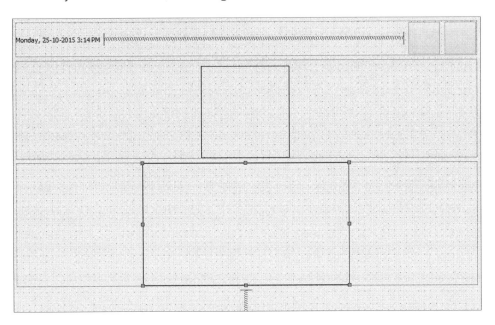

We are not done with the login form yet. Now that we have created the container for the login form, it's time to put more widgets into the form:

1. Place two horizontal layouts into the login form container. We need two layouts as one for the username field and another for the password field.

2. Add a label and a line edit to each of the layouts you just added. Change the text property of the upper label to Username: and the one below as Password:. Then, rename the two line edits as username and password respectively.

3. Add a push button below the password layout and change its text property to Login. After that, rename it as loginButton.

4. You can add a vertical spacer between the password layout and the login button to distance them slightly. After the vertical spacer has been placed, change its `sizeType` property to `Fixed` and change the `Height` to 5.

5. Now, select the `loginForm` container and set all its margins to 35. This is to make the login form look better by adding some space to all its sides.

6. You can also set the `Height` property of the `username`, `password`, and `loginButton` widgets to 25 so that they don't look so cramped.

7. Now your UI should look something like this:

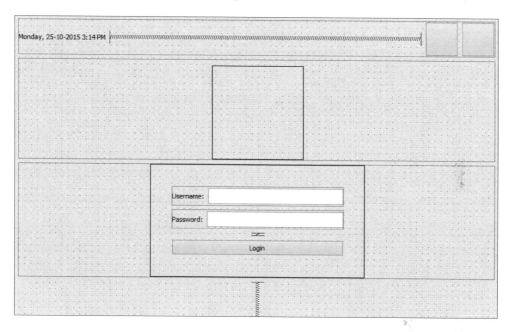

We're not done yet! As you can see, the login form and the logo are both sticking to the top of the main window due to the vertical spacer below them. The logo and the login form should be placed at the center of the main window instead of the top. To fix this problem, use the following steps:

1. Add another vertical spacer between the top panel and the logo's layout. This way it will counter the spacer at the bottom which balances out the alignment.

2. If you think that the logo is sticking too close to the login form, you can also add a vertical spacer between the logo's layout and the login form's layout. Set its `sizeType` property to `Fixed` and the `Height` property to `10`.

3. Right click the top panel's layout and choose **Morph into -> QWidget**. Then, rename it `topPanel`. The reason why the layout has to be converted into `QWidget` is that, we cannot apply style sheets to a layout, as it doesn't have any properties other than margins.

4. Currently you can see there is a little bit of margin around the edges of the main window – we don't want that. To remove the margins, select the `centralWidget` object from the object inspector window, which is right under the `MainWindow` panel, and set all the margin values to zero.

5. At this point, you can run the project by clicking the **Run** button (with the green arrow icon) to see what your program looks like now. If everything went well, you should see something like this:

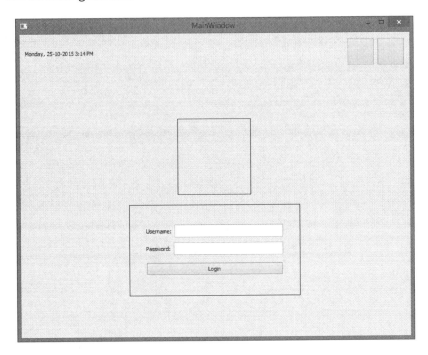

6. After we've done the layout, it's time for us to add some fanciness to the UI using style sheets! Since all the important widgets have been given an object name, it's easier for us to apply the style sheets to it from the main window, since we will only write the style sheets to the main window and let them inherit down the hierarchy tree.

7. Right click on **MainWindow** from the object inspector window and choose **Change Stylesheet**.

8. Add the following code to the style sheet:

    ```
    #centralWidget { background: rgba(32, 80, 96, 100); }
    ```

9. Now you will see that the background of the main window changes its color. We will learn how to use an image for the background in the next section, so the color is just temporary.

10. In Qt, if you want to apply styles to the main window itself, you must apply it to its central widget instead of the main window itself because the window is just a container.

11. Then, we will add a nice gradient color to the top panel:

```
#topPanel { background-color:
   qlineargradient(spread:reflect, x1:0.5, y1:0, x2:0, y2:0,
   stop:0 rgba(91, 204, 233, 100), stop:1 rgba(32, 80, 96,
   100)); }
```

12. After that, we will apply black color to the login form and make it look semi-transparent. After that, we will also make the corners of the login form container slightly rounded by setting the `border-radius` property:

```
#loginForm
{
   background: rgba(0, 0, 0, 80);
   border-radius: 8px;
}
```

13. After we're done applying styles to the specific widgets, we will apply styles to the general types of widgets instead:

```
QLabel { color: white; }
QLineEdit { border-radius: 3px; }
```

14. The preceding style sheets will change all the labels' texts to a white color, which includes the text on the widgets as well because, internally, Qt uses the same type of label on the widgets that have text on it. Also, we made the corners of the line edit widgets slightly rounded.

15. Next, we will apply style sheets to all the push buttons on our UI:

```
QPushButton
{
   color: white;
   background-color: #27a9e3;
   border-width: 0px;
   border-radius: 3px;
}
```

16. The preceding style sheet changes the text of all the buttons to a white color, then sets its background color to blue, and makes its corners slightly rounded as well.

17. To push things even further, we will change the color of the push buttons when we mouse-over it, using the keyword `hover`:

```
QPushButton:hover { background-color: #66c011; }
```

18. The preceding style sheet will change the background color of the push buttons to green when we mouse-over them. We will talk more about this in the following section.

19. You can further adjust the size and margins of the widgets to make them look even better. Remember to remove the border line of the login form by removing the style sheet that we applied directly to it earlier.

20. Now your login screen should look something like this:

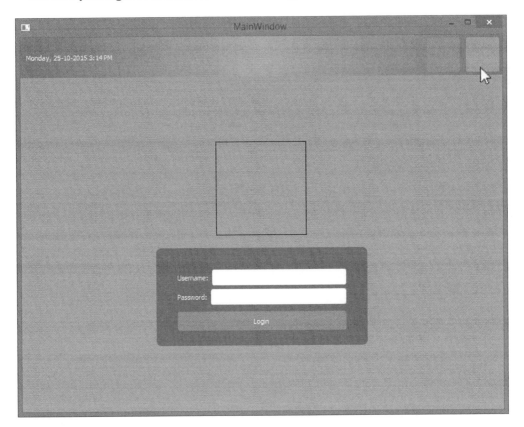

How it works...

This example focuses more on the layout system of Qt. The Qt layout system provides a simple and powerful way of automatically arranging child widgets within a widget to ensure that they make good use of the available space.

The spacer items used in the preceding example help to push the widgets contained in a layout outward to create spacing along the width of the spacer item. To locate a widget to the middle of the layout, put two spacer items to the layout, one on the left side of the widget and another on the right side of the widget. The widget will then be pushed to the middle of the layout by the two spacers.

Using resources in style sheets

Qt provides us with a platform-independent resource system which allows us to store any type of files in our program's executable for later use. There is no limit to the types of files we can store in our executable—images, audio, video HTML, XML, text files, binary files, and so on, are all permitted. This is useful if your application always needs a certain set of files (icons, translation files, and so on) and you don't want to run the risk of losing the files. To achieve this, we must tell Qt which files we want to add to its resource system in the `.qrc` file and Qt will handle the rest during the build process.

How to do it

To add a new `.qrc` file to our project, go to **File | New File or Project**. Then, select **Qt** under the **Files and Classes** category and select **Qt Resources File**. After that, give it a name (that is, `resources`) and click the **Next** button followed by the **Finish** button. The `.qrc` file will not be created and automatically opened by Qt Creator.

You don't have to edit the `.qrc` file directly in the XML format as Qt Creator provides you the user interface to manage your resources. To add images and icons to your project, first you need to make sure that the images and icons are being placed in your project's directory.

While the `.qrc` file is opened in Qt Creator, click the **Add** button followed by **Add Prefix** button. The prefix is used to categorize your resources so that it can be better managed when you have a ton of resources in your project:

1. Rename the prefix you just created `/icons`.

2. Then, create another prefix by clicking **Add** followed by **Add Prefix**.

3. Rename the new prefix `/images`.

4. After that, select the `/icon` prefix and click **Add** followed by **Add Files**.

5. A file selection window will appear; use that to select all the icon files. You can select multiple files at a time by holding the *Ctrl* key on your keyboard while clicking on the files to select them. Click **Open** once you're done.

6. Then, select the `/images` prefix and click the **Add** button followed by the **Add Files** button. The file selection window will pop up again, and this time we will select the background image.

7. Repeat the preceding steps, but this time we will add the logo image to the `/images` prefix.

   Don't forget to save once you're done by pressing *Ctrl + S*. Your `.qrc` file should now look like this:

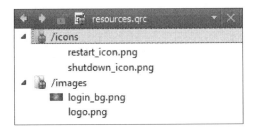

8. After that, open back to our `mainwindow.ui` file; we will now make use of the resources we have just added to our project. First, we will select the restart button located on the top panel. Then, scroll down the property editor until you see the `icon` property. Click the little button with a drop-down arrow icon and click **Choose Resources** from its menu.

9. The **Select Resource** window will then pop up. Click on the `icons` prefix on the left panel and then select the restart icon on the right panel. After that, press **OK**.

10. You will now see a tiny icon appearing on the button. The icon looks very tiny because the default icon size is set at `16x16`. Change the `iconSize` property to `50x50` and you will see the icon appear bigger now.

    Repeat the preceding steps for the shutdown button, except this time we will choose the shutdown icon instead.

11. Once you're done, the two buttons should now look like this:

12. Next, we will use the image we added to the resource file as our logo. First, select the logo widget and remove the style sheet that we added earlier to render its outline.

13. Scroll down the property editor until you see the `pixmap` property.

14. Click the little drop-down button behind the `pixmap` property and select **Choose Resources** from the menu. After that, select the logo image and click **OK**. You will now see the logo size no longer follow the dimension you set previously and follow the actual dimension of the image instead. We cannot change its dimension because this is simply how `pixmap` works.

15. If you want more control over the logo's dimension, you can remove the image from the `pixmap` property and use a style sheet instead. You can use the following code to apply an image to the icon container:

```
border-image: url(:/images/logo.png);
```

16. To obtain the path of the image, right click the image name on the file list window and choose **Copy path**. The path will be saved to your operating system clipboard and now you can just paste it to the preceding style sheet. Using this method will ensure that the image fits exactly the dimension of the widget that you applied the style to. Your logo should now appear like so:

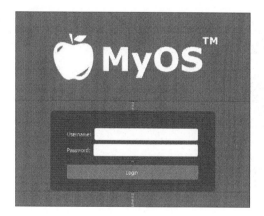

17. Lastly, we will apply the wallpaper image to the background using a style sheet. Since the background dimension will change according to the window size, we cannot use `pixmap` in this case. Instead, we will use the `border-image` property in a style sheet to achieve this. Right click the main window and select **Change styleSheet** to open up the **Edit Style Sheet** window. We will add a new line under the style sheet of the central widget:

```
#centralWidget
{
    background: rgba(32, 80, 96, 100);
    border-image: url(:/images/login_bg.png);
}
```

18. It's really that simple and easy! Your login screen should now look like this:

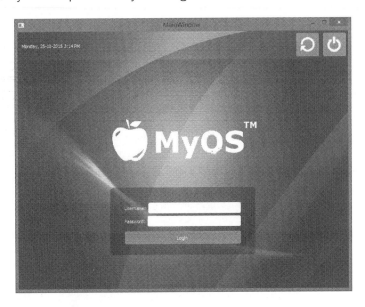

How it works...

The resource system in Qt stores binary files, such as images, translation files, and so on, in the executable when it gets compiled. It reads the resource collection files (`.qrc`) in your project to locate the files that need to be stored in the executable and include them into the build process. A `.qrc` file looks something like this:

```
<!DOCTYPE RCC><RCC version="1.0">
  <qresource>
    <file>images/copy.png</file>
    <file>images/cut.png</file>
    <file>images/new.png</file>
    <file>images/open.png</file>
    <file>images/paste.png</file>
    <file>images/save.png</file>
  </qresource>
</RCC>
```

It uses XML format to store the paths of the resource files which are relative to the directory containing it. Do note that the listed resource files must be located in the same directory as the `.qrc` file, or one of its sub-directories.

Customizing properties and sub-controls

Qt's style sheet system enables us to create stunning and professional-looking UIs with ease. In this example, we will learn how to set custom properties to our widgets and use them to switch between different styles.

How to do it...

1. Let's try out the scenario described in the preceding paragraph by creating a new Qt project. I have prepared the UI for this purpose. The UI contains three buttons on the left side and a tab widget with three pages located at the right side, as shown in the following screenshot:

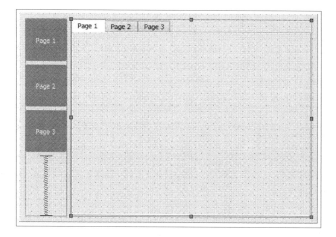

2. The three buttons are blue in color because I've added the following style sheet to the main window (not to the individual button):

```
QPushButton
{
    color: white;
    background-color: #27a9e3;
    border-width: 0px;
    border-radius: 3px;
}
```

3. Next, I will explain to you what pseudo states are in Qt by adding the following style sheet to the main window, which you might be familiar with:

```
QPushButton:hover
{
    color: white;
    background-color: #66c011;
    border-width: 0px;
    border-radius: 3px;
}
```

4. We used the preceding style sheet in the previous tutorial to make the buttons change color when there is a mouse-over. This is made possible by Qt Style Sheet's pseudo state, which in this case is the word `hover` separated from the `QPushButton` class by a colon. Every widget has a set of generic pseudo states, such as `active`, `disabled`, `enabled`, and so on, and also a set of pseudo states which are applicable to their widget type. For example, states such as `open` and `flat` are available for `QPushButton`, but not for `QLineEdit`. Let's add the `pressed` pseudo state to change the buttons' color to yellow when the user clicks on it:

```
QPushButton:pressed
{
    color: white;
    background-color: yellow;
    border-width: 0px;
    border-radius: 3px;
}
```

5. Pseudo states allow the users to load a different set of style sheet based on the condition that applies to it. Qt pushes this concept further by implementing dynamic properties in Qt Style Sheets. This allows us to change the style sheet of a widget when a custom condition has been met. We can make use of this feature to change the style sheet of our buttons based on a custom condition that we can set using custom properties in Qt.

    First, we will add this style sheet to our main window:

```
QPushButton[pagematches=true]
{
    color: white;
    background-color: red;
    border-width: 0px;
    border-radius: 3px;
}
```

6. What it does is basically change the push button's background color to red if the property called `pagematches` returns `true`. Obviously, this property does not exist in the `QPushButton` class. However, we can add it to our buttons by using `QObject::setProperty()`:

    ❑ In your `MainWindow.cpp` source code, add the following code right after `ui->setupUi(this);`:

```
ui->button1->setProperty("pagematches", true);
```

    ❑ The preceding code will add a custom property called `pagematches` to the first button and set its value as `true`. This will make the first button turn red by default.

    ❑ After that, right click on the tab widget and choose **Go to slot**. A window will then pop up; select the **currentChanged(int)** option from the list and click **Ok**. Qt will generate a `slot` function for you, which looks something like this:

```
private slots:
void on_tabWidget_currentChanged(int index);
```

    ❑ The `slot` function will be called whenever we change page of the tab widget. We can then decide what we want it to do by adding our code into the `slot` function. To do that, open up `mainwindow.cpp` and you will see the function's declaration there. Let's add some code to the function:

```
void MainWindow::on_tabWidget_currentChanged(int index)
{
  // Set all buttons to false
  ui->button1->setProperty("pagematches", false);
  ui->button2->setProperty("pagematches", false);
  ui->button3->setProperty("pagematches", false);

  // Set one of the buttons to true
  if (index == 0)
    ui->button1->setProperty("pagematches", true);
  else if (index == 1)
    ui->button2->setProperty("pagematches", true);
  else
    ui->button3->setProperty("pagematches", true);

  // Update buttons style
  ui->button1->style()->polish(ui->button1);
  ui->button2->style()->polish(ui->button2);
  ui->button3->style()->polish(ui->button3);
}
```

7. The preceding code basically does this: when the tab widget switches its current page, it sets the `pagematches` properties of all three buttons to `false`. Just be sure to reset everything before we decide which button should change to red.

8. Then, check the `index` variable supplied by the event signal, which will tell you the index number of the current page. Set the `pagematches` property of one of the buttons to `true` based on the index number.

9. Lastly, refresh the style of all three buttons by calling `polish()`.

Then, build and run the project. You should now see the three buttons changing their color to red whenever you switch the tab widget to a different page. Also, the buttons will change color to green when there is a mouse-over, as well as change their color to yellow when you click on them:

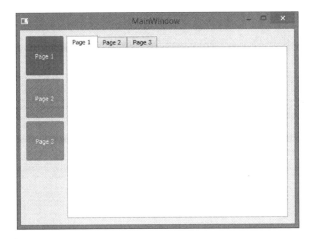

How it works...

Qt provides users the freedom of adding their own custom properties to any type of widget. Custom properties are very useful if you want to change a particular widget when a special condition is met, where Qt doesn't provide such a context by default. This allows the user to extend the usability of Qt and makes it a flexible tool for customized solutions.

For example, if we have a row of buttons on our main window and we need one of them to change its color depending on which page the tab widget is currently showing, then there is no way the buttons would know when they should change their color, because Qt itself has no built-in context for this type of situation. To solve this issue, Qt provides us a method to add our own properties to the widgets, which is using a generic function called `QObject::setProperty()`. To read the custom property, we can use another function called `QObject::property()`.

Next, we will talk about sub-controls in Qt Style Sheets. It's actually quite self-explanatory by looking at the term sub-controls. Often, a widget is not just a single object but a combination of more than one object or control in order to form a more complex widget, and such objects are called sub-controls.

For example, a spin box widget contains an input field, a down button, an up button, an up arrow, and a down arrow, which is quite complicated compared to some other widgets. In this case, Qt grants us more flexibility by allowing us to change every single sub-control using a style sheet, if we wanted to. We can do so by specifying the name of the sub-control behind the widget's class name, separated by a double colon. For instance, if I want to change the image of the down button in a spin box, I can write my style sheet like this:

```
QSpinBox::down-button
{
  image: url(:/images/spindown.png);
  subcontrol-origin: padding;
  subcontrol-position: right bottom;
}
```

That will only apply the image to the down button of my spin box, and not to any other parts of the widget.

By combining custom properties, pseudo states, and sub-controls, Qt provides us with a very flexible method to customize our user interface.

 Visit the following link to learn more about pseudo states and sub-controls in Qt:

`http://doc.qt.io/qt-4.8/stylesheet-reference.html`

Styling in QML

Qt Meta Language or **Qt Modeling Language** (**QML**) is a Javascript-inspired user interface mark-up language used by Qt for designing user interfaces. Qt provides you with Qt Quick components (widgets powered by the QML technology) to easily design touch-friendly UI without C++ programming. We will learn more about how to use QML and Qt Quick components to design our program's UI by following the steps given in the following section.

How to do it...

1. Create a new project by going to **File | New File or Project**. Select **Application** under **Project** category and choose **Qt Quick Application**.

2. Press the **Choose** button, and that will bring you to the next window. Insert a name for your project and click the **Next** button again.

3. Another window will now appear and ask you to choose a minimum required Qt version. Pick the latest version installed on your computer and click **Next**.

4. After that, click **Next** again followed by **Finish**. Qt Creator will now create a new project for you.

5. Once the project is being created, you will see there are some differences compare to a C++ Qt project. You will see two `.qml` files, namely `main.qml` and `MainForm.ui.qml`, inside the project resource. These two files are the UI description files using the QML mark-up language. If you double click `main.qml` file, Qt Creator will open up the script editor and you will see something like this:

```
import QtQuick 2.5
import QtQuick.Window 2.2

Window {
    visible: true
    MainForm {
        anchors.fill: parent
        mouseArea.onClicked: {
            Qt.quit();
        }
    }
}
```

6. This file basically tells Qt to create a window and insert a set of UI called `MainForm` which is actually from the other `.qml` file called `MainForm.ui.qml`. It also tells Qt that when the user clicks on the **mouseArea** widget, the entire program should be terminated.

7. Now, try to open the `MainForm.ui.qml` file by double-clicking on it. This time, Qt Designer (UI editor) will be opened instead, and you will see a completely different UI editor compared to the C++ project we did previously. This editor is also called the Qt Quick Designer, specially designed for editing QML-based UI only.

8. If you open up the `main.cpp` file in your project, you will see this line of code:

```
QQmlApplicationEngine engine;
engine.load(QUrl(QStringLiteral("qrc:/main.qml")));
```

9. The preceding code basically tells Qt's QML engine to load the `main.qml` file when the program starts. If you want to load the other `.qml` file instead of `main.qml`, you know where to look for the code.

10. When `main.qml` is loaded by the QML engine, it will also import `MainForm.ui.qml` into the UI, since `MainForm` is being called in the `main.qml` file. Qt will check if `MainForm` is a valid UI by searching for its `.qml` file based on the naming convention. Basically the concept is similar to the C++ project we did in the previous section, whereby the `main.qml` file acts like the `main.cpp` file and `MainForm.ui.qml` acts like the `MainWindow` class. You can also create other UI templates and use them in `main.qml`. Hopefully this comparison will make it easier to understand how QML works.

11. Now let's open up `MainForm.ui.qml`. You should see three items listed on the navigator window: **Rectangle**, **mouseArea**, and **Text**. When these items are interpreted by the QML engine, it produces the following result on the canvas:

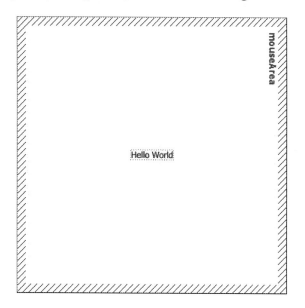

12. The **Rectangle** item is basically the base layout of the window, which cannot be deleted. It is similar to the `centralWidget` we used in the previous section. The **mouseArea** item is an invincible item that gets triggered when the mouse is clicking on it, or when a finger is touching it (for mobile platforms). The mouse area is also used in a button component, which we will be using in a while. The **Text** component is self-explanatory: it is a label that displays a block of text on the application.

13. On the **Navigator** window, we can hide or show an item by clicking on the icon besides the item which resembles an eye. When an item is hidden, it will not show on the canvas nor the compiled application. Just like the widgets in a C++ Qt project, Qt Quick components are arranged in a hierarchy based on the parent-child relationship. All the children items will be placed below the parent item with an indented position. In our case, you can see the **mouseArea** and **Text** items are all positioned slightly to the right compared to the **Rectangle** item, because they are both the children of the **Rectangle** item. We can re-arrange the parent-child relationship as well as their position in the hierarchy by using a click-and-drag method from the navigator window. You can try clicking on the **Text** item and dragging it on top of **mouseArea**. You will then see the **Text** item changes its position and is now located below the **mouseArea** with a wider indentation:

14. We can also re-arrange them by using the arrow buttons located on top of the navigator window, as shown in the preceding screenshot. Anything that happens to the parent item will also affect all its children, such as moving the parent item, hide and show the parent item, and so on.

You can pan around the canvas view by holding the middle mouse button (or mouse scroll) while moving your mouse around. You can also zoom in and out by scrolling your mouse while holding the *Ctrl* key on your keyboard. By default, scrolling your mouse will move the canvas view up and down. However, if your mouse cursor is on top of the horizontal scroll bar of the canvas, scrolling the mouse will move the view to the left and right.

15. Next, delete both the **mouseArea** and **Text** items as we will be learning how to create a user interface from scratch using QML and Qt Quick.

16. After you've done, let's set the **Rectangle** item's size to `800x600`, as we're going to need a bigger space for the widgets.

17. Open up `main.qml` and remove these lines of code:

```
mouseArea.onClicked: {
  Qt.quit();
}
```

This is because the **mouseArea** item no longer exists and it will cause an error when compiling.

18. After that, remove the following code from `MainForm.ui.qml`:

```
property alias mouseArea: mousearea
```

19. This is removed for the same reason as the previous code, because the **mouseArea** item no longer exists.

20. Then, copy the images we used in the previous C++ project over to the QML project's folder, because we are going re-create the same login screen, with QML!

21. Add the images to the resource file so that we can use them for our UI.

22. Once you're done with that, open up Qt Quick Designer again and switch to the resource window. Click and drag the background image directly to the canvas. Then, switch over to the **Layout** tab on the properties pane and click the fill anchor button marked in red circle. This will make the background image always stick to the window size:

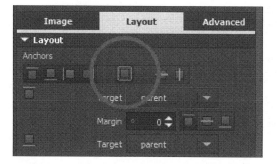

23. Next, click and drag a **Rectangle** component from the library window to the canvas. We will use this as the top panel for our program.

24. For the top panel, enable top anchor, left anchor, and right anchor so that it sticks to the top of the window and follow its width. Make sure all the margins are set to zero.

25. Then, go to the `Color` property of the top panel and select **Gradient** mode. Set the first color to `#805bcce9` and the second color to `#80000000`. This will create a half-transparent panel with a blue gradient.

26. After that, add a text widget to the canvas and make it a child of the top panel. Set its text property to the current date and time (for example, Monday, 26-10-2015 3:14 PM) for display purposes. Then, set the text color to white.

27. Switch over to the **Layout** tab and enable top anchor and left anchor so that the text widget will always stick to the top left corner of the screen.

28. Next, add a mouse area to the screen and set its size to 50x50. Then, make it a child of the top panel by dragging it on top of the top panel in the navigator window.

29. Set the color of the mouse area to blue (#27a9e3) and set its radius to 2 to make its corners slightly rounded. Then, enable top anchor and right anchor to make it stick to the top right corner of the window. Set the top anchor's margin to 8 and right anchor's margin to 10 to give out some space.

30. After that, open up the resources window and drag the shutdown icon to the canvas. Then, make it a child of the mouse area item we created a moment ago. Then, enable the fill anchor to make it fit the size of the mouse area.

31. Phew, that's a lot of steps! Now your items should be arranged like this on the **Navigator** window:

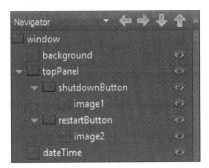

32. The parent-child relationship and the layout anchors are both very important to keep the widgets in the correct positions when the main window changes its size.

33. At this point, your top panel should look something like this:

34. Next, we will be working on the login form. First, add a new rectangle to the canvas by dragging it from the **Library** window. Resize the rectangle to 360x200 and set its radius to 15.

35. Then, set its color to `#80000000`, which will change it to black with `50%` transparency.

36. After that, enable the vertical center anchor and the horizontal center anchor to make it always align to the center of the window. Then, set the margin of the vertical center anchor to `100` so that it moves slightly lower to the bottom to give space to the logo. The following screenshot illustrates the settings of the anchors:

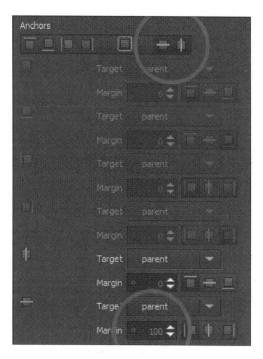

37. Add the text widgets to the canvas. Make them the children of the login form (rectangle widget) and set their text property to `Username:` and `Password:` respectively. Then, change their text color to white and position them accordingly. We don't need to set a margin this time because they will follow the rectangle's position.

38. Next, add two text input widgets to the canvas and place them next to the text widgets we created just now. Make sure the text inputs are also the children of the login form. Since the text inputs don't contain any background color property, we need to add two rectangles to the canvas to use as their background.

39. Add two rectangles to the canvas and make each of them a child of one of the text inputs we created just now. Then, set the radius property to `5` to give them some rounded corners. After that, enable fill anchors on both of the rectangles so that they will follow the size of the text input widgets.

40. After that, we're going to create the login button below the password field. First, add a mouse area to the canvas and make it a child of the login form. Then, resize it to your preferred dimension and move it into place.

41. Since the mouse area also does not contain any background color property, we need to add a rectangle widget and make it a child of the mouse area. Set the color of the rectangle to blue (#27a9e3) and enable the fill anchor so that it fits nicely with the mouse area.

42. Next, add a text widget to the canvas and make it a child of the login button. Change its text color to white and set its text property to Login. Finally, enable the horizontal center anchor and the vertical center anchor to align it to the center of the button.

43. You will now get a login form that looks pretty similar to the one we made in the C++ project:

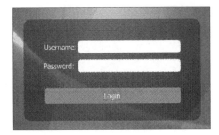

44. After we have done the login form, it's time to add the logo. It's actually very simple. First, open up the resources window and drag the logo image to the canvas.

45. Make it a child of the login form and set its size to 512x200.

46. Position it above the login form and you're done!

47. This is what the entire UI look like when compiled. We have successfully re-created the login screen from the C++ project, but this time we did it with QML and Qt Quick!

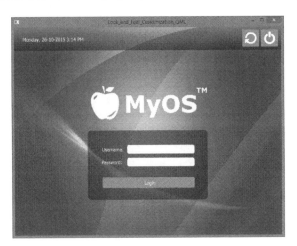

How it works...

Qt Quick editor uses a very different approach for placing widgets in the application compared to the form editor. It's entirely up to the user which method is best suited for him/her.

The following screenshot shows what the Qt Quick Designer looks like:

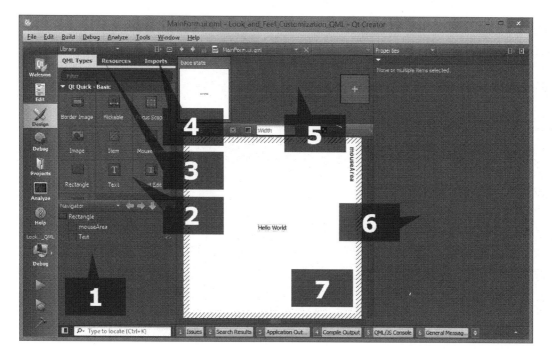

We will now look at the various elements of the editor's UI:

1. **Navigator**: The **Navigator** window displays the items in the current QML file as a tree structure. It's similar to the object operator window in the other Qt Designer we used in previous section.

2. **Library**: The **Library** window displays all the Qt Quick Components or Qt Quick Controls available in QML. You can click and drag it to the canvas window to add to your UI. You can also create your own custom QML components and display it here.

3. **Resources**: The **Resources** window displays all the resources in a list which can then be used in your UI design.

4. **Imports**: The **Imports** window allows you to import different QML modules into your current QML file, such as a bluetooth module, webkit module, positioning module, and so on, to add additional functionality to your QML project.

5. **State pane**: Stat pane displays the different states in the QML project which typically describe UI configurations, such as the UI controls, their properties and behavior, and the available actions.

6. **Properties pane**: Similar to the property editor we used in previous section, this properties pane in QML Designer displays the properties of the selected item. You can also change the properties of the items in the code editor as well.

7. **Canvas**: Canvas is the working area where you create QML components and design applications.

Exposing QML object pointer to C++

Sometimes we want to modify the properties of a QML object through C++ scripting, such as changing the text of a label, hiding/showing the widget, changing its size, and so on. Qt's QML engine allows you to register your QML objects to C++ types which automatically exposes all its properties.

How to do it...

We want to create a label in QML and change its text occasionally. In order to expose the label object to C++, we can do the following steps. First, create a C++ class called `MyLabel` that extends from `QObject` class:

```
mylabel.h:
class MyLabel : public QObject
{
  Q_OBJECT
  public:
    // Object pointer
    QObject* myObject;

    explicit MyLabel(QObject *parent = 0);

    // Must call Q_INVOKABLE so that this function can be used in QML
    Q_INVOKABLE void SetMyObject(QObject* obj);
}
```

In the `mylabel.cpp` source file, define a function called `SetMyObject()` to save the object pointer. This function will later be called in QML:

```
mylabel.cpp:
void MyLabel::SetMyObject(QObject* obj)
{
  // Set the object pointer
  myObject = obj;
}
```

After that, in `main.cpp`, include `MyLabel` header and register it to QML engine using the function `qmlRegisterType()`:

```cpp
#include "mylabel.h"
int main(int argc, char *argv[])
{
    // Register your class to QML
    qmlRegisterType<MyClass>("MyLabelLib", 1, 0, "MyLabel");
}
```

Notice that there are four parameters you need to declare in `qmlRegisterType()`. Besides declaring your class name (`MyLabel`), you also need to declare your library name (`MyLabelLib`) and its version (`1.0`), which will be used for importing your class to QML later on.

Now that the QML engine is fully aware of our custom label class, we can then map it to our label object in QML and import the class library we defined earlier by calling import `MyLabelLib 1.0` in our QML file. Notice that the library name and its version number have to match with the one you declared in `main.cpp`, otherwise it will throw you an error.

After declaring `MyLabel` in QML and setting its ID as `mylabels`, call `mylabel.SetMyObject(myLabel)` to expose its pointer to C/C++ right after the label is being initialized:

```qml
import MyLabelLib 1.0

ApplicationWindow
{
    id: mainWindow
    width: 480
    height: 640

    MyLabel
    {
        id: mylabel
    }

    Label
    {
        id: helloWorldLabel
        text: qsTr("Hello World!")
        Component.onCompleted:
        {
            mylabel.SetMyObject(hellowWorldLabel);
        }
    }
}
```

Please be aware that you need to wait until the label is fully initiated before exposing its pointer to C/C++, otherwise you may cause the program to crash. To make sure it's fully initiated, call `SetMyObject()` within `Component.onCompleted` and not any other places.

Now that the QML label has been exposed to C/C++, we can change any of its properties by calling `setProperty()` function. For instance, we can set its visibility to `true` and change its text to `Bye bye world!`:

```
// QVariant automatically detects your data type
myObject->setProperty("visible", QVariant(true));
myObject->setProperty("text", QVariant("Bye bye world!"));
```

Besides changing the properties, we can also call its functions by calling `QMetaObject::invokeMethod()`:

```
QVariant returnedValue;
QVariant message = "Hello world!";

QMetaObject::invokeMethod(myObject, "myQMLFunction",
Q_RETURN_ARG(QVariant, returnedValue),
Q_ARG(QVariant, message));

qDebug() << "QML function returned:" << returnedValue.toString();
```

Or simply, we can call the `invokedMethod()` function with only two parameters if we do not expect any values to be returned from it:

```
QMetaObject::invokeMethod(myObject, "myQMLFunction");
```

How it works...

QML is designed to be easily extensible through C++ code. The classes in the Qt QML module enable QML objects to be loaded and manipulated from C++, and the nature of the QML engine's integration with Qt's meta object system enables C++ functionality to be invoked directly from QML. To provide some C++ data or functionality to QML, it must be made available from a QObject-derived class.

QML object types can be instantiated from C++ and inspected in order to access their properties, invoke their methods, and receive their signal notifications. This is possible due to the fact that all QML object types are implemented using QObject-derived classes, enabling the QML engine to dynamically load and introspect objects through the Qt meta object system.

2
States and Animations

In this chapter, we will cover the following recipes:

- ▸ Property animation in Qt
- ▸ Using easing curves to control property animation
- ▸ Creating the animation group
- ▸ Creating the nested animation group
- ▸ State machine in Qt
- ▸ States, transitions, and animations in QML
- ▸ Animation widget properties using animators
- ▸ Sprite animation

Introduction

Qt provides an easy way to animate widgets or any other objects that inherit the `QObject` class, through its powerful animation framework. The animation can be used either on its own or used together with the state machine framework, which allows different animations to be played based on the current active state of the widget. Qt's animation framework also supports grouped animation, which allows you to move more than one graphics item simultaneously, or move them in sequence one after the other.

Property animation in Qt

In this example, we will learn how to animate our **Graphical User Interface** (**GUI**) elements using Qt's property animation class, part of its powerful animation framework, which allows us to create fluid looking animation with minimal effort.

How to do it...

1. First, let's create a new Qt Widgets Application project. After that, open up
    `mainwindow.ui` with Qt Designer and place a button on the main window,
    as shown here:

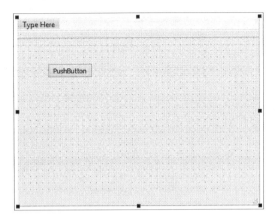

2. Next, open up `mainwindow.cpp` and add the following line of code at the beginning
    of the source code:

    ```
    #include <QPropertyAnimation>
    ```

3. After that, open up `mainwindow.cpp` and add the following code to the constructor:

    ```
    QPropertyAnimation *animation = new QPropertyAnimation
        (ui->pushButton, "geometry");
    animation->setDuration(10000);
    animation->setStartValue(ui->pushButton->geometry());
    animation->setEndValue(QRect(200, 200, 100, 50));
    animation->start();
    ```

How it works...

One of the more common methods to animate a GUI element is through the property
animation class provided by Qt, known as the `QPropertyAnimation` class. This class is
part of the animation framework and it makes use of the timer system in Qt to change the
properties of a GUI element over a given duration.

What we are trying to accomplish here is to animate the button from one position to another,
while at the same time we also enlarge the button size along the way.

By including the `QPropertyAnimation` header in our source code in Step 2, we will
be able to access the `QPropertyAnimation` class provided by Qt and make use of its
functionalities.

The code in Step 3 basically creates a new property animation and applies it to the push button we just created in Qt Designer. We specifically request the property animation class changes the `geometry` properties of the push button and sets its duration to 3,000 milliseconds (3 seconds).

Then, the start value of the animation is set to the initial geometry of the push button, because obviously we want it to start from where we initially place the button in Qt Designer. The end value is then set to what we want it to become; in this case we will move the button to a new position at x: `200`, y: `200` while changing its size to width: `100`, height: `50` along the way.

After that, call `animation->start()` to start the animation.

Compile and run the project and now you should see the button start to move slowly across the main window while expanding in size a bit at a time, until it reaches its destination. You can change the animation duration and the target position and scale by altering the values in the preceding code. It's really that simple to animate a GUI element using Qt's property animation system!

There's more...

Qt provides us with several different sub-systems to create animations for our GUI, including timer, timeline, animation framework, state machine framework, and graphics view framework:

- **Timer**: Qt provides us with repetitive and single-shot timers. When the timeout value is reached, an event callback function will be triggered through Qt's signal-and-slot mechanism. You can make use of a timer to change the properties (color, position, scale, and so on) of your GUI element within a given interval, in order to create an animation.

- **Timeline**: Timeline calls a slot periodically to animate a GUI element. It is quite similar to a repetitive timer, but instead of doing the same thing all the time when the slot is triggered, timeline provides a value to the slot to indicate its current frame index, so that you can do different things (such as offset to a different space of the sprite sheet) based on the given value.

- **Animation framework**: The animation framework makes animating a GUI element easy by allowing its properties to be animated. The animations are controlled by using easing curves. Easing curves describe a function that controls what the speed of the animation should be, resulting in different acceleration and deceleration patterns. The types of easing curve supported by Qt include: linear, quadratic, cubic, quartic, sine, exponential, circular, and elastic.

- **State machine framework**: Qt provides us with classes for creating and executing state graphs, which allow each GUI element to move from one state to another when triggered by signals. The state graph in the state machine framework is hierarchical, which means every state can also be nested inside of other states.

▶ **Graphics view framework**: The graphics view framework is a powerful graphics engine for visualizing and interacting with a large number of custom-made 2D graphical items. You can use the graphics view framework to draw your GUI and have them animated in a totally manual way if you are an experienced programmer.

By making use of all the powerful features mentioned here, we're able to create an intuitive and modern GUI with ease. In this chapter, we will look into the practical approaches to animating GUI elements using Qt.

Using easing curves to control property animation

In this example, we will learn how to make our animation more interesting by utilizing easing curves. We will still use the previous source code, which uses the property animation to animate a push button.

How to do it...

1. Define an easing curve and add it to the property animation before calling the start() function:

```
QPropertyAnimation *animation =
    new QPropertyAnimation(ui->pushButton, "geometry");
animation->setDuration(3000);
animation->setStartValue(ui->pushButton->geometry());
animation->setEndValue(QRect(200, 200, 100, 50));
QEasingCurve curve;
curve.setType(QEasingCurve::OutBounce);
animation->setEasingCurve(curve);
animation->start();
```

2. Call the setLoopCount() function to set how many loops you want it to repeat for:

```
QPropertyAnimation *animation =
    new QPropertyAnimation(ui->pushButton, "geometry");
animation->setDuration(3000);
animation->setStartValue(ui->pushButton->geometry());
animation->setEndValue(QRect(200, 200, 100, 50));
QEasingCurve curve;
Curve.setType(EasingCurve::OutBounce);
animation->setEasingCurve(curve);
animation->setLoopCount(2);
animation->start();
```

3. Call `setAmplitude()`, `setOvershoot()`, and `setPeriod()` before applying the easing curve to the animation:

```
QEasingCurve curve;
curve.setType(QEasingCurve::OutBounce);
curve.setAmplitude(1.00);
curve.setOvershoot(1.70);
curve.setPeriod(0.30);
animation->setEasingCurve(curve);
animation->start();
```

How it works...

In order to let an easing curve control the animation, all you need to do is to define an easing curve and add it to the property animation before calling the `start()` function. You can also try several other types of easing curve and see which one suits you best. Here is an example:

```
animation->setEasingCurve(QEasingCurve::OutBounce);
```

If you want the animation to loop after it has finished playing, you can call the `setLoopCount()` function to set how many loops you want it to repeat for, or set the value to `-1` for an infinite loop:

```
animation->setLoopCount(-1);
```

There are several parameters that you can set to refine the easing curve before applying it to the property animation. These parameters include amplitude, overshoot, and period:

- ▶ **Amplitude**: The higher the amplitude, the higher the bounce or elastic spring effect that will be applied to the animation.

- ▶ **Overshoot**: Some curve functions will produce an overshoot (exceeding its final value) curve due to damping effect. By adjusting the overshoot value, we are able to increase or decrease this effect.

- ▶ **Period**: Setting a small period value will give a high frequency to the curve. A large period will give it a small frequency.

These parameters, however, are not applicable to all curve types. Please refer to the Qt documentation to see which parameter is applicable to which curve type.

There's more...

While the property animation works perfectly fine, sometimes it feels a little boring to look at a GUI element animated at a constant speed. We can make the animation look more interesting by adding an easing curve to control the motion. There are many types of easing curve that you can use in Qt, and here are some of them:

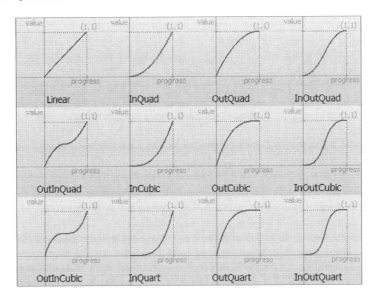

As you can see from the preceding diagram, each easing curve produces a different ease-in and ease-out effect.

 For the full list of easing curves available in Qt, please refer to the Qt documentation at http://doc.qt.io/qt-5/qeasingcurve.html#Type-enum.

Creating an animation group

In this example, we will learn how to use an animation group to manage the states of the animations contained in the group.

How to do it...

1. We will use the previous example, but this time, we add two more push buttons to the main window, like so:

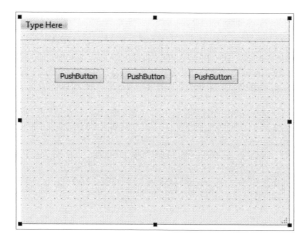

2. Next, define the animation for each of the push buttons in the main window's constructor:

```
QPropertyAnimation *animation1 =
   new QPropertyAnimation(ui->pushButton, "geometry");
animation1->setDuration(3000);
animation1->setStartValue(ui->pushButton->geometry());
animation1->setEndValue(QRect(50, 200, 100, 50));

QPropertyAnimation *animation2 =
   new QPropertyAnimation(ui->pushButton_2, "geometry");
animation2->setDuration(3000);
animation2->setStartValue(ui->pushButton_2->geometry());
animation2->setEndValue(QRect(150, 200, 100, 50));

QPropertyAnimation *animation3 =
   new QPropertyAnimation(ui->pushButton_3, "geometry");
animation3->setDuration(3000);
animation3->setStartValue(ui->pushButton_3->geometry());
animation3->setEndValue(QRect(250, 200, 100, 50));
```

3. After that, create an easing curve and apply the same curve to all three animations:

```
QEasingCurve curve;
curve.setType(QEasingCurve::OutBounce);
curve.setAmplitude(1.00);
curve.setOvershoot(1.70);
curve.setPeriod(0.30);

animation1->setEasingCurve(curve);
animation2->setEasingCurve(curve);
animation3->setEasingCurve(curve);
```

4. Once you have applied the easing curve to all three animations, we will then create an animation group and add all three animations to the group:

```
QParallelAnimationGroup *group = new QParallelAnimationGroup;
group->addAnimation(animation1);
group->addAnimation(animation2);
group->addAnimation(animation3);
```

5. Call the `start()` function from the animation group we just created:

```
group->start();
```

How it works...

Since we are using an animation group now, we no longer call the `start()` function from the individual animation, but instead we will be calling the `start()` function from the animation group we just created.

If you compile and run the example now, you will see all three buttons being played at the same time. This is because we are using the parallel animation group. You can replace it with a sequential animation group and run the example again:

```
QSequentialAnimationGroup *group = new QSequentialAnimationGroup;
```

This time, only a single button will play its animation at a time, while the other buttons will wait patiently for their turn to come.

The priority is set based on which animation is added to the animation group first. You can change the animation sequence by simply rearranging the sequence of an animation being added to the group. For example, if we want button 3 to start the animation first, followed by button 2, and then button 1, the code will look like this:

```
group->addAnimation(animation3);
group->addAnimation(animation2);
group->addAnimation(animation1);
```

Since property animations and animation groups are both inherited from the
`QAbstractAnimator` class, it means that you can also add an animation group
to another animation group to form a more complex, nested animation group.

There's more...

Qt allows us to create multiple animations and group them into an animation group. A group is
usually responsible for managing the state of its animations (that is, it decides when to start,
stop, resume, and pause them). Currently, Qt provides two types of class for animation groups,
`QParallelAnimationGroup` and `QSequentialAnimationGroup`:

- ▸ `QParallelAnimationGroup`: As its name implies, a parallel animation group runs
  all the animations in its group at the same time. The group is deemed finished when
  the longest-lasting animation has finished running.

- ▸ `QSequentialAnimationGroup`: A sequential animation group runs its animations
  in sequence, meaning it will only run a single animation at a time, and only play the
  next animation when the current one has finished.

Creating a nested animation group

One good example of using a nested animation group is when you have several parallel
animation groups and you want to play the groups in a sequential order.

How to do it...

1. We will use the UI from the previous example and add a few more buttons to the main
   window, like so:

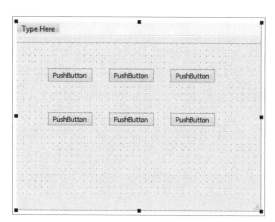

2. First, create all the animations for the buttons, then create an easing curve and apply it to all the animations:

```cpp
QPropertyAnimation *animation1 =
   new QPropertyAnimation(ui->pushButton, "geometry");
animation1->setDuration(3000);
animation1->setStartValue(ui->pushButton->geometry());
animation1->setEndValue(QRect(50, 50, 100, 50));

QPropertyAnimation *animation2 =
   new QPropertyAnimation(ui->pushButton_2, "geometry");
animation2->setDuration(3000);
animation2->setStartValue(ui->pushButton_2->geometry());
animation2->setEndValue(QRect(150, 50, 100, 50));

QPropertyAnimation *animation3 =
   new QPropertyAnimation(ui->pushButton_3, "geometry");
animation3->setDuration(3000);
animation3->setStartValue(ui->pushButton_3->geometry());
animation3->setEndValue(QRect(250, 50, 100, 50));

QPropertyAnimation *animation4 =
   new QPropertyAnimation(ui->pushButton_4, "geometry");
animation4->setDuration(3000);
animation4->setStartValue(ui->pushButton_4->geometry());
animation4->setEndValue(QRect(50, 200, 100, 50));

QPropertyAnimation *animation5 =
   new QPropertyAnimation(ui->pushButton_5, "geometry");
animation5->setDuration(3000);
animation5->setStartValue(ui->pushButton_5->geometry());
animation5->setEndValue(QRect(150, 200, 100, 50));

QPropertyAnimation *animation6 =
   new QPropertyAnimation(ui->pushButton_6, "geometry");
animation6->setDuration(3000);
animation6->setStartValue(ui->pushButton_6->geometry());
animation6->setEndValue(QRect(250, 200, 100, 50));

QEasingCurve curve;
curve.setType(QEasingCurve::OutBounce);
curve.setAmplitude(1.00);
curve.setOvershoot(1.70);
curve.setPeriod(0.30);
```

```
animation1->setEasingCurve(curve);
animation2->setEasingCurve(curve);
animation3->setEasingCurve(curve);
animation4->setEasingCurve(curve);
animation5->setEasingCurve(curve);
animation6->setEasingCurve(curve);
```

3. Create two animation groups, one for the buttons in the upper column and another one for the lower column:

```
QParallelAnimationGroup *group1 = new QParallelAnimationGroup;
group1->addAnimation(animation1);
group1->addAnimation(animation2);
group1->addAnimation(animation3);

QParallelAnimationGroup *group2 = new QParallelAnimationGroup;
group2->addAnimation(animation4);
group2->addAnimation(animation5);
group2->addAnimation(animation6);
```

4. We will create yet another animation group, which will be used to store the two animation groups we created previously:

```
QSequentialAnimationGroup *groupAll =
   new QSequentialAnimationGroup;
groupAll->addAnimation(group1);
groupAll->addAnimation(group2);
groupAll->start();
```

How it works...

What we're trying to do here is to play the animation of the buttons in the upper column first, followed by the buttons in the lower column.

Since both of the animation groups are parallel animation groups, the buttons belonging to the respective groups will be animated at the same time when the start() function is called.

This time, however, the group is a sequential animation group, which means only a single parallel animation group will be played at a time, followed by the other when the first one is finished.

Animation groups are a very handy system that allows us to create very complex GUI animations with simple coding. Qt will handle the difficult part for us so we don't have to.

State machines in Qt

State machines can be used for many purposes, but in this chapter we will only cover topics related to animation.

How to do it...

1. First, we will set up a new user interface for our example program, which looks like this:

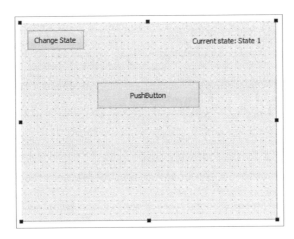

2. Next, we will include some headers in our source code:

```
#include <QStateMachine>
#include <QPropertyAnimation>
#include <QEventTransition>
```

3. After that, in our main window's constructor, add the following code to create a new state machine and two states, which we will be using later:

```
QStateMachine *machine = new QStateMachine(this);
QState *s1 = new QState();
QState *s2 = new QState();
```

4. Then, we will define what we should do within each state, which in this case will be to change the label's text, as well as the button's position and size:

```
QState *s1 = new QState();
s1->assignProperty(ui->stateLabel, "text", "Current state: 1");
s1->assignProperty(ui->pushButton, "geometry", QRect(50, 200, 100,
    50));
```

```
QState *s2 = new QState();
s2->assignProperty(ui->stateLabel, "text", "Current state: 2");
s2->assignProperty(ui->pushButton, "geometry", QRect(200, 50, 140,
    100));
```

5. Once you are done with that, let's proceed by adding event transition classes to our source code:

```
QEventTransition *t1 = new QEventTransition(ui->changeState,
    QEvent::MouseButtonPress);
t1->setTargetState(s2);
s1->addTransition(t1);

QEventTransition *t2 = new QEventTransition(ui->changeState,
    QEvent::MouseButtonPress);
T2->setTargetState(s1);
s2->addTransition(t2);
```

6. Next, add all the states we have just created to the state machine and define state 1 as the initial state. Then, call `machine->start()` to start running the state machine:

```
machine->addState(s1);
machine->addState(s2);

machine->setInitialState(s1);
machine->start();
```

7. If you run the example program now, you will notice everything works fine, except the button is not going through a smooth transition and it simply jumps instantly to the position and size we set previously. This is because we have not used a property animation to create a smooth transition.

8. Go back to the event transition step and add the following lines of code:

```
QEventTransition *t1 =
    new QEventTransition(ui->changeState, QEvent::MouseButtonPress);
t1->setTargetState(s2);
t1->addAnimation(new QPropertyAnimation(ui->pushButton,
    "geometry"));
s1->addTransition(t1);

QEventTransition *t2 = new QEventTransition(ui->changeState,
    QEvent::MouseButtonPress);
t2->setTargetState(s1);
t2->addAnimation(new QPropertyAnimation(ui->pushButton,
    "geometry"));
s2->addTransition(t2);
```

9. You can also add an easing curve to the animation to make it look more interesting:

```
QPropertyAnimation *animation =
    new QPropertyAnimation(ui->pushButton, "geometry");
animation->setEasingCurve(QEasingCurve::OutBounce);
QEventTransition *t1 = new QEventTransition(ui->changeState,
    QEvent::MouseButtonPress);
t1->setTargetState(s2);
t1->addAnimation(animation);
s1->addTransition(t1);

QEventTransition *t2 = new QEventTransition(ui->changeState,
    QEvent::MouseButtonPress);
t2->setTargetState(s1);
t2->addAnimation(animation);
s2->addTransition(t2);
```

How it works...

There are two push buttons and a label on the main window layout. The button at the top-left corner will trigger the state change when pressed, while the label at the top-right corner will change its text to show which state we are currently in, and the button below will animate according to the current state.

The `QEventTransition` classes define what will trigger the transition between one state and another.

In our case, we want the state to change from state 1 to state 2 when the `ui->changeState` button (the one at the upper left) is clicked. After that, we also want to change from state 2 back to state 1 when the same button is pressed again. This can be achieved by creating another event transition class and setting the target state back to state 1. Then, add these transitions to their respective states.

Instead of just assigning the properties directly to the widgets, we tell Qt to use the property animation class to smoothly interpolate the properties toward the target values. It is that simple!

There is no need to set the start value and end value, because we have already called the `assignProperty()` function, which has automatically assigned the end value.

There's more...

The state machine framework in Qt provides classes for creating and executing state graphs. Qt's event system is used to drive the state machines, where transitions between states can be triggered by using signals, then the slots on the other end will be invoked by the signals to perform an action, such as playing an animation.

Once you understand the basics of state machines, you can use them to do other things as well. The state graph in the state machine framework is hierarchical. Just like the animation group in the previous section, states can also be nested inside of other states:

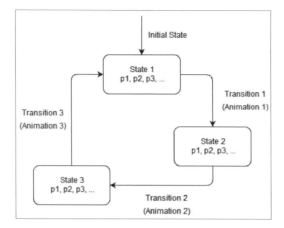

States, transitions, and animations in QML

If you prefer to work with QML instead of C++, Qt also provides similar features in Qt Quick that allow you to easily animate a GUI element with the minimum lines of code. In this example, we will learn how to achieve this with QML.

How to do it...

1. First we will create a new **Qt Quick Application** project and set up our user interface like so:

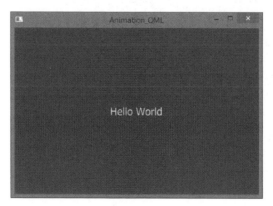

2. Here is what my `main.qml` file looks like:

```
import QtQuick 2.3
import QtQuick.Window 2.2

Window {
    visible: true
    width: 480;
    height: 320;

    Rectangle {
        id: background;
        anchors.fill: parent;
        color: "blue";
    }

    Text {
        text: qsTr("Hello World");
        anchors.centerIn: parent;
        color: "white";
        font.pointSize: 15;
    }
}
```

3. Add the color animation to the `Rectangle` object:

```
Rectangle {
    id: background;
    anchors.fill: parent;
    color: "blue";
    SequentialAnimation on color
    {
        ColorAnimation { to: "yellow"; duration: 1000 }
        ColorAnimation { to: "red"; duration: 1000 }
        ColorAnimation { to: "blue"; duration: 1000 }
        loops: Animation.Infinite;
    }
}
```

4. Then, add a number animation to the text object:

```
Text {
    text: qsTr("Hello World");
    anchors.centerIn: parent;
    color: "white";
    font.pointSize: 15;
    SequentialAnimation on opacity {
```

```
        NumberAnimation { to: 0.0; duration: 200}
        NumberAnimation { to: 1.0; duration: 200}
        loops: Animation.Infinite;
    }
}
```

5. Next, add another number animation to it:

```
Text {
    text: qsTr("Hello World");
    anchors.centerIn: parent;
    color: "white";
    font.pointSize: 15;
    SequentialAnimation on opacity {
        NumberAnimation { to: 0.0; duration: 200}
        NumberAnimation { to: 1.0; duration: 200}
        loops: Animation.Infinite;
    }
    NumberAnimation on rotation {
        from: 0;
        to: 360;
        duration: 2000;
        loops: Animation.Infinite;
    }
}
```

6. Define two states, one called the PRESSED state and another called the RELEASED
   state. Then, set the default state to RELEASED:

```
Rectangle {
    id: background;
    anchors.fill: parent;

    state: "RELEASED";
    states: [
        State {
            name: "PRESSED"
            PropertyChanges { target: background; color: "blue"}
        },
        State {
            name: "RELEASED"
            PropertyChanges { target: background; color: "red"}
        }
    ]
}
```

7. After that, create a mouse area within the `Rectangle` object so that we can click on it:

```
MouseArea {
    anchors.fill: parent;
    onPressed: background.state = "PRESSED";
    onReleased: background.state = "RELEASED";
}
```

8. Add some transitions to the `Rectangle` object:

```
transitions: [
    Transition {
        from: "PRESSED"
        to: "RELEASED"
        ColorAnimation { target: background; duration: 200}
    },
    Transition {
        from: "RELEASED"
        to: "PRESSED"
        ColorAnimation { target: background; duration: 200}
    }
]
```

How it works...

The main window consists of a blue rectangle and static text that says Hello World.

We want the background color to change from blue to yellow, then to red, and back to blue in a loop. This can be easily achieved using the color animation type in QML.

What we're doing at Step 3 is basically creating a sequential animation group within the `Rectangle` object, then creating three different color animations within the group, which will change the color of the object every 1,000 milliseconds (1 second). We also set the animations to loop infinitely.

In Step 4, we want to use the number animation to animate the alpha value of the static text. We created another sequential animation group within the `Text` object and created two number animations to animate the alpha value from 0 to 1 and back. Then, we set the animations to loop infinitely.

Then in Step 5, we rotate the Hello World text by adding another number animation to it.

In Step 6, we wanted to make the `Rectangle` object change from one color to another when we click on it. When the mouse is released, the `Rectangle` object will change back to its initial color. To achieve that, first we need to define the two states, one called the PRESSED state and another called the RELEASED state. Then, we set the default state to RELEASED.

Now, when you compile and run the example, the background will instantly change color to blue when pressed and change back to red when the mouse is released. That works great and we can further enhance it by giving it a little transition when switching color. This can be easily achieved by adding transitions to the `Rectangle` object.

There's more...

In QML, there are eight different types of property animation you can use:

- **Anchor animation**: Animates changes in anchor values
- **Color animation**: Animates changes in color values
- **Number animation**: Animates changes in qreal-type values
- **Parent animation**: Animates changes in parent values
- **Path animation**: Animates an item along a path
- **Property animation**: Animates changes in property values
- **Rotation animation**: Animates changes in rotation values
- **Vector3d animation**: Animates changes in QVector3d values

Just like the C++ version, these animations can also be grouped together in an animation group to play the animations in sequence or in parallel. You can also control the animations using easing curves and determine when to play these animations using state machines, just like what we have done in the previous section.

Animating widget properties using animators

In this recipe, we will learn how to animate the properties of our GUI widgets using the animator feature provided by QML.

How to do it...

1. Create a rectangle object and add a scale animator to it:

```
Rectangle {
  id: myBox;
  width: 50;
  height: 50;
  anchors.horizontalCenter: parent.horizontalCenter;
  anchors.verticalCenter: parent.verticalCenter;
  color: "blue";

  ScaleAnimator {
    target: myBox;
```

```
        from: 5;
        to: 1;
        duration: 2000;
        running: true;
    }
}
```

2. Add a rotation animator and set the running value in the parallel animation group, but not in any of the individual animators:

```
ParallelAnimation {
    ScaleAnimator {
        target: myBox;
        from: 5;
        to: 1;
        duration: 2000;
    }
    RotationAnimator {
        target: myBox;
        from: 0;
        to: 360;
        duration: 1000;
    }
    running: true;
}
```

3. Add an easing curve to the scale animator:

```
ScaleAnimator {
    target: myBox;
    from: 5;
    to: 1;
    duration: 2000;
    easing.type: Easing.InOutElastic;
    easing.amplitude: 2.0;
    asing.period: 1.5;
    running: true;
}
```

How it works...

The animator type can be used just like any other animation type. We want to scale a rectangle from a size of 5 to a size of 1 within 2,000 milliseconds (2 seconds).

We created a blue `Rectangle` object and added a scale animator to it. We set the initial value to 5 and the final value to 1. Then, we set the animation duration to 2000 and set the running value to `true` so that it will be played when the program starts.

Just like the animation types, animators can also be put into groups (that is, parallel animation groups or sequential animation groups). An animation group will also be treated as an animator by QtQuick and be run on the scene graph's rendering thread whenever possible.

In Step 2, we want to group two different animators into a parallel animation group so that they run together at the same time.

We will keep the scale animator we have created previously and add another rotation animator to rotate the `Rectangle` object. This time, set the running value in the parallel animation group, but not in any of the individual animators.

Just like the C++ version, QML also supports easing curves and they can be easily applied to any of the animations or animator types.

There is something called animator in QML, which is similar but different from the ordinary animation type. Animator types are a special type of animation that operate directly on Qt Quick's scene graph, rather than the QML objects and their properties like regular animation types do.

The value of the QML property will be updated after the animation has finished. However, the property is not updated while the animation is running. The benefits of using the animator type is that the performance is slightly better because it doesn't run on the UI thread, but operates directly on the scene graph's rendering thread.

Sprite animation

In this example, we will learn how to create sprite animation in QML.

How to do it...

1. First of all, we'll need to add our sprite sheet to Qt's resource system so that it can be used in the program. Open up `qml.qrc` and click the **Add | Add Files** buttons. Select your sprite sheet image and save the resource file by pressing *Ctrl + S*.

2. After that, create a new empty window in `main.qml`:

```
import QtQuick 2.3
import QtQuick.Window 2.2

Window {
  visible: true
  width: 420
  height: 380
  Rectangle {
    anchors.fill: parent
    color: "white"
  }
}
```

3. Once you're done with that, we will start creating an `AnimatedSprite` object in QML:

```
import QtQuick 2.3
import QtQuick.Window 2.2

Window {
  visible: true;
  width: 420;
  height: 380;
  Rectangle {
    anchors.fill: parent;
    color: "white";
  }

  AnimatedSprite {
    id: sprite;
    width: 128;
    height: 128;
    anchors.centerIn: parent;
    source: "qrc:///horse_1.png";
    frameCount: 11;
    frameWidth: 128;
    frameHeight: 128;
    frameRate: 25;
    loops: Animation.Infinite;
    running: true;
  }
}
```

4. Add a mouse area to the window and check for the `onClicked` event:

```
MouseArea {
  anchors.fill: parent;
  onClicked: {
    if (sprite.paused)
      sprite.resume();
    else
      sprite.pause();
  }
}
```

5. If you compile and run the example program now, you will see a little pony running in the middle of the window. How fun!

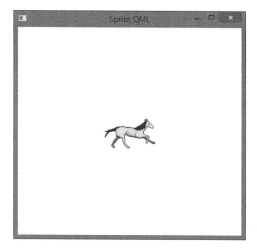

6. Next, we want to try and do something cool. We will make the horse run across the window and loop infinitely while playing its running animation!

    First, we need to remove the `anchors.centerIn:` parent from QML and replace it with x and y values:

```
AnimatedSprite {
  id: sprite;
  width: 128;
  height: 128;
  x: -128;
  y: parent.height / 2;
  source: "qrc:///horse_1.png";
  frameCount: 11;
  frameWidth: 128;
  frameHeight: 128;
```

```
        frameRate: 25;
        loops: Animation.Infinite;
        running: true;
    }
```

7. After that, add a number animation to the sprite object and set its properties like this:

```
NumberAnimation {
    target: sprite;
    property: "x";
    from: -128;
    to: 512;
    duration: 3000;
    loops: Animation.Infinite;
    running: true;
}
```

8. Compile and run the example program now and you will see the pony go crazy and start running across the window!

How it works...

In this recipe, we placed the animated sprite object in the middle of the window and set its image source to the sprite sheet that we had just added to the project resource.

Then, we counted how many frames there are in the sprite sheet that belong to the running animation, which in this case was 11 frames. We also told Qt about the dimension of each frame of the animation, which in this case was 128 x 128. After that, we set the frame rate to 25 to get a decent speed and then set it to loop infinitely. We then set the running value to true so that the animation will be played by default when the program starts running.

Then in Step 4, we wanted to be able to pause the animation and resume it by clicking on the window. We simply check whether the sprite is current paused when clicking on the mouse area. If the sprite animation has been paused, then resume the animation; otherwise, pause the animation.

In Step 6, we replaced anchors.centerIn with x and y values so that the animated sprite object is not anchored to the center of the window, which would have made it impossible to move around.

Then, we created a number animation within the animated sprite to animate its x property. We set the start value to somewhere outside the window on the left side, and set the end value to somewhere outside the window on the right side. After that, we set the duration to 3,000 milliseconds (3 seconds) and made it loop infinitely.

Lastly, we also set the running value to true so that it will play the animation by default when the program starts running.

There's more...

Sprite animation is used extensively, especially in game development. Sprites are used for character animation, particle animation, and even GUI animation. A sprite sheet consists of many images combined into one, which can then be chopped down and displayed on the screen one at a time. The transitions between different images (or sprites) from the sprite sheet creates the illusion of animation, which we usually refer to as sprite animation. Sprite animation can be easily achieved in QML using the `AnimatedSprite` type.

> In this example program, I'm using a free and open source image created by bluecarrot16 under the CC-BY 3.0 / GPL 3.0 / GPL 2.0 / OGA-BY 3.0 license. The image can be obtained legally at `http://opengameart.org/content/lpc-horse`.

3
QPainter and 2D Graphics

In this chapter, we will cover the following recipes:

- ▸ Drawing basic shapes on screen
- ▸ Exporting shapes to an SVG file
- ▸ Coordinate transformation
- ▸ Displaying images on screen
- ▸ Applying image effects to graphics
- ▸ Creating a basic paint program
- ▸ 2D Canvas in QML

Introduction

In this chapter, we will learn how to render 2D graphics on screen with Qt. Internally, Qt uses a low-level class called `QPainter` to render its widgets on the main window. Qt allows us to access and use the `QPainter` class for drawing vector graphics, text, 2D images, and even 3D graphics. You can make use of the `QPainter` class to create your own custom widgets or to create programs that rely heavily on computer graphics rendering such as video games, photo editors, 3D modeling tools, and so on.

Drawing basic shapes on screen

In this section, we will learn how to draw simple vector shapes (line, rectangle, circle, and so on) and display text on the main window using the QPainter class. We will also learn how to change the drawing style of the vector shapes using the QPen class.

How to do it...

First, let's create a new **Qt Widgets Application** project:

1. Open up mainwindow.ui and remove the menu bar, main tool bar, and status bar so that we get a clean, empty main window. Right-click on the bar widgets and select **Remove Menu Bar** from the pop-up menu:

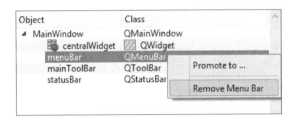

2. Then, open up mainwindow.h and add the following code to include the QPainter header file:

    ```
    #include <QMainWindow>
    #include <QPainter>
    ```

3. Then, declare the paintEvent() event handler below the class destructor:

    ```
    public:
    explicit MainWindow(QWidget *parent = 0);
    ~MainWindow();
    virtual void paintEvent(QPaintEvent *event);
    ```

4. Next, open up mainwindow.cpp and define the paintEvent() event handler:

    ```
    void MainWindow::paintEvent(QPaintEvent *event)
    {
    }
    ```

5. After that, we will add text to the screen using the QPainter class inside the paintEvent() event handler. We set the text font settings before drawing it on the screen at the position (20, 30):

    ```
    QPainter textPainter(this);
    textPainter.setFont(QFont("Times", 14, QFont::Bold));
    textPainter.drawText(QPoint(20, 30), "Testing");
    ```

6. Then, we will draw a straight line that starts from (50, 60) and ends at (100, 100):

```
QPainter linePainter(this);
linePainter.drawLine(QPoint(50, 60), QPoint(100, 100));
```

7. We can also easily draw a rectangle shape by calling the drawRect() function using a QPainter class. This time however, we also apply a background pattern to the shape before drawing it:

```
QPainter rectPainter(this);
rectPainter.setBrush(Qt::BDiagPattern);
rectPainter.drawRect(QRect(40, 120, 80, 30));
```

8. Next, declare a QPen class, set its color to red, and set its drawing style to Qt::DashDotLine. Then, apply the QPen class to QPainter and draw an ellipse shape at (80, 200) with a horizontal radius of 50 and a vertical radius of 20:

```
QPen ellipsePen;
ellipsePen.setColor(Qt::red);
ellipsePen.setStyle(Qt::DashDotLine);

QPainter ellipsePainter(this);
ellipsePainter.setPen(ellipsePen);
ellipsePainter.drawEllipse(QPoint(80, 200), 50, 20);
```

9. We can also use QPainterPath class to define a shape before passing it over to the QPainter class for rendering:

```
QPainterPath rectPath;
rectPath.addRect(QRect(150, 20, 100, 50));

QPainter pathPainter(this);
pathPainter.setPen(QPen(Qt::red, 1, Qt::DashDotLine, Qt::FlatCap,
Qt::MiterJoin));
pathPainter.setBrush(Qt::yellow);
pathPainter.drawPath(rectPath);
```

10. You can also draw any other shapes by using QPainterPath, such as an ellipse:

```
QPainterPath ellipsePath;
ellipsePath.addEllipse(QPoint(200, 120), 50, 20);

QPainter ellipsePathPainter(this);
ellipsePathPainter.setPen(QPen(QColor(79, 106, 25), 5,
Qt::SolidLine, Qt::FlatCap, Qt::MiterJoin));
ellipsePathPainter.setBrush(QColor(122, 163, 39));
ellipsePathPainter.drawPath(ellipsePath);
```

11. `QPainter` can also be used to draw an image file onto the screen. In the following example, we load an image file called `tux.png` and draw it on the screen at position `(100, 150)`:

```
QImage image;
image.load("tux.png");

QPainter imagePainter(this);
imagePainter.drawImage(QPoint(100, 150), image);
```

12. The final result should look something like this:

How it works...

If you want to draw something on screen using `QPainter`, basically all you need to do is tell it what type of graphics it should be drawing (text, vector shape, image, polygon, and so on) with its position and size.

QPen determines what the outline of the graphic should look like, such as its color, line width, line style (solid, dashed, dotted, and so on), cap style, join style, and so on.

On the other hand, `QBrush` sets the style of the background of the graphics, such as the background color, pattern (solid color, gradient, dense brush, crossing diagonal lines, and so on) and pixmap.

The options for the graphics should be set before calling the draw function (`drawLine()`, `drawRect()`, `drawEllipse()`, and so on).

If your graphics do not appear on screen and you see warnings such as `QPainter::setPen: Painter not active` and `QPainter::setBrush: Painter not active` appearing on the application output window in Qt Creator, it means that the `QPainter` class is not currently active and your program will not trigger its paint event. To solve this problem, set the main window as the parent of the `QPainter` class. Usually, if you're writing code in the `mainwindow.cpp` file, all you need to do is to put `this` in the bracket when initializing `QPainter`. For example:

```
QPainter linePainter(this);
```

`QImage` can load images from both the computer directories and from the program resources.

There's more...

Think of `QPainter` as a robot with a pen and an empty canvas. You just have to tell the robot what type of shape it should be drawing and its location on the canvas, then the robot will do its job based on your description. To make your life easier, the `QPainter` class also provides numerous functions such as `drawArc()`, `drawEllipse()`, `drawLine()`, `drawRect()`, `drawPie()`, and so on that allow you to easily render a predefined shape.

In Qt, all the widget classes (including the main window) have an event handler called `QWidget::paintEvent()`. This event handler will be triggered whenever the operating system thinks that the main window should re-draw its widgets. Many things can lead to that decision, such as the main window being scaled, a widget changing its state (that is, a button being pressed), or functions such as `repaint()` or `update()` being invoked manually in the code. Different operating system may behave differently when it comes to deciding whether or not to trigger the update event on the same set of conditions. If you're making a program that requires continuous and consistent graphical updates, call `repaint()` or `update()` manually with a timer.

Exporting shapes to SVG files

Scalable Vector Graphics (**SVG**) is an XML-based language for describing two-dimensional vector graphics. Qt provides classes for saving vector shapes into an SVG file. This feature can be used to create a simple vector graphics editor similar to Adobe Illustrator and Inkscape.

In the next example, we will continue using the same project file from the previous example.

How to do it...

Let's learn how to create a simple program that displays SVG graphics on screen:

1. First of all, let's create a menu bar by right-clicking the main window widget on the hierarchy window and selecting **Create Menu Bar** option from the pop-up menu. After that, add a **File** option to the menu bar and a **Save as SVG** action underneath it:

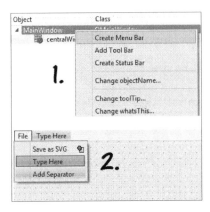

2. After that, you will see an item called `actionSave_as_SVG` in the **Action Editor** window at the bottom of the Qt Creator window. Right-click on the item and choose **Go to slot...** from the pop-up menu. A window will now appear, which carries a list of slots available for the particular action. Choose the default signal called `triggered()` and click the **OK** button:

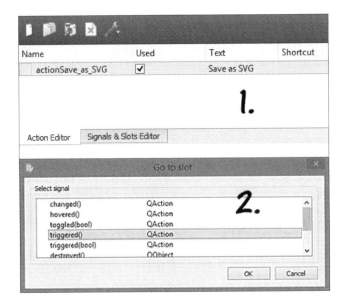

3. Once you have clicked the **OK** button, Qt Creator will switch over to the script editor. You will realize that a slot called `on_actionSave_as_SVG_triggered()` has been automatically added to your main window class. At the bottom of your `mainwindow.h`, you will see something like this:

```
void MainWindow::on_actionSave_as_SVG_triggered()
{
}
```

The preceding function will be called when you clicked on the **Save as SVG** option from the menu bar. We will write our code within this function to save all the vector graphics into an SVG file.

4. To do that, we need to first of all include a class header called `QSvgGenerator` at the top of our source file. This header is very important as it's required for generating SVG files. Then, we also need to include another class header called `QFileDialog`, which will be used to open the save dialog:

```
#include <QtSvg/QSvgGenerator>
#include <QFileDialog>
```

5. We also need to add the SVG module to our project file, like so:

```
QT += core gui svg
```

6. Then, create a new function called `paintAll()` within `mainwindow.h`, like so:

```
public:
    explicit MainWindow(QWidget *parent = 0);
    ~MainWindow();

    virtual void paintEvent(QPaintEvent *event);
    void paintAll(QSvgGenerator *generator = 0);
```

7. After that, in `mainwindow.cpp`, move all the code from `paintEvent()` to the `paintAll()` function. Then, replace all the individual `QPainter` objects with a single, unified `QPainter` for drawing all the graphics. Also, call the `begin()` function before drawing anything and call the `end()` function after finishing drawing. The code should look like this:

```
void MainWindow::paintAll(QSvgGenerator *generator)
{
    QPainter painter;

    if (engine)
        painter.begin(engine);
    else
        painter.begin(this);
```

generator   *errata* (handwritten annotations: `generator` pointing to `engine`)

```
painter.setFont(QFont("Times", 14, QFont::Bold));
painter.drawText(QPoint(20, 30), "Testing");

painter.drawLine(QPoint(50, 60), QPoint(100, 100));

painter.setBrush(Qt::BDiagPattern);
painter.drawRect(QRect(40, 120, 80, 30));

QPen ellipsePen;
ellipsePen.setColor(Qt::red);
ellipsePen.setStyle(Qt::DashDotLine);

painter.setPen(ellipsePen);
painter.drawEllipse(QPoint(80, 200), 50, 20);

QPainterPath rectPath;
rectPath.addRect(QRect(150, 20, 100, 50));

painter.setPen(QPen(Qt::red, 1, Qt::DashDotLine, Qt::FlatCap,
    Qt::MiterJoin));
painter.setBrush(Qt::yellow);
painter.drawPath(rectPath);

QPainterPath ellipsePath;
ellipsePath.addEllipse(QPoint(200, 120), 50, 20);

painter.setPen(QPen(QColor(79, 106, 25), 5, Qt::SolidLine,
    Qt::FlatCap, Qt::MiterJoin));
painter.setBrush(QColor(122, 163, 39));
painter.drawPath(ellipsePath);

QImage image;
image.load("tux.png");

painter.drawImage(QPoint(100, 150), image);

painter.end();
}
```

8. Since we have moved all the code from `paintEvent()` to `paintAll()`, we shall now call the `paintAll()` function inside `paintEvent()`, like so:

```
void MainWindow::paintEvent(QPaintEvent *event)
{
    paintAll();
}
```

9. Then, we will write the code for exporting the graphics to an SVG file. The code will be written inside the slot function called `on_actionSave_as_SVG_triggered()`, which was generated by Qt. We start by calling the save file dialog and obtain the directory path with the desired file name from the user:

```
void MainWindow::on_actionSave_as_SVG_triggered()
{
    QString filePath = QFileDialog::getSaveFileName(this, "Save
        SVG", "", "SVG files (*.svg)");

    if (filePath == "")
        return;
}
```

10. After that, create a `QSvgGenerator` object and save the graphics to an SVG file by passing the `QSvgGenerator` object to the `paintAll()` function:

```
void MainWindow::on_actionSave_as_SVG_triggered()
{
    QString filePath = QFileDialog::getSaveFileName(this, "Save
        SVG", "", "SVG files (*.svg)");

    if (filePath == "")
        return;

    QSvgGenerator generator;
    generator.setFileName(filePath);
    generator.setSize(QSize(this->width(), this->height()));
    generator.setViewBox(QRect(0, 0, this->width(),
        this->height()));
    generator.setTitle("SVG Example");
    generator.setDescription("This SVG file is generated by Qt.");

    paintAll(&generator);
}
```

11. Compile and run the program now and you should be able to export the graphics by going to **File | Save as SVG**:

How it works...

By default, QPainter will use the paint engine from its parent object to draw the graphics assigned to it. If you don't assign any parent to QPainter, you can manually assign a paint engine to it, which is what we have done in this example.

The reason why we placed the code into paintAll() is because we want to reuse the same code for two different purposes: for displaying the graphics on the window and exporting the graphics to an SVG file. Notice the default value of the generator variable in the paintAll() function is set to 0, which means no QSvgGenerator object is required to run the function unless specified. Later on, in the paintAll() function, we check whether the generator object exists. If it does exist, use it as the paint engine for the painter, like so:

```
if (engine)
    painter.begin(engine);
else
    painter.begin(this);
```

→ generator *errata*

Otherwise, pass the main window to the `begin()` function (since we're writing the code in `mainwindow.cpp`, we can directly use `this` to refer to main window's pointer) so that it will use the paint engine of the main window itself, which means the graphics will be drawn onto the surface of the main window.

In this example, it's required to use a single `QPainter` object to save the graphics into the SVG file. If you use multiple `QPainter` objects, the resulting SVG file will contain multiple XML header definitions and thus the file will be deemed to be invalid by any graphics editor software out there.

`QFileDialog::getSaveFileName()` will open up the native save file dialog for the user to choose the save directory and set a desired file name. Once the user is done with that, the full path will be returned as a string and we will be able to pass that information to the `QSvgGenerator` object to export the graphics.

Notice that in the previous screenshot, the penguin in the SVG file has been cropped. This is because the canvas size of the SVG was set to follow the size of the main window. To help the poor penguin getting its body back, scale the window bigger before exporting the SVG file.

There's more...

Scalable Vector Graphics (**SVG**) defines the graphics in XML format. Since it is vector graphics, SVG graphics do not lose any quality if they are zoomed or resized.

SVG allows three types of graphic object: vector graphics, raster graphics, and text. Graphical objects, including PNG and JPEG raster images, can be grouped, styled, transformed, and composited into previously rendered objects.

You can check out the full specification of SVG graphics at `https://www.w3.org/TR/SVG`.

Coordinate transformation

In this example, we will learn how to use coordinate transformation and a timer to create a real-time clock display.

How to do it...

To create our first graphical clock display, let's follow these steps:

1. First, create a new **Qt Widgets Application** project. Then, open up `mainwindow.ui` and remove the menu bar, tool bar, and status bar.

2. After that, open up `mainwindow.h` and include the following headers:

```
#include <QTime>
#include <QTimer>
#include <QPainter>
```

3. Then, declare the `paintEvent()` function, like so:

```
public:
    explicit MainWindow(QWidget *parent = 0);
    ~MainWindow();

    virtual void paintEvent(QPaintEvent *event);
```

4. In `mainwindow.cpp`, create three arrays to store the shapes of the hour hand, minute hand, and second hand, where each of the arrays contains three sets of coordinates:

```
void MainWindow::paintEvent(QPaintEvent *event)
{
    static const QPoint hourHand[3] =
    {
        QPoint(4, 4),
        QPoint(-4, 4),
        QPoint(0, -40)
    };

    static const QPoint minuteHand[3] =
    {
        QPoint(4, 4),
        QPoint(-4, 4),
        QPoint(0, -70)
    };

    static const QPoint secondHand[3] =
    {
        QPoint(2, 2),
        QPoint(-2, 2),
        QPoint(0, -90)
    };
}
```

5. After that, add the following code below the arrays to create the painter and move it to the center of the main window. Also, we adjust the size of the painter so that it fits nicely in the main window, even when the window is being resized:

```
int side = qMin(width(), height());
```

```
QPainter painter(this);
painter.setRenderHint(QPainter::Antialiasing);
painter.translate(width() / 2, height() / 2);
painter.scale(side / 250.0, side / 250.0);
```

6. Once you are done with that, we will start drawing the dials by using a `for` loop. Each dial is rotated by an increment of 6 degrees, so 60 dials would complete a full circle. Also, the dial at every 5 minutes will look slightly longer:

```
for (int i = 0; i < 60; ++i)
{
  if ((i % 5) != 0)
    painter.drawLine(92, 0, 96, 0);
  else
    painter.drawLine(86, 0, 96, 0);
  painter.rotate(6.0);
}
```

7. Then, we proceed with drawing the hands of the clock. Each hand's rotation is calculated according to the current time and its respective unit over 360 degrees:

```
QTime time = QTime::currentTime();

// Draw hour hand
painter.save();
painter.rotate((time.hour() * 360) / 12);
painter.setPen(Qt::NoPen);
painter.setBrush(Qt::black);
painter.drawConvexPolygon(hourHand, 3);
painter.restore();

// Draw minute hand
painter.save();
painter.rotate((time.minute() * 360) / 60);
painter.setPen(Qt::NoPen);
painter.setBrush(Qt::black);
painter.drawConvexPolygon(minuteHand, 3);
painter.restore();

// Draw second hand
painter.save();
painter.rotate((time.second() * 360) / 60);
painter.setPen(Qt::NoPen);
painter.setBrush(Qt::black);
painter.drawConvexPolygon(secondHand, 3);
painter.restore();
```

8. Last but not least, create a timer to refresh the graphics every second so that the program will work like a real clock!

```
MainWindow::MainWindow(QWidget *parent) :
    QMainWindow(parent), ui(new Ui::MainWindow)
{
    ui->setupUi(this);

    QTimer* timer = new QTimer(this);
    timer->start(1000);
    connect(timer, SIGNAL(timeout()), this, SLOT(update()));
}
```

9. Compile and run the program now and you should see something like this:

How it works...

Each of the arrays contain three `QPoint` data, which form the shape of an elongated triangle. The arrays are then passed to the painter and rendered as a convex polygon using the `drawConvexPolygon()` function.

Before drawing each of the clock hands, we use `painter.save()` to save the state of the `QPainter` object and then proceed with drawing the hand using coordinate transformation. Once we're done with the drawing, we restore the painter to its previous state by calling `painter.restore()`. This function will undo all the transformations before `painter.restore()` so that the next clock hand will not inherit the transformations of the previous one. Without using `painter.save()` and `painter.restore()`, we will have to manually change back the position, rotation, and scale before drawing the next hand.

A good example of not using `painter.save()` and `painter.restore()` is when drawing the dials. Since each dial's rotation is an increment of 6 degrees from the previous one, we don't need to save the painter's state at all. We just have to call `painter.rotate(6.0)` in a loop and each dial will inherit the previous dial's rotation. We also use a modulus operator (`%`) to check whether the unit represented by the dial can be divided by 5. If it can, then we draw it slightly longer.

Without using a timer to constantly call the `update()` slot, the clock will not function properly. This is because `paintEvent()` will not be called by Qt when there is no change to the state of the parent widget, which in this case is the main window. Therefore, we need to manually tell Qt that we need to refresh the graphics by calling `update()` every second.

We used the `painter.setRenderHint(QPainter::Antialiasing)` function to enable anti-aliasing when rendering the clock. Without anti-aliasing, the graphics will look very jagged and pixelated:

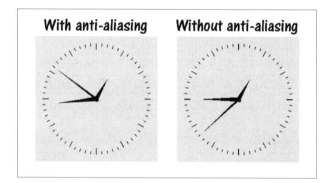

There's more...

The `QPainter` class uses the coordinate system to determine the position and size of the graphics before rendering them on screen. This information can be altered to make the graphics appear at a different position, rotation, and size. This process of altering the coordinate information of a graphic is what we called coordinate transformation. There are several types of transformation, among them are translation, rotation, scaling and shearing:

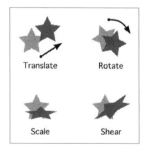

Qt uses a coordinate system that has its origin at the top-left corner, meaning the x values increase to the right and the y values increase downwards. This coordinate system might be different from the coordinate system used by the physical device, such as a computer screen. Qt handles this automatically by using the `QPaintDevice` class, which maps Qt's logical coordinates to the physical coordinates.

`QPainter` provides four transform operations to perform different types of transformation:

- `QPainter::translate()`: Offset the graphic's position by a given set of units
- `QPainter::rotate()`: Rotate the graphics around the origin in a clockwise direction
- `QPainter::scale()`: Offset the graphic's size by a given factor
- `QPainter::shear()`: Twist the graphic's coordinate system around the origin

Displaying images on screen

Qt not only allows us to draw shapes and images on screen, but it also allows us to overlay multiple images on top of each other and combine the pixel information from all the layers using different types of algorithms to create very interesting results. In this example, we will learn how to overlay images on top of each other and apply different composition effects to them.

How to do it...

Let's create a simple demo that shows the effect of different image compositions by following these steps:

1. First, set up a new **Qt Widgets Application** project and remove the menu bar, tool bar, and status bar.

2. Next, add the QPainter class header to `mainwindow.h`:

   ```
   #include <QPainter>
   ```

3. After that, declare the `paintEvent()` virtual function like so:

   ```
   virtual void paintEvent(QPaintEvent* event);
   ```

4. In `mainwindow.cpp`, we will first load several image files using the `QImage` class:

   ```
   void MainWindow::paintEvent(QPaintEvent* event)
   {
     QImage image;
     image.load("checker.png");
   ```

```
    QImage image2;
    image2.load("tux.png");

    QImage image3;
    image3.load("butterfly.png");
}
```

5. Then, create a `QPainter` object and use it to draw two pairs of images, where one image is on top of another:

```
QPainter painter(this);
painter.drawImage(QPoint(10, 10), image);
painter.drawImage(QPoint(10, 10), image2);
painter.drawImage(QPoint(300, 10), image);
painter.drawImage(QPoint(300, 40), image3);
```

6. Compile and run the program now and you should see something like this:

7. Next, we will set the composition mode before drawing each image on screen:

```
QPainter painter(this);

painter.setCompositionMode(QPainter::CompositionMode_Difference);
painter.drawImage(QPoint(10, 10), image);
painter.setCompositionMode(QPainter::CompositionMode_Multiply);
painter.drawImage(QPoint(10, 10), image2);

painter.setCompositionMode(QPainter::CompositionMode_Xor);
painter.drawImage(QPoint(300, 10), image);
painter.setCompositionMode(QPainter::CompositionMode_SoftLight);
painter.drawImage(QPoint(300, 40), image3);
```

8. Compile and run the program again and you will now see something like this:

How it works...

When drawing images with Qt, the sequence of calling the drawImage() function will determine which image is being rendered first and which one is rendered later. This will affect the depth order of the images and yield different outcomes.

In the previous example, we called drawImage() four times to draw four different images on screen. The first drawImage() renders checker.png and the second drawImage() renders tux.png (the penguin). The image that gets rendered later will always appear in front of the others, which is why the penguin is showing in front of the checker box. The same goes for the butterfly and the checker on the right. The reason why you can still see the checker even though the butterfly is rendered in front of it is because the butterfly image is not fully opaque.

Now let's invert the render sequence and see what happens. We will try to render the penguin first, followed by the checker box. The same goes for the other pair of images on the right: the butterfly gets rendered first, followed by the checker box:

To apply a composition effect to the image, we'll have to set the painter's composition mode before drawing the image, by calling the `painter.setCompositionMode()` function. You can pick a desired composition mode from the auto-complete menu by typing `QPainter::CompositionMode`.

In the previous example, we applied `QPainter::CompositionMode_Difference` to the checker box on the left, which inverted its color. Next, we applied `QPainter::CompositionMode_Overlay` to the penguin which makes it blend with the checker and we're able to see both images overlaying each other.

On the right-hand side, we applied `QPainter::CompositionMode_Xor` to the checker, where if differences exist between the source and destination, colors are shown; otherwise, it will be rendered black. Since it's comparing differences with the white background, the non-transparent part of the checker becomes completely black. We also applied `QPainter::CompositionMode_SoftLight` to the butterfly image. This blends the pixels with the background with reduced contrast.

If you want to disable the composition mode you have just set for the previous rendering before proceeding to the next, simply set it back to the default mode, which is `QPainter::CompositionMode_SourceOver`.

There's more...

For example, we can overlay multiple images on top of each other and use Qt's image composition feature to merge them together and calculate the resulting pixels on screen, based on the composition mode we used. This is often used in image editing software such as Photoshop and GIMP to composite image layers.

There are more than 30 types of composition mode available in Qt. Some of the most commonly used modes are:

- **Clear**: The pixels in the destination are set to fully transparent, independent of the source.
- **Source**: The output is the source pixel. This mode is the inverse of `CompositionMode_Destination`.
- **Destination**: The output is the destination pixel. This means that the blending has no effect. This mode is the inverse of `CompositionMode_Source`.
- **Source Over**: Often referred to as alpha blending. The alpha of the source is used to blend the pixel on top of the destination. This is the default mode used by `QPainter`.
- **Destination Over**: The alpha of the destination is used to blend it on top of the source pixels. This mode is the inverse of `CompositionMode_SourceOver`.
- **Source In**: The output is the source, where the alpha is reduced by that of the destination.
- **Destination In**: The output is the destination, where the alpha is reduced by that of the source. This mode is the inverse of `CompositionMode_SourceIn`.
- **Source Out**: The output is the source, where the alpha is reduced by the inverse of the destination.
- **Destination Out**: The output is the destination, where the alpha is reduced by the inverse of the source. This mode is the inverse of `CompositionMode_SourceOut`.
- **Source Atop**: The source pixel is blended on top of the destination, with the alpha of the source pixel reduced by the alpha of the destination pixel.
- **Destination Atop**: The destination pixel is blended on top of the source, with the alpha of the source pixel reduced by the alpha of the destination pixel. This mode is the inverse of `CompositionMode_SourceAtop`.
- **Xor**: This is short for **Exclusive OR**, which is an advanced blending mode that is primarily used for image analysis. The source, whose alpha is reduced by the inverse of the destination alpha, is merged with the destination, whose alpha is reduced by the inverse of the source alpha.

The following image shows the outcome of overlaying two images with different composition modes:

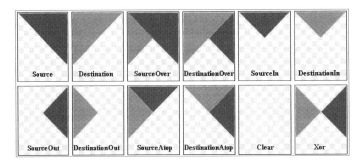

Applying image effects to graphics

Qt provides an easy way to add image effects to any graphics drawn using the `QPainter` class. In this example, we will learn how to apply different images effects, such as drop shadow, blur, colorize, and opacity effects, to a graphic before displaying it on screen.

How to do it...

Let's learn how to apply image effects to text and graphics by following these steps:

1. Create a new **Qt Widgets Application** and remove the menu bar, tool bar, and status bar.

2. Create a new resource file by going to **File | New File or Project** and adding all the images required by the project:

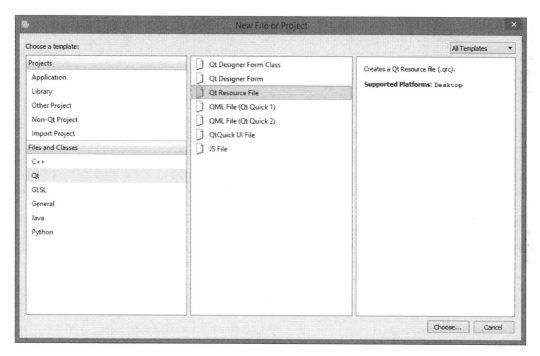

3. Next, open up `mainwindow.ui` and add four labels to the window. Two of the labels will be text and the two others we will load with the images we have just added to the resource file:

4. You may already notice the font sizes are way bigger than the default size. That can be achieved by adding a style sheet to the label widget, for example:

```
font: 26pt "MS Shell Dlg 2";
```

5. After that, open up `mainwindow.cpp` and include the following headers at the top of the source code:

```
#include <QGraphicsBlurEffect>
#include <QGraphicsDropShadowEffect>
#include <QGraphicsColorizeEffect>
#include <QGraphicsOpacityEffect>
```

6. Then, within the constructor of the `MainWindow` class, add the following code to create a drop shadow effect, and apply it to one of the labels:

```
MainWindow::MainWindow(QWidget *parent) :
  QMainWindow(parent), ui(new Ui::MainWindow)
{
  ui->setupUi(this);

  QGraphicsDropShadowEffect* shadow = new
    QGraphicsDropShadowEffect();
  shadow->setXOffset(4);
  shadow->setYOffset(4);
  ui->label->setGraphicsEffect(shadow);
}
```

7. Next, we will create a colorized effect and apply it to one of the images, in this case the butterfly. We also set the effect color to red:

```
QGraphicsColorizeEffect* colorize = new QGraphicsColorizeEffect();
colorize->setColor(QColor(255, 0, 0));
ui->butterfly->setGraphicsEffect(colorize);
```

8. Once we're done with that, create a blur effect and set its radius to `12`. Then, apply the graphics effect to the other label:

```
QGraphicsBlurEffect* blur = new QGraphicsBlurEffect();
blur->setBlurRadius(12);
ui->label2->setGraphicsEffect(blur);
```

9. Lastly, create an alpha effect and apply it to the penguin image. We set the opacity value to `0.2`, which means 20% opacity:

```
QGraphicsOpacityEffect* alpha = new QGraphicsOpacityEffect();
alpha->setOpacity(0.2);
ui->penguin->setGraphicsEffect(alpha);
```

10. Compile and run the program now and you should be able to see something like this:

How it works...

Each of the graphic effects is a class of its own that inherits the `QGraphicsEffect` parent class. You can create your own custom effect by creating a new class that inherits `QGraphicsEffect` and re-implementing some of the functions in it.

Each effect has its own set of variables that are specifically created for it. For example, you can set the color of the colorized effect, but there is no such variable in the blur effect. This is because each effect is vastly different from the others, which is also why it needs to be a class of its own rather than using the same class for all the different effects.

It's only possible to add a single graphics effect to a widget at a time. If you add more than one effect, only the last one will be applied to the widget as it replaces the previous one. Other than that, be aware that if you create a graphics effect, say the drop shadow effect, you can't assign it to two different widgets as it will only get assigned to the last widget you applied it to. If you need to apply the same type of effect to several different widgets, create a few graphics effects of the same type and apply each of them to their respective widgets.

There's more...

Currently Qt supports blur, drop shadow, colorize, and opacity effects. These effects can be used by calling the following classes: QGraphicsBlurEffect, QGraphicsDropShadowEffect, QGraphicsColorizeEffect, and QGraphicsOpacityEffect. All these classes are inherited from the QGraphicsEffect class. You can also create your own custom image effect by creating a subclass of QGrapicsEffect (or any other existing effects) and re-implementing the draw() function.

The graphics effect changes only the bounding rectangle of the source. If you want to increase the margin of the bounding rectangle, re-implement the virtual boundingRectFor() function, and call updateBoundingRect() to notify the framework whenever this rectangle changes.

Creating a basic paint program

Since we have learned so much about the QPainter class and how to use it to display graphics on screen, I guess it's time for us to do something fun so that we can put our knowledge into practice.

In this recipe, we will learn how to make a basic paint program that allows us to draw lines on a canvas with different brush sizes and colors. We will also learn how to use the QImage class and the mouse events in order to construct the paint program.

How to do it...

Let us start our fun project through the following steps:

1. Again, we start by creating a new **Qt Widgets Application** project and removing the tool bar and status bar. We will keep the menu bar this time.

2. After that, set up the menu bar like so:

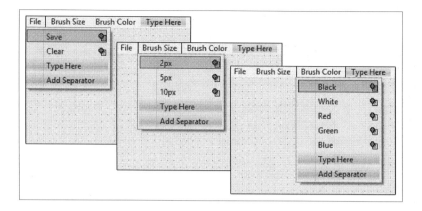

3. We will leave the menu bar as it is for the moment and let's proceed to `mainwindow.h`. First, include the following header files as it's required for the project:

```
#include <QPainter>
#include <QMouseEvent>
#include <QFileDialog>
```

4. Next, declare the variables that we'll be using for this project, like so:

```
private:
Ui::MainWindow *ui;

QImage image;
bool drawing;
QPoint lastPoint;
int brushSize;
QColor brushColor;
```

5. Then, declare the event callback functions, which are inherited from the `QWidget` class. These functions will be triggered by Qt when the respective event happens. We will override these functions and tell Qt what to do when these events get called:

```
public:
    explicit MainWindow(QWidget *parent = 0);
    ~MainWindow();

    virtual void mousePressEvent(QMouseEvent *event);
    virtual void mouseMoveEvent(QMouseEvent *event);
    virtual void mouseReleaseEvent(QMouseEvent *event);
    virtual void paintEvent(QPaintEvent *event);
    virtual void resizeEvent(QResizeEvent *event);
```

6. After that, go to `mainwindow.cpp` and add the following code to the class constructor for setting up some of the variables:

```
MainWindow::MainWindow(QWidget *parent) :
  QMainWindow(parent), ui(new Ui::MainWindow)
{
  ui->setupUi(this);

  image = QImage(this->size(), QImage::Format_RGB32);
  image.fill(Qt::white);

  drawing = false;
  brushColor = Qt::black;
  brushSize = 2;
}
```

7. Next, we will construct the `mousePressEvent()` event and tell Qt what to do when the left mouse button is pressed:

```
void MainWindow::mousePressEvent(QMouseEvent *event)
{
  if (event->button() == Qt::LeftButton)
  {
    drawing = true;
    lastPoint = event->pos();
  }
}
```

8. Then, we will construct the `mouseMoveEvent()` event and tell Qt what to do when the mouse is moving. In this case, we want to draw the lines on the canvas if the left mouse button is being held:

```
void MainWindow::mouseMoveEvent(QMouseEvent *event)
{
  if ((event->buttons() & Qt::LeftButton) && drawing)
  {
    QPainter painter(&image);
    painter.setPen(QPen(brushColor, brushSize, Qt::SolidLine,
      Qt::RoundCap, Qt::RoundJoin));
    painter.drawLine(lastPoint, event->pos());

    lastPoint = event->pos();
    this->update();
  }
}
```

9. After that, we will also construct the `mouseReleaseEvent()` event, which will be triggered when the mouse button is released:

```
void MainWindow::mouseReleaseEvent(QMouseEvent *event)
{
  if (event->button() == Qt::LeftButton)
  {
    drawing = false;
  }
}
```

10. Once you're done with that, we will proceed to the `paintEvent()` event, which is surprisingly simple compared to the other examples we have seen in previous sections:

```
void MainWindow::paintEvent(QPaintEvent *event)
{
  QPainter canvasPainter(this);
  canvasPainter.drawImage(this->rect(), image, image.rect());
}
```

11. Remember we have a menu bar sitting around doing nothing? Let's right-click on each of the actions below the GUI editor and select **Go to slot...** in the pop-up menu. We want to tell Qt what to do when each of these options on the menu bar is selected:

12. Then, select the default slot called `triggered()` and press the **OK** button. Qt will automatically generate a new slot function in both your `mainwindow.h` and `mainwindow.cpp`. Once you are done with all the actions, you should see something like this in your `mainwindow.h`:

```
private slots:
    void on_actionSave_triggered();
    void on_actionClear_triggered();
    void on_action2px_triggered();
    void on_action5px_triggered();
    void on_action10px_triggered();
    void on_actionBlack_triggered();
    void on_actionWhite_triggered();
    void on_actionRed_triggered();
    void on_actionGreen_triggered();
    void on_actionBlue_triggered();
```

13. Next, we will tell Qt what to do when each of these slots is triggered:

```
void MainWindow::on_actionSave_triggered()
{
    QString filePath = QFileDialog::getSaveFileName(this,
        "Save Image", "", "PNG (*.png);;JPEG (*.jpg *.jpeg);;All files
        (*.*)");

    if (filePath == "")
        return;

    image.save(filePath);
}
void MainWindow::on_actionClear_triggered()
{
    image.fill(Qt::white);
    this->update();
}
void MainWindow::on_action2px_triggered()
{
    brushSize = 2;
}
void MainWindow::on_action5px_triggered()
{
    brushSize = 5;
}
void MainWindow::on_action10px_triggered()
{
    brushSize = 10;
```

```
}
void MainWindow::on_actionBlack_triggered()
{
  brushColor = Qt::black;
}

void MainWindow::on_actionWhite_triggered()
{
  brushColor = Qt::white;
}
void MainWindow::on_actionRed_triggered()
{
  brushColor = Qt::red;
}
void MainWindow::on_actionGreen_triggered()
{
  brushColor = Qt::green;
}
void MainWindow::on_actionBlue_triggered()
{
  brushColor = Qt::blue;
}
```

14. If we compile and run the program now, we will get a simple but usable paint program:

How it works...

In this example, we created a `QImage` widget when the program started. This widget acts as the canvas and it will follow the size of the window whenever the window gets resized.

In order to draw something on the canvas, we will need to use the mouse events provided by Qt. These events will tell us the position of the cursor and we will be able to use this information to change the pixels on the canvas.

We use a Boolean variable called `drawing` to let the program know whether it should start drawing when a mouse button is pressed. In this case, when the left mouse button is pressed, the variable `drawing` will be set to `true`. We also save the current cursor position to the `lastPoint` variable when the left mouse button is pressed, so that Qt will know where it should start drawing.

When the mouse moves, the `mouseMoveEvent()` event will be triggered by Qt. This is where we need to check whether the `drawing` variable is set to `true`. If it is, then `QPainter` can start drawing the lines onto the `QImage` widget based on the brush settings that we provide.

The brush settings consist of the brush color as well as the brush size. These settings are being saved as variables and can be altered by selecting a different setting from the menu bar.

Please remember to call the `update()` function when the user is drawing on the canvas. Otherwise, the canvas will remain empty even though we have changed the pixel information of the canvas. We also have to call the `update()` function when we select **File | Clear** from the menu bar to reset our canvas.

In this example, we use `QImage::save()` to save the image file, which is very easy and straightforward. We use the file dialog to let the user decide where to save the image and its desired file name. Then, we pass the information to `QImage` and it will do the rest by itself. If we don't specify the file format to the `QImage::save()` function, `QImage` will try to figure it out by looking at the extension of the desired file name.

2D canvas in QML

In all the previous examples of this chapter, we have discussed the methods and techniques used to render 2D graphics with Qt's C++ API. However, we have yet to learn how to achieve similar results using the powerful QML script.

How to do it...

In this project, we'll be do something quite different:

1. As usual, the first step we should do is to create a new project by going to **File | New File or Project** and selecting **Qt Quick Application** as the project template.

2. Once you are done creating the new project, open up `qml.qrc` from the `Resource` folder in the project pane by right-clicking on it and selecting **Open in Editor**. Then, remove `MainForm.ui.qml` from your project's resources, as we don't need it for this project:

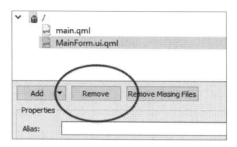

3. Next, open up `main.qml`, which is listed under `qml.rc` in the project pane. After that, remove the entire section that references `MainForm`. Now what is left is only the `Window` object in `main.qml`. After that, set an ID for the window and adjust its width and height to higher values, like so:

```
import QtQuick 2.5
import QtQuick.Window 2.2

Window
{
    id: myWindow
    visible: true
    width: 540
    height: 380
}
```

4. Then, add a `Canvas` object under `myWindow` and call it `myCanvas`. After that, we make its width and height the same as `myWindow`:

```
Window
{
    id: myWindow
    visible: true
    width: 540
    height: 380
```

```
        Canvas
        {
          id: myCanvas
          width: myWindow.width
          height: myWindow.height
        }
    }
```

5. Next, we define what will happen when the `onPaint` event is triggered; in this case, we will draw a cross on the window:

```
Canvas
{
  id: myCanvas
  width: myWindow.width
  height: myWindow.height

  onPaint:
  {
    var context = getContext('2d')
    context.fillStyle = 'white'
    context.fillRect(0, 0, width, height)
    context.lineWidth = 2
    context.strokeStyle = 'black'

    // Draw cross
    context.beginPath()
    context.moveTo(50, 50)
    context.lineTo(100, 100)
    context.closePath()
    context.stroke()

    context.beginPath()
    context.moveTo(100, 50)
    context.lineTo(50, 100)
    context.closePath()
    context.stroke()
  }
}
```

6. After that, we add the following code to draw a tick besides the cross:

```
// Draw tick
context.beginPath()
context.moveTo(150, 90)
context.lineTo(158, 100)
```

```
context.closePath()
context.stroke()

context.beginPath()
context.moveTo(180, 100)
context.lineTo(210, 50)
context.closePath()
context.stroke()
```

7. Then, draw a triangle shape by adding the following code:

```
// Draw triangle
context.lineWidth = 4
context.strokeStyle = "red"
context.fillStyle = "salmon"

context.beginPath()
context.moveTo(50,150)
context.lineTo(150,150)
context.lineTo(50,250)
context.closePath()
context.fill()
context.stroke()
```

8. After that, draw a half circle and a full circle with the following code:

```
// Draw circle
context.lineWidth = 4
context.strokeStyle = "blue"
context.fillStyle = "steelblue"

var pi = 3.141592653589793

context.beginPath()
context.arc(220, 200, 60, 0, pi, true)
context.closePath()
context.fill()
context.stroke()

context.beginPath()
context.arc(220, 280, 60, 0, 2 * pi, true)
context.closePath()
context.fill()
context.stroke()
```

9. Finally, we draw a 2D image from a file:

```
// Draw image
context.drawImage("tux.png", 280, 10, 256, 297)
```

10. However, the preceding code alone will not successfully render an image on screen because you must also load the image file beforehand. Add the following code within the `Canvas` object to ask QML to load the image file when the program is started, then call the `requestPaint()` signal when the image is loaded so that the `onPaint()` event slot will be triggered:

```
Component.onCompleted:
{
   loadImage("tux.png")
}

onImageLoaded:requestPaint();
onPaint:
{
   // The code we added previously
}
```

11. Build and run the program now and you should get the following result:

4

OpenGL Implementation

In this chapter, we will cover the following recipes:

- ▶ Setting up OpenGL in Qt
- ▶ Hello World!
- ▶ Rendering 2D shapes
- ▶ Rendering 3D shapes
- ▶ Texturing in OpenGL
- ▶ Lighting and texture filter in OpenGL
- ▶ Moving an object using keyboard controls
- ▶ 3D Canvas in QML

Introduction

In this chapter, we will learn how to use **Open Graphics Library** (**OpenGL**), a powerful rendering **Application Program Interface** (**API**), and combine it with Qt. OpenGL is a cross-language, cross platform API for drawing 2D and 3D graphics on screen through the **Graphics Processing Unit** (**GPU**) within our computer's graphics chip. In this chapter, we will be learning OpenGL 2.x instead of 3.x, because the fixed-function pipeline is easier for beginners to grasp compared to the newer programmable pipeline. Qt supports both versions, so there should be no problem switching over to OpenGL 3.x and above once you have learned the basic concepts of OpenGL rendering.

Setting up OpenGL in Qt

In this recipe, we will learn how to set up OpenGL in Qt.

How to do it...

1. First, let's create a new Qt widgets application by going to **File | New File or Project**.

2. Next, we will remove the `mainwindow.ui` file because we are not going to use it in this example. Right-click on the `mainwindow.ui` file and select **Remove File** from the drop-down menu. Then, a message box will appear and ask for your confirmation. Tick **Delete file permanently** and press the **OK** button.

3. After that, open up your project file (`.pro`) and add the OpenGL module to your project by adding an `opengl` keyword behind `QT +=`, like so:

   ```
   QT += core gui opengl
   ```

4. You also need to add another line in your project file so that it will load both the OpenGL and **GLu** (**OpenGL Utilities**) libraries during startup. Without these two libraries, you program will not be able to run:

   ```
   LIBS += -lopengl32 -lglu32
   ```

5. Then, open up `mainwindow.h` and remove several things from it:

   ```
   #ifndef MAINWINDOW_H
   #define MAINWINDOW_H
   #include <QMainWindow>

   namespace Ui {
     class MainWindow;
   }
   class MainWindow : public QMainWindow
   {
     Q_OBJECT
     public:
       explicit MainWindow(QWidget *parent = 0);
       ~MainWindow();
     private:
       Ui::MainWindow *ui;
   };
   #endif // MAINWINDOW_H
   ```

6. Next, add the following code to your `mainwindow.h`:

   ```
   #ifndef MAINWINDOW_H
   #define MAINWINDOW_H
   ```

```
#include <QOpenGLWindow>

class MainWindow : public QOpenGLWindow
{
  Q_OBJECT
  public:
    explicit MainWindow(QWidget *parent = 0);
    ~MainWindow();

  protected:
    virtual void initializeGL();
    virtual void resizeGL(int w, int h);
    virtual void paintGL();
    void paintEvent(QPaintEvent *event);
    void resizeEvent(QResizeEvent *event);
};

#endif // MAINWINDOW_H
```

7. Once you have done that, we will proceed to the source file, which is `mainwindow.cpp`. Functions that we have just added to the header, such as `initializeGL()`, `resizeGL()`, and so on, can be left empty for now; we will only use these in the next section:

```
#include "mainwindow.h"
#include "ui_mainwindow.h"

MainWindow::MainWindow(QWidget *parent) :
  QMainWindow(parent),
  ui(new Ui::MainWindow)
MainWindow::MainWindow(QWidget *parent)
{
  ui->setupUi(this);
  setSurfaceType(QWindow::OpenGLSurface);
}

MainWindow::~MainWindow()
{
  delete ui;
}
void MainWindow::initializeGL()
{
  void MainWindow::resizeGL(int w, int h)
  {
  }
```

```
void MainWindow::paintGL()
{
}
void MainWindow::paintEvent(QPaintEvent *event)
{
}
void MainWindow::resizeEvent(QResizeEvent *event)
{
}
```

8. Lastly, set a title for the main window and resize it to 640x480 by adding the following code to your `main.cpp` file:

```
#include "mainwindow.h"
#include <QApplication>

int main(int argc, char *argv[])
{
  QApplication a(argc, argv);
  MainWindow w;
  w.setTitle("OpenGL Hello World!");
  w.resize(640, 480);
  w.show();
  return a.exec();
}
```

9. If you compile and run the project now, you will see an empty window with a black background. Don't worry about it, your program is now running on OpenGL!

How it works...

The OpenGL module must be added to the project file (`.pro`) in order to access header files that are related to OpenGL, such as QtOpenGL, QOpenGLFunctions, and so on. We used the `QOpenGLWindow` class instead of `QMainWindow` for the main window because it's designed to easily create windows that perform OpenGL rendering, and it offers better performance compared to QOpenGLWidget due to the fact that it has no dependencies in its widget module. We must call `setSurfaceType(QWindow::OpenGLSurface)` to tell Qt we prefer to use OpenGL to render the images to screen, instead of QPainter. The `QOpenGLWindow` class provides several virtual functions (`initializeGL()`, `resizeGL()`, `paintGL()`, and so on) for us to conveniently set up OpenGL and perform graphics rendering.

There's more...

OpenGL is a cross-language, cross-platform API for drawing 2D and 3D graphics on screen through the **Graphics Processing Unit (GPU)** within our computer's graphics chip.

Computer graphics technology has been evolving rapidly over the years, so rapidly that the software industry can hardly keep up with its pace. In 2008, Khronos Group, the company that maintains and develops OpenGL, announced the release of the OpenGL 3.0 specification, which created a huge uproar and controversy throughout the industry. That was mainly because OpenGL 3.0 was supposed to deprecate the entire fixed-function pipeline from the OpenGL API, and it was simply an impossible task for the big players to make the sudden switch overnight from a fixed-function pipeline to a programmable pipeline. This resulted in two different major versions of OpenGL being maintained concurrently by the Khronos Group, namely OpenGL 2.x and 3.x.

In this chapter, we will be learning OpenGL 2.x instead of 3.x, because the fixed-function pipeline is easier for beginners to grasp than the programmable pipeline. It's very straightforward and less confusing for learning the basics of computer graphics programming. Qt supports both versions, so there should be no problem switching over to OpenGL 3.x (and above) once you have learned the basic concepts of OpenGL rendering.

Qt uses OpenGL internally whenever it sees fit. Moreover, the new Qt Quick 2 renderer is based on OpenGL and is now a core part of Qt's graphical offering. That makes OpenGL more compatible with Qt than any other graphics APIs, such as DirectX.

Hello world!

In this recipe, we will learn about the pipeline of OpenGL and how to render a simple shape to the window. We will continue from the example project used in the previous recipe.

How to do it...

1. First of all, go to `mainwindow.h` and add the following headers at the top of the source code:

```
#include <QSurfaceFormat>
#include <QOpenGLFunctions>
#include <QtOpenGL>
#include <GL/glu.h>
```

2. Next, declare two private variables in `mainwindow.h`:

```
private:
    QOpenGLContext* context;
    QOpenGLFunctions* openGLFunctions;
```

3. After that, move over to `mainwindow.cpp` and set the surface format to compatibility profile. We also set the OpenGL version to 2.1 and create the OpenGL context using the format we just declared. Then, use the context we just created to access the OpenGL functions that are relevant only to the OpenGL version we have just set, by calling `context->functions()`:

```
MainWindow::MainWindow(QWidget *parent)
{
    setSurfaceType(QWindow::OpenGLSurface);
    QSurfaceFormat format;
    format.setProfile(QSurfaceFormat::CompatibilityProfile);
    format.setVersion(2, 1); // OpenGL 2.1
    setFormat(format);

    context = new QOpenGLContext;
    context->setFormat(format);
    context->create();
    context->makeCurrent(this);

    openGLFunctions = context->functions();
}
```

4. Next, we will start adding some code to the `paintGL()` function:

```
void MainWindow::paintGL()
{
    // Initialize clear color (cornflower blue)
    glClearColor(0.39f, 0.58f, 0.93f, 1.f);

    // Clear color buffer
    glClear(GL_COLOR_BUFFER_BIT);
```

```
// Render quad
glBegin(GL_QUADS);
  glVertex2f(-0.5f, -0.5f);
  glVertex2f(0.5f, -0.5f);
  glVertex2f(0.5f, 0.5f);
  glVertex2f(-0.5f, 0.5f);
glEnd();

glFlush();
}
```

5. Nothing will appear on the screen yet until we call `paintGL()` in the `paintEvent()` function:

```
void MainWindow::paintEvent(QPaintEvent *event)
{
  paintGL();
}
```

6. If you compile and run the project now, you should be able to see a white rectangle being drawn in front of a blue background:

How it works...

We must set the OpenGL version to 2.1 and the surface format to compatibility profile so that we can access the fixed-function pipeline, which no longer exists in the newer version. Alternatively, you can set the surface format to `QSurfaceFormat::CoreProfile` if you want to use OpenGL 3.x and above.

We called `glClearColor()` and `glClear(GL_COLOR_BUFFER_BIT)` to remove the previous `render buffer` (or in layman's terms, the previous frame) and fill the entire canvas with the color we provided. We will repeat this step after an image has been rendered so that it clears the entire screen before we proceed to the next frame. We called `glBegin(GL_QUAD)` to tell OpenGL we are about to draw a quad on the screen. After that, we provided the positions of all the vertices (or points) to OpenGL so that it will know how the quad should be positioned on the screen by calling `glVertex2f()` four times, because a quad can only be constructed by connecting four different points. Then, we called `glEnd()` to inform OpenGL that we are done with the quad.

Always call `glFlush()` once you are done drawing images on screen so that OpenGL clears away all the unwanted information from the memory to give space to the next drawing.

Lastly, we must call `paintGL()` in the `paintEvent()` function, or else nothing will be drawn on the screen. Just like what we have learned in the previous chapters, all drawings happen within the `paintEvent()` function, and it will only be called by Qt when it thinks it's necessary to refresh the screen. To force Qt to update the screen, call `update()` manually.

Rendering 2D shapes

Since we have already learned how to draw our first rectangle on the screen, we will further enhance it in this section. We will take the previous example and continue from there.

How to do it...

1. First, go to the `paintGL()` function in `mainwindow.cpp` and replace the quad in the previous example with new code. This time, we draw a quad together with a triangle:

```cpp
void MainWindow::paintGL()
{
    // Initialize clear color (cornflower blue)
    glClearColor(0.39f, 0.58f, 0.93f, 1.f);

    // Clear color buffer
    glClear(GL_COLOR_BUFFER_BIT);
```

```
glBegin(GL_QUADS);
glVertex2f(-0.5f, -0.5f);
glVertex2f(0.5f, -0.5f);
glVertex2f(0.5f, 0.5f);
glVertex2f(-0.5f, 0.5f);
glEnd();

glBegin(GL_QUADS);
    glColor3f(1.f, 0.f, 0.f); glVertex2f(-0.8f, -0.8f);
    glColor3f(1.f, 1.f, 0.f); glVertex2f(0.3f, -0.8f);
    glColor3f(0.f, 1.f, 0.f); glVertex2f(0.3f, 0.3f);
    glColor3f(0.f, 0.f, 1.f); glVertex2f(-0.8f, 0.3f);
glEnd();

glBegin(GL_TRIANGLES);
    glColor3f(1.f, 0.f, 0.f); glVertex2f(-0.4f, -0.4f);
    glColor3f(0.f, 1.f, 0.f); glVertex2f(0.8f, -0.1f);
    glColor3f(0.f, 0.f, 1.f); glVertex2f(-0.1f, 0.8f);
glEnd();

glFlush();
}
```

2. Next, in the `resizeGL()` function, add the following code to adjust the viewport and orthographic view so that the rendered image correctly follows the window's aspect ratio:

```
void MainWindow::resizeGL(int w, int h)
{
    // Initialize Projection Matrix
    glMatrixMode(GL_PROJECTION);
    glLoadIdentity();

    glViewport(0, 0, w, h);

    qreal aspectRatio = qreal(w) / qreal(h);
    glOrtho(-1 * aspectRatio, 1 * aspectRatio, -1, 1, 1, -1);
}
```

3. Then, in the `resizeEvent()` function, call the `resize()` function and force the main window to refresh the screen:

```
void MainWindow::resizeEvent(QResizeEvent *event)
{
    resizeGL(this->width(), this->height());
    this->update();
}
```

4. After that, in the `initializeGL()` function, we call `resizeGL()` once so that the aspect ratio of the first rendered image is correct (before any window resize event is triggered):

```
void MainWindow::initializeGL()
{
    resizeGL(this->width(), this->height());
}
```

5. Once you're done with that, compile and run the program. You should see something like this:

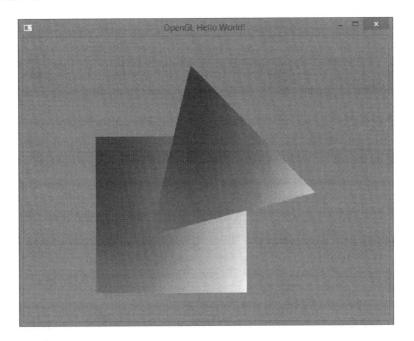

How it works...

The geometric primitive types supported by OpenGL are points, lines, linestrips, line loops, polygons, quads, quad strips, triangles, triangle strips, and triangle fans. In this example, we drew a quad and a triangle, where each of the shapes is provided with a set of vertices and colors so that OpenGL knows how the shapes should be rendered. The rainbow color is created by giving a different color to each of the vertices. OpenGL will automatically interpolate the colors between each vertex and display it onscreen. The shape that gets rendered later will always appear in front of other shapes. In this case, the triangle is being rendered later and hence it appears in front of the rectangle.

We need to calculate the aspect ratio of the main window every time it's resized, so that the rendered image will not be stretched and result in an odd appearance. Always reset the projection matrix by calling `glMatrixMode()` and `glLoadIdentity()` before calling `glViewport()` and `glOrtho()` so that the shapes are being rendered correctly when resizing the main window. Without resetting the projection matrix, we will be using the matrices from the previous frame and hence producing the wrong projection.

 Remember to call `update()` when the window is being resized, otherwise the screen will not be updated.

Render 3D shapes

We have learned how to draw simple 2D shapes onscreen in the previous section. However, to fully utilize the OpenGL API, we also need to learn how to use it to render 3D images. In a nutshell, 3D images are simply an illusion created using 2D shapes stacked in a way that makes them look like 3D.

The main ingredient here is the depth value, which determines which shapes should appear in front or at the back of the other shapes. The primitive shape that is positioned behind another surface (with a shallower depth than another shape) will not be rendered (or partially rendered). OpenGL provides a simple way to achieve this, without too much technical hassle.

How to do it...

1. First, add the `QTimer` header to your `mainwindow.h`:

   ```
   #include <QTimer>
   ```

2. Then, add a private variable to your `MainWindow` class:

   ```
   private:
      QOpenGLContext* context;
      QOpenGLFunctions* openGLFunctions;
      float rotation;
   ```

3. We also add a public slot to `mainwindow.h` for later use:

   ```
   public slots:
      void updateAnimation();
   ```

4. After that, enable depth testing by adding `glEnable(GL_DEPTH_TEST)` to the `initializeGL()` function in `mainwindow.cpp`:

```
void MainWindow::initializeGL()
{
    //  Enable Z-buffer depth test
    glEnable(GL_DEPTH_TEST);
    resizeGL(this->width(), this->height());
}
```

5. Next, we will alter the `resizeGL()` function so that it uses the perspective view instead of the orthogonal view:

```
void MainWindow::resizeGL(int w, int h)
{
    // Set the viewport
    glViewport(0, 0, w, h);
    qreal aspectRatio = qreal(w) / qreal(h);

    // Initialize Projection Matrix
    glMatrixMode(GL_PROJECTION);
    glLoadIdentity();

    glOrtho(-1 * aspectRatio, 1 * aspectRatio, -1, 1, 1, -1);
    gluPerspective(75, aspectRatio, 0.1, 400000000);

    // Initialize Modelview Matrix
    glMatrixMode(GL_MODELVIEW);
    glLoadIdentity();
}
```

6. After that, we need to alter the `paintGL()` function as well. First, add `GL_DEPTH_BUFFER_BIT` to the `glClear()` function, because we also need to clear the depth information for the previous frame before we proceed to render the next frame. Then, remove the code we used in the previous example, which rendered a quad and a triangle on the screen:

```
void MainWindow::paintGL()
{
    // Initialize clear color (cornflower blue)
    glClearColor(0.39f, 0.58f, 0.93f, 1.f);

    // Clear color buffer
    glClear(GL_COLOR_BUFFER_BIT);
    glClear(GL_COLOR_BUFFER_BIT | GL_DEPTH_BUFFER_BIT);
```

```
glBegin(GL_QUADS);
glColor3f(1.f, 0.f, 0.f); glVertex2f(-0.8f, -0.8f);
glColor3f(1.f, 1.f, 0.f); glVertex2f(0.3f, -0.8f);
glColor3f(0.f, 1.f, 0.f); glVertex2f(0.3f, 0.3f);
glColor3f(0.f, 0.f, 1.f); glVertex2f(-0.8f, 0.3f);
glEnd();

glBegin(GL_TRIANGLES);
glColor3f(1.f, 0.f, 0.f); glVertex2f(-0.4f, -0.4f);
glColor3f(0.f, 1.f, 0.f); glVertex2f(0.8f, -0.1f);
glColor3f(0.f, 0.f, 1.f); glVertex2f(-0.1f, 0.8f);
glEnd();

glFlush();
}
```

7. Then, before calling `glFlush()`, we will add the following code to draw a 3D cube:

```
// Reset modelview matrix
glMatrixMode(GL_MODELVIEW);
glLoadIdentity();

// Transformations
glTranslatef(0.0, 0.0, -3.0);
glRotatef(rotation, 1.0, 1.0, 1.0);

// FRONT
glBegin(GL_POLYGON);
  glColor3f(0.0, 0.0, 0.0);
  glVertex3f(0.5, -0.5, -0.5); glVertex3f(0.5, 0.5, -0.5);
  glVertex3f(-0.5, 0.5, -0.5); glVertex3f(-0.5, -0.5, -0.5);
glEnd();

// BACK
glBegin(GL_POLYGON);
  glColor3f(0.0, 1.0, 0.0);
  glVertex3f(0.5, -0.5, 0.5); glVertex3f(0.5, 0.5, 0.5);
  glVertex3f(-0.5, 0.5, 0.5); glVertex3f(-0.5, -0.5, 0.5);
glEnd();

// RIGHT
glBegin(GL_POLYGON);
  glColor3f(1.0, 0.0, 1.0);
  glVertex3f(0.5, -0.5, -0.5); glVertex3f(0.5, 0.5, -0.5);
  glVertex3f(0.5, 0.5, 0.5); glVertex3f(0.5, -0.5, 0.5);
```

```
          glEnd();

          // LEFT
          glBegin(GL_POLYGON);
            glColor3f(1.0, 1.0, 0.0);
            glVertex3f(-0.5, -0.5, 0.5); glVertex3f(-0.5, 0.5, 0.5);
            glVertex3f(-0.5, 0.5, -0.5); glVertex3f(-0.5, -0.5, -0.5);
          glEnd();

          // TOP
          glBegin(GL_POLYGON);
            glColor3f(0.0, 0.0, 1.0);
            glVertex3f(0.5, 0.5, 0.5); glVertex3f(0.5, 0.5, -0.5);
            glVertex3f(-0.5, 0.5, -0.5); glVertex3f(-0.5, 0.5, 0.5);
          glEnd();

          // BOTTOM
          glBegin(GL_POLYGON);
            glColor3f(1.0, 0.0, 0.0);
            glVertex3f(0.5, -0.5, -0.5); glVertex3f(0.5, -0.5, 0.5);
            glVertex3f(-0.5, -0.5, 0.5); glVertex3f(-0.5, -0.5, -0.5);
          glEnd();
```

8. Once you are done with that, add a timer to the construction of the `MainWindow` class, like so:

```
MainWindow::MainWindow(QWidget *parent)
{
  setSurfaceType(QWindow::OpenGLSurface);
  QSurfaceFormat format;
  format.setProfile(QSurfaceFormat::CompatibilityProfile);
  format.setVersion(2, 1); // OpenGL 2.1
  setFormat(format);

  context = new QOpenGLContext;
  context->setFormat(format);
  context->create();
  context->makeCurrent(this);

  openGLFunctions = context->functions();

  QTimer *timer = new QTimer(this);
  connect(timer, SIGNAL(timeout()), this,
    SLOT(updateAnimation()));
  timer->start(100);

  rotation = 0;
}
```

9. Lastly, we increase the rotation variable by 10 every time the updateAnimation()
   slot is called by the timer. We also manually call the update() function to update
   the screen:

```
void MainWindow::updateAnimation()
{
    rotation += 10;
    this->update();
}
```

10. If you compile and run the program now, you should see a spinning cube in your
    main window!

How it works...

In any 3D rendering, depth is very important and thus we need to enable the depth testing
feature in OpenGL by calling glEnable(GL_DEPTH_TEST). When we clear the buffer, we
also must specify GL_DEPH_BUFFER_BIT so that the depth information is also being cleared,
in order for the next image to be rendered correctly.

We use `gluPerspective()` to set up a perspective projection matrix so that the graphics appear to have depth and distance. The opposite to the perspective view is the orthographic view, which is the default view in OpenGL, and we have used it in our previous example. Orthographic projection is a form of parallel projection where objects appear to be flat and do not suggest depth and distance:

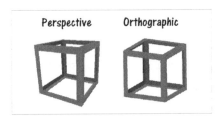

In this example, we used a timer to increase the rotation value by 10 every 100 milliseconds (0.1 second). The rotation value is then applied to the cube by calling `glRotatef()` before supplying the vertex data to OpenGL. We also called `glTranslatef()` to move the cube slightly to the back so that it's not too close to the camera view.

Remember to call `update()` manually so that the screen gets refreshed, otherwise the cube will not be animated.

Texturing in OpenGL

OpenGL allows us to map an image (also referred to as a texture) to a 3D shape or polygon. This process is also called texture mapping. Qt appears to be the best combination with OpenGL in this case because it provides an easy way to load images that belong to one of the common formats (BMP, JPEG, PNG, TARGA, TIFF, and so on) and you don't have to implement it by yourself. We will use the previous example with a spinning cube and try to map it with a texture!

How to do it...

1. First of all, open up `mainwindow.h` and add the following header to it:

    ```
    #include <QGLWidget>
    ```

2. Next, declare an array that stores the texture IDs created by OpenGL. We will be using it later when it comes to rendering:

    ```
    private:
        QOpenGLContext* context;
        QOpenGLFunctions* openGLFunctions;

        float rotation;
        GLuint texID[1];
    ```

3. After that, open up `mainwindow.cpp` and add the following code to `initializeGL()` to load the texture file:

```
void MainWindow::initializeGL()
{
  // Enable Z-buffer depth test
  glEnable(GL_DEPTH_TEST);

  // Enable texturing
  glEnable(GL_TEXTURE_2D);

  QImage image("bricks");
  QImage texture = QGLWidget::convertToGLFormat(image);

  glGenTextures(1, &texID[0]);
  glBindTexture(GL_TEXTURE_2D, texID[0]);

  glTexParameteri(GL_TEXTURE_2D, GL_TEXTURE_MIN_FILTER, GL_
    NEAREST);
  glTexParameteri(GL_TEXTURE_2D, GL_TEXTURE_MAG_FILTER, GL_
    NEAREST);

  glTexImage2D(GL_TEXTURE_2D, 0, GL_RGBA, texture.width(),
    texture.height(), 0, GL_RGBA, GL_UNSIGNED_BYTE,
  texture.bits());

  // Make sure render at the correct aspect ratio
  resizeGL(this->width(), this->height());
}
```

4. Then, add the following code to the `paintGL()` function to apply the texture to the 3D cube:

```
glEnable(GL_TEXTURE_2D);
glBindTexture(GL_TEXTURE_2D, texID[0]);

// FRONT
glBegin(GL_POLYGON);
  glColor3f(0.0, 0.0, 0.0);
  glTexCoord2f(0.0f, 0.0f); glVertex3f(0.5, -0.5, -0.5);
  glTexCoord2f(1.0f, 0.0f); glVertex3f(0.5, 0.5, -0.5);
  glTexCoord2f(1.0f, 1.0f); glVertex3f(-0.5, 0.5, -0.5);
  glTexCoord2f(0.0f, 1.0f); glVertex3f(-0.5, -0.5, -0.5);
glEnd();
```

```
// BACK
glBegin(GL_POLYGON);
  glColor3f(0.0, 1.0, 0.0);
  glTexCoord2f(1.0f, 0.0f); glVertex3f(0.5, -0.5, 0.5);
  glTexCoord2f(1.0f, 1.0f); glVertex3f(0.5, 0.5, 0.5);
  glTexCoord2f(0.0f, 1.0f); glVertex3f(-0.5, 0.5, 0.5);
  glTexCoord2f(0.0f, 0.0f); glVertex3f(-0.5, -0.5, 0.5);
glEnd();

// RIGHT
glBegin(GL_POLYGON);
  glColor3f(1.0, 0.0, 1.0);
  glTexCoord2f(0.0f, 1.0f); glVertex3f(0.5, -0.5, -0.5);
  glTexCoord2f(0.0f, 0.0f); glVertex3f(0.5, 0.5, -0.5);
  glTexCoord2f(1.0f, 0.0f); glVertex3f(0.5, 0.5, 0.5);
  glTexCoord2f(1.0f, 1.0f); glVertex3f(0.5, -0.5, 0.5);
glEnd();

// LEFT
glBegin(GL_POLYGON);
  glColor3f(1.0, 1.0, 0.0);
  glTexCoord2f(1.0f, 1.0f); glVertex3f(-0.5, -0.5, 0.5);
  glTexCoord2f(0.0f, 1.0f); glVertex3f(-0.5, 0.5, 0.5);
  glTexCoord2f(0.0f, 0.0f); glVertex3f(-0.5, 0.5, -0.5);
  glTexCoord2f(1.0f, 0.0f); glVertex3f(-0.5, -0.5, -0.5);
glEnd();

// TOP
glBegin(GL_POLYGON);
  glColor3f(0.0, 0.0, 1.0);
  glTexCoord2f(1.0f, 0.0f); glVertex3f(0.5, 0.5, 0.5);
  glTexCoord2f(1.0f, 1.0f); glVertex3f(0.5, 0.5, -0.5);
  glTexCoord2f(0.0f, 1.0f); glVertex3f(-0.5, 0.5, -0.5);
  glTexCoord2f(0.0f, 0.0f); glVertex3f(-0.5, 0.5, 0.5);
glEnd();

// Red side - BOTTOM
glBegin(GL_POLYGON);
  glColor3f(1.0, 0.0, 0.0);
  glTexCoord2f(0.0f, 0.0f); glVertex3f( 0.5, -0.5, -0.5);
  glTexCoord2f(1.0f, 0.0f); glVertex3f( 0.5, -0.5, 0.5);
  glTexCoord2f(1.0f, 1.0f); glVertex3f(-0.5, -0.5, 0.5);
  glTexCoord2f(0.0f, 1.0f); glVertex3f(-0.5, -0.5, -0.5);
glEnd();

glDisable(GL_TEXTURE_2D);
```

5. If you compile and run the program now, you should see a brick cube rotating around the screen!

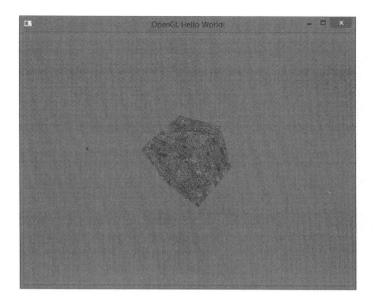

How it works...

The variable `GLuint texID[1]` is an array that stores the texture ID generated by OpenGL when we call `glGenTexture()`, which OpenGL uses to allocate the texture from the memory during rendering. In this case, we set the size of the array to 1 because we are only using a single texture in this example. We must tell OpenGL to enable texturing by calling `glEnable(GL_TEXTURE_2D)` before doing anything related to texturing. We used two `QImage` classes to load the texture, the first one called `image` was used to load the image file, and the second one called `texture` was used to convert the image to an OpenGL-compatible format. Then we called `glGenTextures()` to generate an empty texture using OpenGL, and after that, we called `glBindTexture()` to select that particular texture. This step was needed so that the functions called after that will be applied to the texture that we just selected.

Next, we called `glTexParameteri()` twice to set both the texture minifying and texture magnification settings to point sampling. This will tell OpenGL how the texture should be rendered. More about that later. After that, we called `glTexImage2D()` to supply the pixel information from the texture file loaded by Qt to the empty OpenGL texture we just created. Call `glEnabled(GL_TEXTURE_2D)` and `glBindTexture()` to enable texturing in OpenGL and select the texture we wanted to use before we start rendering the 3D cube. Then, we must call `glTexCoord2f()` before calling `glVertex3f()` to tell OpenGL how the texture should be mapped. We supply the coordinates for the texture and OpenGL will figure out the rest for us.

Once you're done, call `glDisable(GL_TEXTURE_2D)` to disable texturing.

Lighting and texture filter in OpenGL

In this example, we will learn how to apply different types of filtering effects such as point sampling, bilinear interpolation, and trilinear interpolation to the textures we use in OpenGL.

How to do it...

1. Again, we will use the previous example and add a light near the spinning cube. Open up `mainwindow.cpp` and add the following code to the `initializeGL()` function:

```
// Trilinear interpolation
glTexParameterf(GL_TEXTURE_2D, GL_TEXTURE_MIN_FILTER, GL_LINEAR_
MIPMAP_LINEAR);
glTexParameterf(GL_TEXTURE_2D, GL_TEXTURE_MAG_FILTER, GL_LINEAR);

glTexParameteri(GL_TEXTURE_2D, GL_GENERATE_MIPMAP, GL_TRUE);

glTexImage2D(GL_TEXTURE_2D, 0, GL_RGBA, texture.width(), texture.
  height(), 0, GL_RGBA, GL_UNSIGNED_BYTE, texture.bits());

// Enable smooth shading
glShadeModel(GL_SMOOTH);

// Lighting
glEnable(GL_LIGHT1);
GLfloat lightAmbient[] = { 0.5f, 0.5f, 0.5f, 1.0f };
GLfloat lightDiffuse[] = { 1.0f, 1.0f, 1.0f, 1.0f };
GLfloat lightPosition[] = { 3.0f, 3.0f, -5.0f, 1.0f };
glLightfv(GL_LIGHT1, GL_AMBIENT, lightAmbient);
glLightfv(GL_LIGHT1, GL_DIFFUSE, lightDiffuse);
glLightfv(GL_LIGHT1, GL_POSITION, lightPosition);

// Make sure render at the correct aspect ratio
resizeGL(this->width(), this->height());
```

2. Next, go to the `paintGL()` function and add the following code:

```
glEnable(GL_LIGHTING);

// FRONT
glBegin(GL_POLYGON);
  glNormal3f(0.0f, 0.0f, 1.0f);
  glTexCoord2f(0.0f, 0.0f); glVertex3f(0.5, -0.5, -0.5);
```

```
    glTexCoord2f(1.0f, 0.0f); glVertex3f(0.5, 0.5, -0.5);
    glTexCoord2f(1.0f, 1.0f); glVertex3f(-0.5, 0.5, -0.5);
    glTexCoord2f(0.0f, 1.0f); glVertex3f(-0.5, -0.5, -0.5);
glEnd();

// BACK
glBegin(GL_POLYGON);
  glNormal3f(0.0f, 0.0f,-1.0f);
    glTexCoord2f(1.0f, 0.0f); glVertex3f(0.5, -0.5, 0.5);
    glTexCoord2f(1.0f, 1.0f); glVertex3f(0.5, 0.5, 0.5);
    glTexCoord2f(0.0f, 1.0f); glVertex3f(-0.5, 0.5, 0.5);
    glTexCoord2f(0.0f, 0.0f); glVertex3f(-0.5, -0.5, 0.5);
glEnd();

// RIGHT
glBegin(GL_POLYGON);
  glNormal3f(0.0f, 1.0f, 0.0f);
    glTexCoord2f(0.0f, 1.0f); glVertex3f(0.5, -0.5, -0.5);
    glTexCoord2f(0.0f, 0.0f); glVertex3f(0.5, 0.5, -0.5);
    glTexCoord2f(1.0f, 0.0f); glVertex3f(0.5, 0.5, 0.5);
    glTexCoord2f(1.0f, 1.0f); glVertex3f(0.5, -0.5, 0.5);
glEnd();

// LEFT
glBegin(GL_POLYGON);
  glNormal3f(0.0f,-1.0f, 0.0f);
    glTexCoord2f(1.0f, 1.0f); glVertex3f(-0.5, -0.5, 0.5);
    glTexCoord2f(0.0f, 1.0f); glVertex3f(-0.5, 0.5, 0.5);
    glTexCoord2f(0.0f, 0.0f); glVertex3f(-0.5, 0.5, -0.5);
    glTexCoord2f(1.0f, 0.0f); glVertex3f(-0.5, -0.5, -0.5);
glEnd();

// TOP
glBegin(GL_POLYGON);
  glNormal3f(1.0f, 0.0f, 0.0f);
    glTexCoord2f(1.0f, 0.0f); glVertex3f(0.5, 0.5, 0.5);
    glTexCoord2f(1.0f, 1.0f); glVertex3f(0.5, 0.5, -0.5);
    glTexCoord2f(0.0f, 1.0f); glVertex3f(-0.5, 0.5, -0.5);
    glTexCoord2f(0.0f, 0.0f);glVertex3f(-0.5, 0.5, 0.5);
glEnd();

// Red side - BOTTOM
glBegin(GL_POLYGON);
  glNormal3f(-1.0f, 0.0f, 0.0f);
```

```
        glTexCoord2f(0.0f, 0.0f); glVertex3f(0.5, -0.5, -0.5);
        glTexCoord2f(1.0f, 0.0f); glVertex3f(0.5, -0.5, 0.5);
        glTexCoord2f(1.0f, 1.0f); glVertex3f(-0.5, -0.5, 0.5);
        glTexCoord2f(0.0f, 1.0f); glVertex3f(-0.5, -0.5, -0.5);
    glEnd();

    glDisable(GL_LIGHTING);
```

3. If you compile and run the program now, you should see the lighting in action!

How it works...

In the fixed pipeline, it's extremely easy to add lights to your scene. First, we need to choose which shading model we want OpenGL to use. In our case, we chose the smooth shading model by calling glShaderModel(GL_SMOOTH). Alternatively, you can also pick the flat shading model by calling glShaderModel(GL_FLAT):

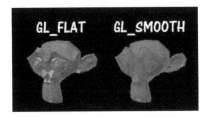

After that, enable the first light in OpenGL by calling `glEnable(GL_LIGHT1)`. Since there is a limited number of lights allowed in the fixed pipeline, the names of the lights are all static: `GL_LIGHT1`, `GL_LIGHT2`, `GL_LIGHT3`, and so on. Next, we created three arrays that store the color of the ambient light, the color of the diffuse light, and the position of the diffuse light. Ambient light is the environment lighting, which affects the entire scene and has no position. Diffuse light, on the other hand, has a position and area of light influence. We then supply this information to OpenGL by calling the `glLightfv()` functions. Then, in `paintGL()`, we must enable the lighting by calling `glEnable(GL_LIGHTING)` before we start rendering the cube. Without it, you won't see any lighting effects applied to the cube.

Other than that, we also need to add a surface normal value to every surface of the cube. Surface normal indicates where the surface is facing and is used for lighting calculations. Don't forget to disable lighting once you're done with it by calling `glDisable(GL_LIGHTING)`.

Besides adding a light to the scene, we also changed the texture filtering setting to trilinear interpolation by calling `glTexParameteri()`, which makes the texture looks smoother. You can also try out the other two types of filtering, point filtering and bilinear filtering, by uncommenting the code.

The following image shows the distinction between three different types of filtering:

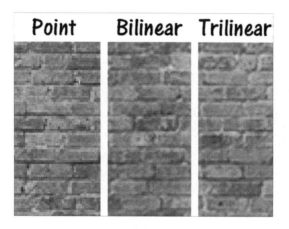

Bilinear and trilinear filtering require a mipmap in order to work, which we can ask OpenGL to generate by calling `glTexParameteri(GL_TEXTURE_2D, GL_GENERATE_MIPMAP, GL_TRUE)`. Mipmaps are pre-calculated, optimized sequences of textures, each of which is a progressively lower resolution representation of the same image. OpenGL will switch the texture of an object to a lower resolution mipmap when moving further away from the camera, which is effective for avoiding visual artifacts.

There's more...

In a 3D scene, lighting is a very important aspect that helps to define the 3D shape of an object. A light doesn't just make the surfaces facing the light become brighter, but it also makes other surfaces that are blocked become darker.

In OpenGL, at least in the fixed-function pipeline, you can only add a limited number of lights to the scene. The number of lights is limited by the graphics chip – some support up to four lights, some support up to eight, and some support up to 16. However, since the fixed-function pipeline is slowly being phased out and people are starting to use the programmable pipeline, this problem has been solved. In the programmable pipeline, you can have any number of lights in the scene; however, the lighting model will need to be coded entirely by you in the shaders, which is not an easy task.

In the fixed-function pipeline, if you want to add more lights than what your graphics chip supports, what you can do is to turn off lights that are further away from the camera view and only turn on a few that are closer to your camera view. The disadvantage of this method is that you may see the lights popping on and off while walking along a maze, for example.

Moving an object using keyboard controls

In this topic we'll be looking at is how to move an object in OpenGL using keyboard controls. Qt provides an easy way to detect keyboard events using virtual functions, namely `keyPressEvent()` and `keyReleaseEvent()`. We will be using the previous example and adding to it.

How to do it...

1. Open up `mainwindow.h` and declare two floating point numbers called `moveX` and `moveZ`:

```
private:
    QOpenGLContext* context;
    QOpenGLFunctions* openGLFunctions;

    float rotation;
    GLuint texID[1];

    float moveX;
    float moveZ;
```

2. After that, declare the `keyPressEvent()` function, like so:

```
public:
    explicit MainWindow(QWidget *parent = 0);
    ~MainWindow();

    void keyPressEvent(QKeyEvent *event);
```

3. Then, open up `mainwindow.cpp` and set the default values for the two variables we just declared:

```
MainWindow::MainWindow(QWidget *parent)
{
    setSurfaceType(QWindow::OpenGLSurface);

    QSurfaceFormat format;
    format.setProfile(QSurfaceFormat::CompatibilityProfile);
    format.setVersion(2, 1); // OpenGL 2.1
    setFormat(format);

    context = new QOpenGLContext;
    context->setFormat(format);
    context->create();
    context->makeCurrent(this);

    openGLFunctions = context->functions();

    QTimer *timer = new QTimer(this);
    connect(timer, SIGNAL(timeout()), this,
      SLOT(updateAnimation()));
    timer->start(100);

    rotation = 0;

    moveX = 0;
    moveZ = 0;
}
```

4. Next, we will implement the keyPressEvent() function:

```
void MainWindow::keyPressEvent(QKeyEvent *event)
{
  if (event->key() == Qt::Key_W)
  {
    moveZ -= 0.2;
  }

  if (event->key() == Qt::Key_S)
  {
    moveZ += 0.2;
  }

  if (event->key() == Qt::Key_A)
  {
    moveX -= 0.2;
  }

  if (event->key() == Qt::Key_D)
  {
    moveX += 0.2;
  }
}
```

5. After that, we call glTranslatef() before drawing the 3D cube and putting both moveX and moveZ into the function. Also, we disabled the rotation so that it's easier to see the movement:

```
// Transformations
glTranslatef(0.0, 0.0, -3.0);
glRotatef(rotation, 1.0, 1.0, 1.0);
glTranslatef(moveX, 0.0, moveZ);

// Texture mapping
glEnable(GL_TEXTURE_2D);
glBindTexture(GL_TEXTURE_2D, texID[0]);

glEnable(GL_LIGHTING);
```

6. If you compile and run the program now, you should be able to move the cube around by pressing *W*, *A*, *S* and *D*:

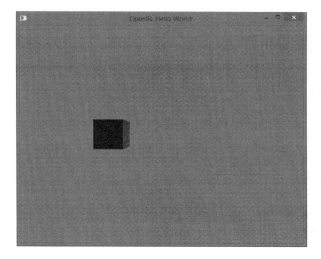

How it works...

Basically, what we did here was add or subtract the `moveX` and `moveZ` values when a key is pressed. In `keyPressEvent()`, we checked whether the keyboard button pressed was *W*, *A*, *S*, or *D*. Then, we add or subtract 0.2 from the variables accordingly. To get the full list of key names used by Qt, visit `http://doc.qt.io/qt-5/qt.html#Key-enum`.

When we hold down the same key and don't release it, Qt will repeat the key press event after an interval. The keyboard input interval varies between different operating systems. You can set the interval by calling `QApplication::setKeyboardInterval()`, but this may not work in every operating system. We called `glTranslatef(moveX, 0.0, moveZ)` before drawing the cube, which moves the cube around when we press *W*, *A*, *S*, or *D*.

3D canvas in QML

In this recipe, we will learn how to render 3D images using Qt's powerful QML scripting language.

How to do it...

1. Let's start this example by creating a new project in Qt Creator. This time around, we will create **Qt Canvas 3D Application** and not the other options that we chose in all previous examples:

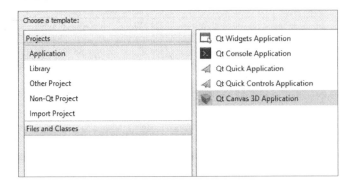

2. After that, Qt Creator will ask you whether to create a project that is based on `three.js`. Leave the option checked and press the **Next** button to proceed:

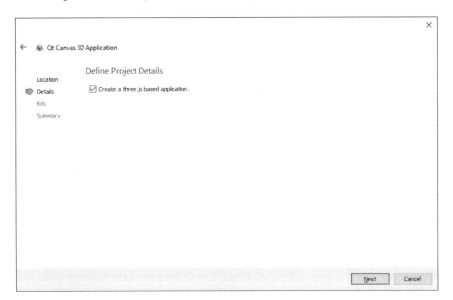

3. Once the project is created, you will notice there are some JavaScript (.js) files already added to your project's resources. This is normal as the Qt Canvas 3D application uses JavaScript and WebGL technology to render 3D images on screen. In this case, it's running a WebGL-based rendering library called three.js, which makes our programming job simpler and easier compare to writing pure WebGL code:

4. Next, add an image file to our project resources as we'll be using it in this example. Open up qml.qrc with Qt Creator by right-clicking on it in the **Projects** pane and select **Open in Editor**. Once the resources file is opened by Qt Creator, click the **Add** button, followed by the **Add File** button, then select the image file you want from your computer. In my case, I've added a bricks.png image, which will be used as the surface texture for our 3D object:

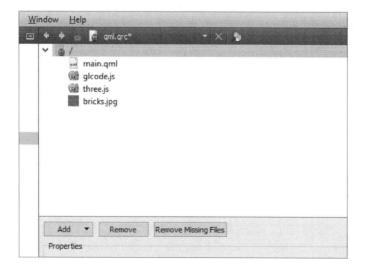

5. After that, open up `glcode.js` using Qt Creator. You will see there is already plenty of code written in the file. What ithis does is basically render a simple 3D cube on screen using the `three.js` library. You can build the project right away and run it to see what it looks like. However, we will change the code a little bit to customize its output.

6. In the `initializeGL()` function, we'll add a directional light to the scene, load the texture file we just added to our project resources, and then apply the texture to the material that defines the surface properties of the 3D cube. Also, we will make the scale of the cube slightly bigger by setting its scale to 3 in all dimensions:

```
function initializeGL(canvas) {
    scene = new THREE.Scene();
    camera = new THREE.PerspectiveCamera(75, canvas.width / canvas.
        height, 0.1, 1000);
    camera.position.z = 5;

    var directionalLight = new THREE.DirectionalLight(0xffffff);
    directionalLight.position.set(1, 1, 1).normalize();
    scene.add(directionalLight);

    var texture = THREE.ImageUtils.loadTexture('bricks.jpg');

    var material = new THREE.MeshBasicMaterial({ map: texture });
    var cubeGeometry = new THREE.BoxGeometry(3, 3, 3);
    cube = new THREE.Mesh(cubeGeometry, material);
    cube.rotation.set(0.785, 0.785, 0.0);
    scene.add(cube);

    renderer = new THREE.Canvas3DRenderer(
        { canvas: canvas, antialias: true, devicePixelRatio: canvas.
          devicePixelRatio });
    renderer.setSize(canvas.width, canvas.height);
}
```

7. Then, in the `paintGL()` function, add an extra line of code to rotate the 3D cube before rendering the scene:

```
function paintGL(canvas) {
    cube.rotation.y -= 0.005;
    renderer.render(scene, camera);
}
```

8. I personally find the window size is a little too large, so I also changed the width and height of the window in `main.qml` file:

```
import QtQuick 2.4
import QtCanvas3D 1.0
import QtQuick.Window 2.2
```

```
import "glcode.js" as GLCode

Window {
  title: qsTr("Qt_Canvas_3D")
  width: 480
  height: 320
  visible: true

  Canvas3D {
    id: canvas3d
    anchors.fill: parent
    focus: true

    onInitializeGL: {
      GLCode.initializeGL(canvas3d);
    }

    onPaintGL: {
      GLCode.paintGL(canvas3d);
    }

    onResizeGL: {
      GLCode.resizeGL(canvas3d);
    }
  }
}
```

9. Once you're done, let's build and run the project. You should be able to see a 3D cube with a brick texture, spinning slowly on the screen:

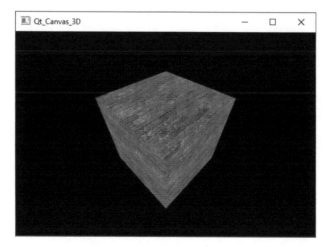

How it works...

Originally, `three.js` was a cross-browser JavaScript library/API that used WebGL technology to display animated 3D computer graphics in a web browser. Qt Canvas 3D, however, also uses web technology, specifically the WebGL technology, to render 3D images like it would on a web browser. This means that not only is `three.js` supported on Qt Canvas 3D, but all the different types of library that are based on WebGL technology will work flawlessly on Qt Canvas 3D. However, Qt Canvas 3D only works on QML-based projects and does not work in C++.

 If you're interested to learn more about `three.js`, check out their website at `http://threejs.org`.

5

Building a Touch Screen Application with Qt5

In this chapter, we will cover the following recipes:

- ▸ Setting up Qt for mobile applications
- ▸ Designing a basic user interface with QML
- ▸ Touch events
- ▸ Animation in QML
- ▸ Displaying information using model views
- ▸ Integrating QML and C++

Introduction

Qt is not only a cross-platform software development kit for PC platforms, it also supports mobile platforms such as iOS and Android. The developers of Qt introduced Qt Quick back in 2010, which provides an easy way to build custom user interfaces that are highly dynamic, where users can easily create fluid transitions and effects with only minimal coding. Qt Quick uses a declarative scripting language called **QML**, which is similar to the JavaScript language used in web development. Advanced users can also create custom functions in C++ and port them over to Qt Quick to enhance its functionality. At the moment, Qt Quick supports multiple platforms such as Windows, Linux, Mac, iOS, and Android.

Setting up Qt for mobile applications

In this example, we will learn how to set up our Qt project in Qt Quick and enable it to be build and exported to mobile devices.

How to do it...

1. First of all, let's create a new project by going to **File | New File or New Project**. Then, a window will pop up for you to choose a project template. Select **Qt Quick Application** and click the **Choose** button:

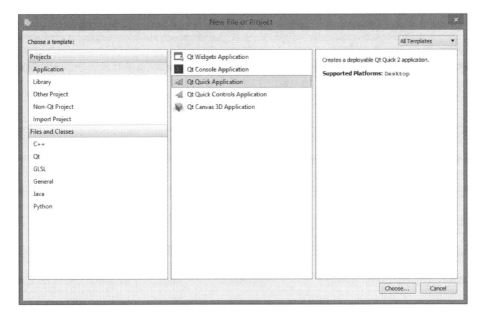

2. After that, insert the project name and select the project location. Click the **Next** button and it will ask you to select the minimum Qt version required for your project. Please make sure that you select a version that exists on your computer, otherwise you won't be able to run it properly. Once you have done that, proceed by clicking the **Next** button.

3. Then, Qt Creator will ask you which **kit** you want to use for your project. These "kits" are basically different compilers that you can use to compile your project for different platforms. Since we're doing an application for a mobile platform, we will enable the Android kit (or the iOS kit if you're running a Mac) in order to build and export your app to your mobile device. Do note that you need to configure the Android kit if you're using it for the first time, so that Qt can find the directory of the Android SDK. Click **Next** once you're done with it:

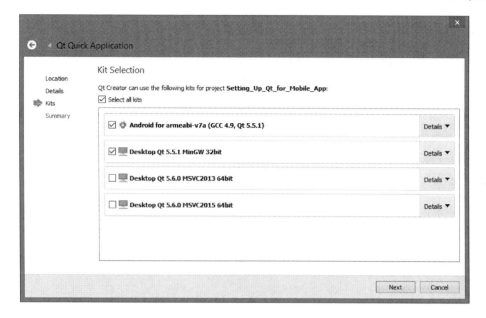

4. Once the project has been created, Qt Creator will automatically open up a file from your project, called `main.qml`. You will see something like this on screen, which is very different from your usual C/C++ project:

```
import QtQuick 2.3
import QtQuick.Window 2.2

Window {
  visible: true

  MouseArea {
    anchors.fill: parent
    onClicked: {
      Qt.quit();
    }
  }

  Text {
    text: qsTr("Hello World")
    anchors.centerIn: parent
  }
}
```

5. Build and run the project now by clicking on the green arrow button located at the bottom-left corner of your Qt Creator. If you set the default kit to **Desktop**, a window will pop up which looks something like this:

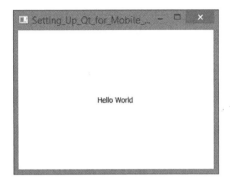

6. We can switch between different kits by going to the **Projects** interface and selecting the kit you want your project to be built with. You can also manage all the kits available on your computer, or add a new kit to your project from the **Projects** interface:

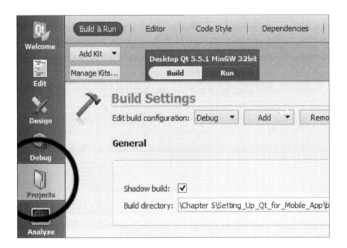

7. If this is your first time building and running your project, you need to create a template for the Android kit under the **Build** settings. Once you have clicked the **Create Templates** button, Qt will generate all the files required to run your app on an Android device. If you don't plan to use Gradle in your project, disable the option **Copy the Gradles files to Android directory**. Otherwise, you may encounter problems when trying to compile and deploy your app to your mobile device:

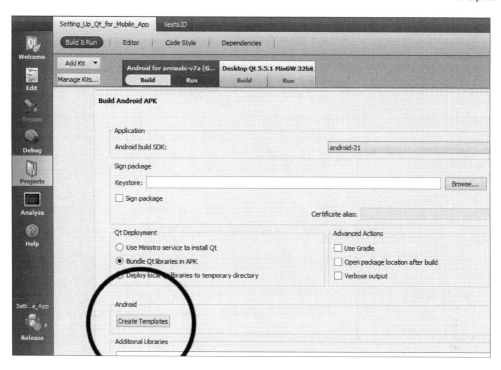

8. Once you have created the template, press the **Run** button and now you should see a window popping up, asking which device it should export to:

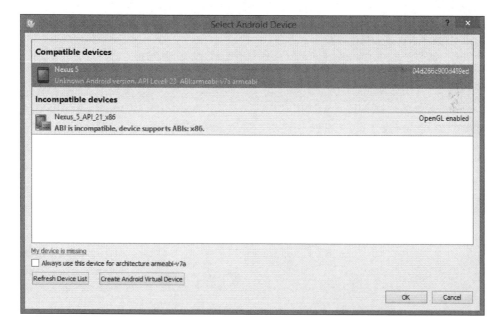

9. Select the device that is currently connected to your computer and press the **OK** button. Wait for a while for it to build the project, and you should see something like this on your mobile device:

How it works...

A Qt Quick application project is quite different from a form application project. You will be writing QML script most of the time instead of writing C/C++ code.

The **Android Software Development Kit (SDK)**, **Android Native Development Kit (NDK)**, **Java Development Kit (JDK)**, and **Apache Ant** are required to build and export your app to the Android platform. Alternatively, you can also use Gradle instead of Apache Ant for your Android kit. All you need to do is to enable the **Use Gradle instead of Ant** option and provide Qt with Gradle's installation path. Note that Android Studio is currently not supported by Qt Creator:

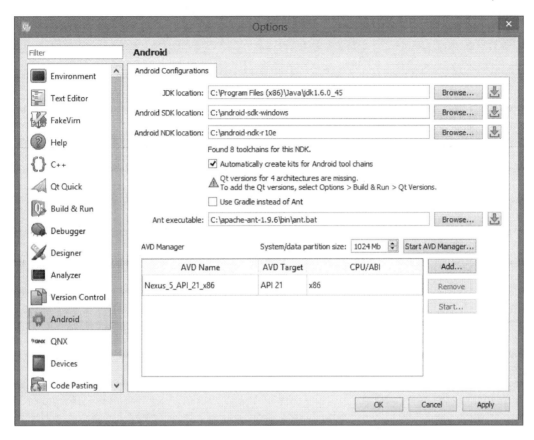

If you're running the app on an Android device, make sure that you have enabled USB Debugging Mode. To enable USB Debugging Mode, you need to first enable the developer options on your Android device by going to **Settings | About Phone** and tap the **Build Number** seven times. After that, go to **Settings | Developer Options** and you will see the **Android Debugging** option in the menu. Enable that option and you can now export your app to your device for testing.

To build for the iOS platform, you need to run Qt Creator on a Mac and make sure the latest XCode is installed on your Mac as well.

To test your app on an iOS device, you need to register a developer account with Apple, register your device at the developer portal, and install the provisioning to your XCode, which is a lot trickier than Android. You will be given access to the developer portal once you have obtained a developer account from Apple.

Designing a basic user interface with QML

In this example, we will learn how to use Qt Quick Designer to design our program's user interface.

How to do it...

1. First of all, create a new Qt Quick application project, just like we did in the previous recipe. You can also use the previous project files if you wish to.

2. You will see two QML files in your project resources—main.qml and MainForm. ui.qml. The former is where we implement the logic for our application, and the latter is where we design our user interface. We will start with the UI design, so let's open up MainForm.ui.qml. Once it's been opened by Qt Creator, you will see an entirely different UI editor compared to the one we used in previous chapters. This editor is called the Qt Quick Designer, which is used specifically to design UI for Qt Quick projects. The components of this editor are described as follows:

   - **Library**: The **Library** window displays all the predefined QML types that you can add to your UI canvas. You can also import custom Qt Quick components from the **Import** tab and display them here.

   - **Navigator**: The **Navigator** window displays the items in the current QML file in a tree structure.

   - **Connections**: You can use the tools provided in the **Connections** window to connect objects to signals, specify dynamic properties for objects, and create bindings between the properties of two objects.

   - **State**: The **State** window displays the different states of an item. You can add a new state for an item by clicking on the **+** button on the right of the **State** window.

   - **Canvas**: The canvas is where you design your program's user interface. You can drag and drop a Qt Quick component from the **Library** window onto the canvas and instantly see what it will look like in the program.

   - **Properties**: This is where you change the properties of a selected item.

3. Select everything under the **Rectangle** object (**mouseArea** and **Text**) in the **Navigator** window and delete them.

4. We're about to make a simple login screen. From the **Library** window, drag two text widgets onto the canvas.

5. Set the text properties of both the text widgets to **Username:** and **Password:**

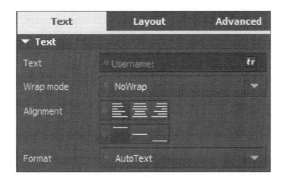

6. Drag two rectangles from the **Library** window to the canvas, then drag two text input widgets onto the canvas and parent each of them to the rectangles you just added to the canvas. Set the `border` property of the rectangles to `1` and the `radius` to `5`. Then, set the `echo mode` of one of the text fields to `Password`.

7. Now we're going to manually create a button widget by combining a mouse area widget with a rectangle and a text widget. Drag a mouse area widget onto the canvas, then drag a rectangle and a text widget onto the canvas and parent them both to the mouse area. Set the color of the rectangle to `#bdbdbd`, then set its `border` property to `1` and its `radius` to `5`. Then, set the `text` to `Login` and make sure the size of the mouse area is the same as the rectangle.

8. After that, drag another rectangle onto the canvas to act as the container for the login form so that it will look neat. Set its `border color` to `#5e5858` and its `border` property to `2`. Then, set its `radius` property to `5` to make its corners look a little rounded.

9. Make sure the rectangle that we added in the previous step is positioned at the top of the hierarchy in the **Navigator** window so that it appears behind all the other widgets. You can arrange the widget positions within the hierarchy by pressing the arrow buttons located at the top of the **Navigator** window:

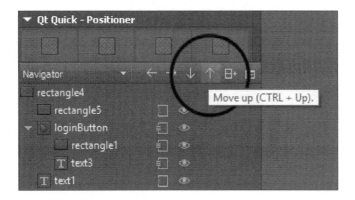

10. Next, we will export three widgets—mouse area and the two text input widgets—as alias properties of the root item so that later on we can access these widgets from the `main.qml` file. The widgets can be exported by clicking on the small icon behind the widget name and making sure the icon changes to the **On** status:

11. By now, your UI should look something like this:

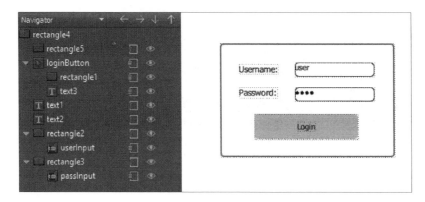

12. Now let's open up `main.qml`. Qt Creator will not open this file in Qt Quick Designer by default, but instead, it will be opened with the Script Editor. This is because all the UI design-related tasks were done in `MainForm.ui.qml`, and `main.qml` is only for defining the logic and functions that will be applied to the UI. You can, however, open it with Qt Quick Designer to preview the UI by clicking on the **Design** button located in the side bar on the left of the editor.

13. At the top of the script, add the third line to import the dialog module to `main.qml`, like so:

```
import QtQuick 2.5
import QtQuick.Window 2.2
import QtQuick.Dialogs 1.2
```

14. After that, replace the code below it with this:

```
Window {
    visible: true
    width: 360
    height: 360
```

```
MainForm {
  anchors.fill: parent
  loginButton.onClicked: {
    messageDialog.text = "Username is " +
      userInput.text + " and password is " +
      passInput.text
    messageDialog.visible = true
  }
}

MessageDialog {
  id: messageDialog
  title: "Fake login"
  text: ""
  onAccepted: {
    console.log("You have clicked the login button")
    Qt.quit()
  }
}
}
```

15. Build and run this program on your PC and you should get a simple program that shows a message box when you click on the **Login** button:

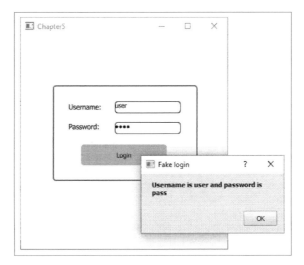

How it works...

Since Qt 5.4, a new file extension called `.ui.qml` has been introduced. The QML engine handles it like the normal `.qml` files, but forbids any logic implementation to be written in it. It serves as the UI definition template, which can be reused in different `.qml` files. The separation of UI definition and logic implementation improves the maintainability of QML code and creates a better workflow.

All the widgets under **Qt Quick – Basic** are the most basic widgets that we can use to mix and match and create a new type of widget. In the previous example, we have learned how to put three widgets together—a text, a mouse area, and a rectangle, to form a button widget.

If you're lazy, however, you can import pre-made modules to your Qt Quick project by going to the **Imports** tab in the **Library** window and clicking the **<Add Import>** button. Then, select the module you want to add to your project from the drop-down list. You can also create your own Qt Quick module once you have advanced in both QML scripting and C++ programming:

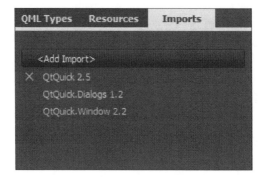

We imported `QtQuick.dialogs` module in `main.qml` and created a message box that displays the user name and password filled in by the user when the **Login** button is pressed, so that we can prove that the UI function is working. If the widgets are not exported from `MainForm.ui.qml`, we will not be able to access its properties in `main.qml`.

At this point, we can export the program to iOS and Android, but the UI may not look accurate on some of the devices that have higher resolution or higher **Density-per-Pixel (DPI)** unit. We will cover this issue later on in this chapter.

Touch events

In this section, we will learn how to develop a touch-driven application that runs on mobile devices using Qt Quick.

How to do it...

1. First of all, create a new Qt Quick application project.

2. In Qt Creator, right-click on `qml.qrc` and select **Open in Editor**. Then, click **Add | Add Files** and add `tux.png` to the project:

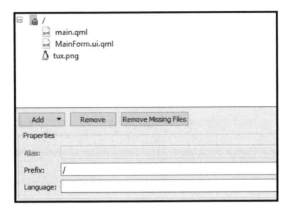

3. Next, open up `MainForm.ui.qml`. Drag an image widget from the **Library** window to the canvas. Then, set the source of the image to `tux.png` and set its `fillmode` to `PreserveAspectFit`. After that, set its `width` to `200` and its `height` to `220`.

4. Make sure both the mouse area widget and the image widget are exported as alias properties of the root item by clicking on the small icon besides their respective widget name.

5. After that, switch over to the Script Editor by clicking on the **Edit** button on the side bar located at the left side of the editor. We need to change the mouse area widget to a multi-point touch area widget, like so:

```
MultiPointTouchArea {
  id: touchArea
  anchors.fill: parent
  touchPoints: [
    TouchPoint { id: point1 },
    TouchPoint { id: point2 }
  ]
}
```

6. We also set the `Image` widget to be automatically placed at the center of the window by default:

```
Image {
    id: tux
    x: (window.width / 2) - (tux.width / 2)
    y: (window.height / 2) - (tux.height / 2)
    width: 200
    height: 220
    fillMode: Image.PreserveAspectFit
    source: "tux.png"
}
```

The final UI should look something like this:

7. Once you're done with that, let's open up `main.qml`. First, clear everything within the `MainForm` object except `anchors.fill: parent`, like so:

```
import QtQuick 2.5
import QtQuick.Window 2.2

Window {
    visible: true

    MainForm {
        anchors.fill: parent
    }
}
```

8. After that, declare several variables within the `MainForm` object that will be used to rescale the image widget. If you want to know more about the `property` keyword used in the following code, check out the *There's more...* section at the end of this example:

```
property int prevPointX: 0
property int prevPointY: 0
property int curPointX: 0
property int curPointY: 0

property int prevDistX: 0
property int prevDistY: 0
property int curDistX: 0
property int curDistY: 0

property int tuxWidth: tux.width
property int tuxHeight: tux.height
```

9. Next, we will define what will happen when our finger touches the multi-point area widget. In this case, we will save the positions of the first and second touch points if more than one finger touches the multi-point touch area. We also save the width and height of the image widget so that later on we can use these variables to calculate the scale of the image when the fingers start to move:

```
touchArea.onPressed:
{
  if (touchArea.touchPoints[1].pressed)
  {
    if (touchArea.touchPoints[1].x < touchArea.touchPoints[0].x)
      prevDistX = touchArea.touchPoints[1].x -
        touchArea.touchPoints[0].x
    else
      prevDistX = touchArea.touchPoints[0].x -
        touchArea.touchPoints[1].x

    if (touchArea.touchPoints[1].y < touchArea.touchPoints[0].y)
      prevDistY = touchArea.touchPoints[1].y -
        touchArea.touchPoints[0].y
    else
      prevDistY = touchArea.touchPoints[0].y -
        touchArea.touchPoints[1].y
```

```
    tuxWidth = tux.width
    tuxHeight = tux.height
  }
}
```

The following image shows the example of touch points being registered when two fingers are touching the screen, within the touchArea boundary. `touchArea.touchPoints[0]` is the first registered touch point and `touchArea.touchPoints[1]` is the second. We then calculate the X and Y distance between the two touch points and save them as `prevDistX` and `prevDistY`:

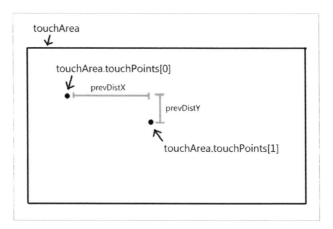

10. After that, we will define what will happen when our fingers move while remaining in contact with the screen and still within the boundary of the touch area. At this point, we will calculate the scale of the image by using the variables we saved in the previous step. At the same time, if we detect that only a single touch is found, then we will move the image instead of altering its scale:

```
touchArea.onUpdated:{
  if (!touchArea.touchPoints[1].pressed)
  {
    tux.x += touchArea.touchPoints[0].x -
      touchArea.touchPoints[0].previousX
    tux.y += touchArea.touchPoints[0].y -
      touchArea.touchPoints[0].previousY
  }
  else
  {
    if (touchArea.touchPoints[1].x <
      touchArea.touchPoints[0].x)
```

```
    curDistX = touchArea.touchPoints[1].x -
      touchArea.touchPoints[0].x
  else
    curDistX = touchArea.touchPoints[0].x -
      touchArea.touchPoints[1].x

  if (touchArea.touchPoints[1].y <
    touchArea.touchPoints[0].y)
    curDistY = touchArea.touchPoints[1].y -
      touchArea.touchPoints[0].y
  else
    curDistY = touchArea.touchPoints[0].y -
      touchArea.touchPoints[1].y

  tux.width = tuxWidth + prevDistX - curDistX
  tux.height = tuxHeight + prevDistY - curDistY
  }
}
```

The following image shows the example of moving touch points - touchArea.touchPoints[0] moved from point A to point B while touchArea.touchPoints[1] moved from point C to point D. We can then determine how many units have the touch points moved by looking at the differences between the previous X, Y variables with the current ones:

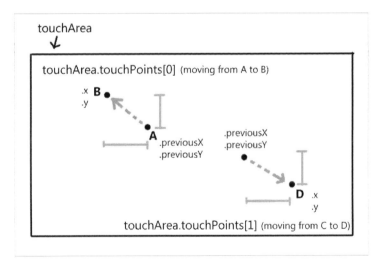

11. You can now build and export the program to your mobile device. You will not be able to test this program on a platform that does not support multi-touch. Once the program is running on the mobile device (or desktop/laptop that supports multi-touch), try two things: put only one finger on the screen and move it around, and put two fingers on the screen and move them in opposite directions. What you should see is that the penguin will be moved to another place if you use only one finger, and it will be scaled up or down if you use two fingers:

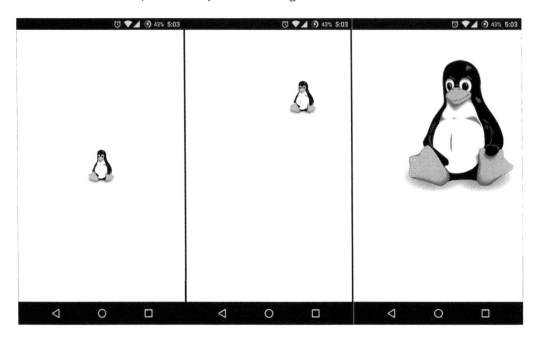

How it works...

When a finger touches the screen of the device, the multi-point touch area widget triggers the onPressed event and registers the position of each of the touch points in an internal array. We can get this data by telling Qt which touch point you want to get access to. The first touch will bear the index number of 0, the second touch will be 1, and so on. We will then save this data into variables so that we can retrieve it later to calculate the scaling of the penguin image.

When one or more fingers remain in contact with the screen while moving, a multi-point touch area will trigger the onUpdate event. We will then check how many touches there are—if only one touch is found, we will just move the penguin image based on how much our finger has moved. If there is more than one touch, we will compare the distance between the two touches and compare this with the previous variables we have saved, to determine how much we should rescale the image.

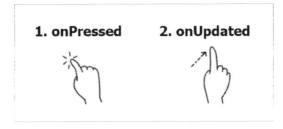

We must also check whether the first touch is on the left side of the second touch or the right side. This way we can prevent the image from being scaled in the inverse direction of the finger movement and producing an inaccurate result.

As for the movement of the penguin, we will just get the difference between the current touch position and the previous one, add that to the coordinate of the penguin, and it's done. A single touch event is usually a lot simpler and more straightforward than a multi-touch event.

There's more...

In Qt Quick, all its components have built-in properties such as width, height, color, and so on that are attached to the components by default. However, Qt Quick also allows you to create your own custom properties and attach them to the components you declared in your QML script. A custom property of an object type may be defined in an object declaration in a QML document by adding the `property` keyword before the type keyword, for example:

```
property int myValue;
```

You can also bind the custom property to a value by using a colon (`:`) before the value, like so:

```
property int myValue: 100;
```

To learn more about the property types supported by Qt Quick, check out this link: `http://doc.qt.io/qt-5/qtqml-typesystem-basictypes.html`

Animation in QML

Qt allows us to easily animate a UI component without writing a bunch of code. In this example, we will learn how to make our program's UI more interesting by applying animations to it.

How to do it...

1. Once again, we will start everything from scratch. Therefore, create a new Qt Quick application project in Qt Creator and open up `MainForm.ui.qml`.

2. Go to the **Imports** tab in the **Library** window and add a Qt Quick module called **QtQuick.Controls** to your project.

3. After that, you will see a new category appear in the **QML Types** tab called **Qt Quick - Controls**, which contains many new widgets that can be placed on the canvas.

4. Next, drag three button widgets to the canvas and set their height to 45. Then, go to the **Layout** tab on the **Properties** window and enable both the left and right anchors for all the three button widgets. Make sure the target for the anchors are set to **Parent** and the margins remain as 0. This will make the buttons resize horizontally according to the width of the main window. After that, set the y value of the first button to 0, the second to 45, and the third to 90. The UI should now look like this:

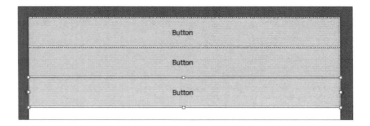

5. Now, open up `qml.qrc` with the Editor and add `fan.png` to the project:

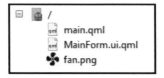

6. Then, add two mouse area widgets to the canvas. After that, drag a rectangle widget and an image widget on the canvas. Parent the rectangle and image to the mouse areas we have just added before this.

7. Set the color of the rectangle to `#0000ff` and apply `fan.png` to the image widget. Your UI should now look like this:

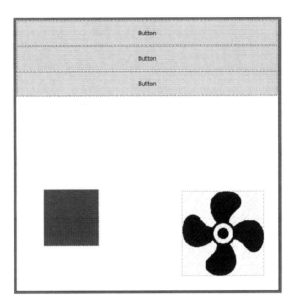

8. After that, export all the widgets in your `MainForm.ui.qml` as alias properties of the root item by clicking on the icons located to the right of the widget name:

9. Next, we will apply animation and logic to the UI but we won't be doing it in `MainForm.ui.qml`. Instead, we will do it all in `main.qml`.

10. In `main.qml`, remove the default code for the mouse area and add in a width and height for the window so that we get more space to preview:

```
import QtQuick 2.5
import QtQuick.Window 2.2
```

```
Window {
   visible: true
   width: 480
   height: 550

   MainForm {
      anchors.fill: parent
   }
}
```

11. After that, add the code that defines the behavior of the buttons in the `MainForm` widget:

```
button1 {
   Behavior on y { SpringAnimation { spring: 2;
      damping: 0.2 } }

   onClicked: {
      button1.y = button1.y + (45 * 3)
   }
}

button2 {
   Behavior on y { SpringAnimation { spring: 2;
      damping: 0.2 } }

   onClicked: {
      button2.y = button2.y + (45 * 3)
   }
}

button3 {
   Behavior on y { SpringAnimation { spring: 2;
      damping: 0.2 } }

   onClicked: {
      button3.y = button3.y + (45 * 3)
   }
}
```

12. Then, follow this with the behavior of the `fan` image and the mouse area widget it is attached to:

```
fan {
   RotationAnimation on rotation {
      id: anim01
      loops: Animation.Infinite
```

```
      from: 0
      to: -360
      duration: 1000
    }
  }

  mouseArea1 {
    onPressed: {
      if (anim01.paused)
        anim01.resume()
      else
        anim01.pause()
    }
  }
```

13. Last but not least, add the behavior of the rectangle and the mouse area widget it's attached to:

```
rectangle2 {
    id: rect2
    state: "BLUE"
    states: [
        State {
            name: "BLUE"
            PropertyChanges {
                target: rect2
                color: "blue"
            }
        },
        State {
            name: "RED"
            PropertyChanges {
                target: rect2
                color: "red"
            }
        }
    ]
}

mouseArea2 {

    SequentialAnimation on x {
        loops: Animation.Infinite
        PropertyAnimation { to: 150; duration: 1500 }
        PropertyAnimation { to: 50; duration: 500 }
    }

    onClicked: {
        if (rect2.state == "BLUE")
            rect2.state = "RED"
        else
            rect2.state = "BLUE"
    }
}
```

14. If you compile and run the program now, you should see three buttons at the top of the window and a moving rectangle at the bottom left, followed by a spinning fan at the bottom right. If you click any of the buttons, they will move slightly downward with a nice, smooth animation. If you click on the rectangle, it will change color from blue to red. Meanwhile, the fan image will pause its animation if you click on it while it's animating, and it will resume the animation if you click on it again:

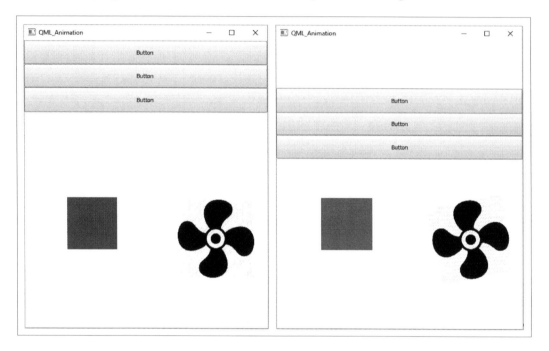

How it works...

Most of the animation elements supported by the C++ version of Qt, such as transition, sequential animation, parallel animation, and so on, are also available in Qt Quick. If you are familiar with the Qt animation framework in C++, you should be able to grasp this pretty easily.

In this example, we added a spring animation element to all three buttons that specifically tracked their respective *y*-axes. If Qt detects that the y value has changed, the widget will not instantly pop to the new position, but instead it will be interpolated, move across the canvas, and perform a little shaking animation when reaching its destination, which simulates the spring effect. We just have to write one line of code and leave the rest to Qt.

As for the fan image, we added a rotation animation element to it and set the `duration` to `1000` milliseconds, which means it will complete a full rotation in one second. We also set it to loop its animation infinitely. When we clicked on the mouse area widget it's attached to, we just called `pause()` or `resume()` to enable or disable the animation.

Next, for the rectangle widget, we added two states to it, one called `BLUE` and one called `RED`, each of which carries a `color` property that will be applied to the rectangle upon state change. At the same time, we added a sequential animation group to the mouse area widget that the rectangle is attached to, and then added two property animation elements to the group. You can also mix different types of group animation; Qt can handle this very well.

Displaying information using Model View

Qt includes a Model View framework that maintains separation between the way data is organized and managed, and the way that it is presented to the user. In this section, we will learn how to make use of the model view, in particular by using the list view to display information and at the same time apply our own customization to make it look slick.

How to do it...

1. Create a new Qt Quick application project and open up `qml.qrc` with Qt Creator. Add six images, `home.png`, `map.png`, `profile.png`, `search.png`, `settings.png`, and `arrow.png`, to the project:

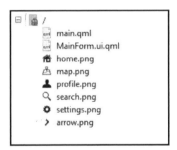

2. After that, open up `MainForm.ui.qml`. Delete all the default widgets on the canvas and drag a **List View** widget from under the **Qt Quick - Views** category in the Library window onto the canvas. Then, set its **Anchors** setting to **Fill the parent size** by clicking on the button located in the middle of the **Layout** window:

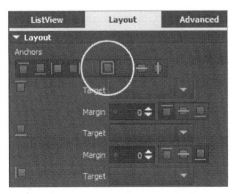

3. Next, switch over to the Script Editor, as we will define what the list view will look like:

```
import QtQuick 2.4

Rectangle {
    id: rectangle1

    property alias listView1: listView1
    property double sizeMultiplier: width / 480

    ListView {
        id: listView1
        y: 0
        height: 160
        orientation: ListView.Vertical
        boundsBehavior: Flickable.StopAtBounds
        anchors.fill: parent
        delegate: Item {
            width: 80 * sizeMultiplier
            height: 55 * sizeMultiplier
            Row {
                id: row1
                Rectangle {
                    width: listView1.width
                    height: 55 * sizeMultiplier
                    gradient: Gradient {
                        GradientStop { position: 0.0; color: "#ffffff" }
                        GradientStop { position: 1.0; color: "#f0f0f0" }
                    }
                    opacity: 1.0

                    MouseArea {
                        id: mouseArea
                        anchors.fill: parent
                    }

                    Image {
                        anchors.verticalCenter: parent.verticalCenter
                        x: 15 * sizeMultiplier
                        width: 30 * sizeMultiplier
                        height: 30 * sizeMultiplier
                        source: icon
                    }

                    Text {
                        text: title
                        font.family: "Courier"
                        font.pixelSize: 17 * sizeMultiplier
                        x: 55 * sizeMultiplier
                        y: 10 * sizeMultiplier
                    }
```

```
                    Text {
                        text: subtitle
                        font.family: "Verdana"
                        font.pixelSize: 9 * sizeMultiplier
                        x: 55 * sizeMultiplier
                        y: 30 * sizeMultiplier
                    }

                    Image {
                        anchors.verticalCenter: parent.verticalCenter
                        x: parent.width - 35 * sizeMultiplier
                        width: 30 * sizeMultiplier
                        height: 30 * sizeMultiplier
                        source: "arrow.png"
                    }
                }
            }
        }
    model: ListModel {
        ListElement {
            title: "Home"
            subtitle: "Go back to dashboard"
            icon: "home.png"
        }

        ListElement {
            title: "Map"
            subtitle: "Help navigate to your destination"
            icon: "map.png"
        }

        ListElement {
            title: "Profile"
            subtitle: "Customize your profile picture"
            icon: "profile.png"
        }

        ListElement {
            title: "Search"
            subtitle: "Search for nearby places"
            icon: "search.png"
        }

        ListElement {
            title: "Settings"
            subtitle: "Customize your app settings"
            icon: "settings.png"
        }
    }
  }
}
```

4. After that, open up `main.qml` and replace the code with this:

```
import QtQuick 2.4
import QtQuick.Window 2.2

Window {
  visible: true
  width: 480
  height: 480

  MainForm {
    anchors.fill: parent

    MouseArea {
      onPressed: row1.opacity = 0.5
      onReleased: row1.opacity = 1.0
    }
  }
}
```

5. Build and run the program, and now your program should look like this:

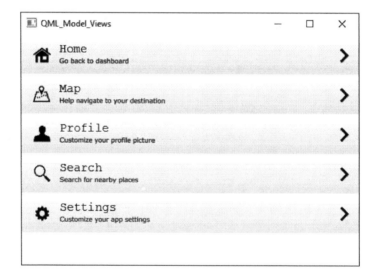

How it works...

Qt Quick allows us to customize the look of each row of the list view with ease. The `delegate` defines what each row will look like and the `model` is where you store the data that will be displayed on the list view.

In this example, we added a background with a gradient on each row, then we also added an icon on each side of the item, a title, a description, and a mouse area widget that makes each row of the list view clickable. The delegate is not static, as we allow the model to change the title, description, and the icon to make each row look unique.

In `main.qml`, we defined the behavior of the mouse area widget, which will halve its own opacity value lower when pressed and return to fully opaque when released. Since all other elements, such as title, icon, and so on, are all the children of the mouse area widget, they all will also automatically follow their parent widget's behavior and become semi-transparent.

Also, we have finally solved the display problem on mobile devices with high resolution and DPI. It's a very simple trick—first, we defined a variable called `sizeMultiplier`. The value of `sizeMultiplier` is the result of dividing the width of the window by a predefined value, say `480`, which is the current window width we used for the PC. Then, multiply `sizeMultiplier` by all the widget variables that have to do with size and position, including font size. Do note that in this case, you should use the `pixelSize` property for text instead of `pointSize`, so that you will get the correct display when multiplying by `sizeMultiplier`. The following screenshot shows you what the app looks like on the mobile device with and without `sizeMultiplier`:

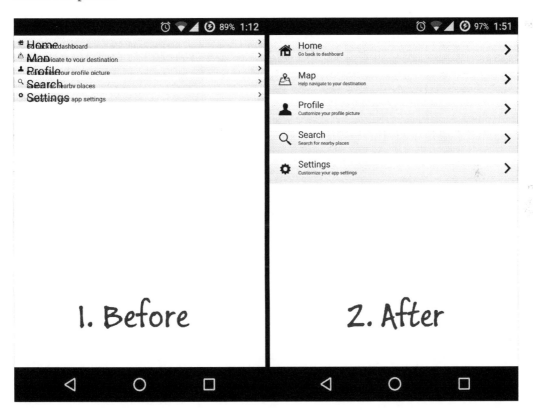

Notice that you may get a messed up UI in the editor once you multiply everything with the `sizeMultiplier` variable. This is because the `width` variable may return as `0` in the editor. Hence, by multiplying `0` by `480`, you may get the result `0`, which makes the entire UI to look funny. However, it will look fine when running the actual program. If you want to preview the UI on the editor, temporarily set the `sizeMultiplier` to `1`.

Integrating QML and C++

Qt supports bridging between C++ classes with the QML engine. This combination allows developers to take advantage of both the simplicity of QML and the flexibility of C++. You can even integrate features that are not supported by Qt from an external library, then pass the resulting data to Qt Quick to be displayed in the UI. In this example, we will learn how to export our UI components from QML to the C++ framework and manipulate their properties before displaying them on screen.

How to do it...

1. Once again, we will start everything from scratch. Therefore, create a new Qt Quick application project in Qt Creator and open up `MainForm.ui.qml`.

2. We can keep the mouse area and text widget, but place the text widget at the bottom of the window. Change the **Text** property of the text widget to **Change this text using C++** and set its font size to `18`. After that, go to the **Layout** tab and enable both **Vertical center anchor** and **Horizontal center anchor** to ensure it's always somewhere in the middle of the window, regardless of how you rescale the window. Set the **Margin** for the **Vertical center anchor** to `120`:

3. Next, drag a **Rectangle** widget from the **Library** window to the canvas and set its color to #ff0d0d. Set its **Width** and **Height** to 200 and enable both the vertical and horizontal center anchor. After that, set the **Margin** of the horizontal center anchor to -14. Your UI should now look something like this:

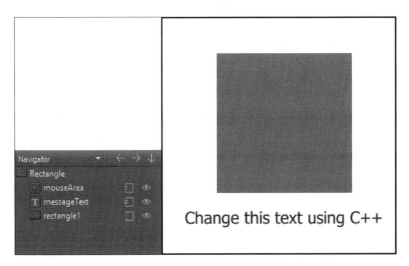

4. Once you are done with that, right-click on your project directory in Qt Creator and choose **Add New**. Then, a window will pop up and let you pick a file template. Select **C++ Class** and press **Choose...**. After that, it will ask you to define the C++ class by filling in the information for the class. In this case, insert **MyClass** in the **Class Name** field and select **QObject** as the **Base class**. Then, make sure **Include QObject** option is ticked and you can now click the **Next** button, follow by the **Finish** button. Two files—myclass.h and myclass.cpp—will now be created and added to your project:

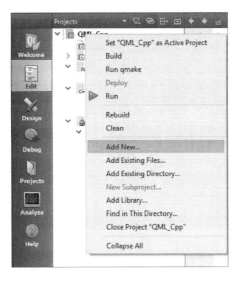

5. Now, open up `myclass.h` and add a variable and function below the class constructor, like so:

```
#ifndef MYCLASS_H
#define MYCLASS_H
#include <QObject>

class MyClass : public QObject
{
  Q_OBJECT
  public:
    explicit MyClass(QObject *parent = 0);

    // Object pointer
    QObject* myObject;

    // Must call Q_INVOKABLE so that this function can be used in
QML
    Q_INVOKABLE void setMyObject(QObject* obj);

  signals:

  public slots:
};

#endif // MYCLASS_H
```

6. After that, open up `myclass.cpp` and define the `setMyObject()` function:

```
#include "myclass.h"

MyClass::MyClass(QObject *parent) : QObject(parent)
{
}

void MyClass::setMyObject(QObject* obj)
{
  // Set the object pointer
  myObject = obj;
}
```

7. We can now close `myclass.cpp` and open up `main.qml`. At the top of the file, add in the third line, which imports the custom library we just created in C++:

```
import QtQuick 2.4
import QtQuick.Window 2.2
import MyClassLib 1.0
```

8. Then, define `MyClass` in the `Window` object and call its function `setMyObject()` within the `MainForm` object, like so:

```
Window {
   visible: true
   width: 480
   height: 320

   MyClass
   {
      id: myclass
   }

   MainForm {
      anchors.fill: parent
      mouseArea.onClicked: {
         Qt.quit();
      }
      Component.onCompleted:
         myclass.setMyObject(messageText);
   }
}
```

9. Lastly, open up `main.cpp` and register the custom class to the QML engine. We also change the properties of the text widget and the rectangle here using C++ code:

```
#include <QGuiApplication>
#include <QQmlApplicationEngine>
#include <QtQml>
#include <QQuickView>
#include <QQuickItem>
#include <QQuickView>
#include "myclass.h"
```

```
int main(int argc, char *argv[])
{
    // Register your class to QML
    qmlRegisterType<MyClass>("MyClassLib", 1, 0, "MyClass");

    QGuiApplication app(argc, argv);

    QQmlApplicationEngine engine;
    engine.load(QUrl(QStringLiteral("qrc:/main.qml")));

    QObject* root = engine.rootObjects().value(0);

    QObject* messageText =
        root->findChild<QObject*>("messageText");
    messageText->setProperty("text", QVariant("C++ is now in
        control!"));
    messageText->setProperty("color", QVariant("green"));

    QObject* square = root->findChild<QObject*>("square");
    square->setProperty("color", QVariant("blue"));

    return app.exec();
}
```

10. Build and run the program now, and you should see the colors of the rectangle and the text are completely different from what you defined earlier in Qt Quick. This is because their properties have been changed by the C++ code:

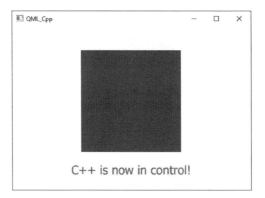

How it works...

QML is designed to be easily extensible through C++ code. The classes in the Qt QML module enable QML objects to be loaded and manipulated from C++.

Only classes that are inherited from the `QObject` base class can be integrated with QML, as it is part of the Qt ecosystem. Once the class has been registered with the QML engine, we get the root item from the QML engine and use it to find the objects we want to manipulate. After that, use the `setProperty()` function to change any of the properties belong to the widget.

Notice that the `Q_INVOKABLE` macro is required in front of the function that you intend to call in QML. Without it, Qt will not expose the function to Qt Quick and you will not be able to call it.

6
XML Parsing Made Easy

In this chapter, we will cover the following recipes:

- ▸ Processing XML data using stream reader
- ▸ Writing XML data using stream writer
- ▸ Processing XML data using the QDomDocument class
- ▸ Writing XML data using the QDomDocument class
- ▸ Using Google's Geocoding API

Introduction

XML is the file extension of a type of file format called **Extensible Markup Language**, which is used to store information in a structured format. The XML format is used extensively for the Web, as well as other applications. HTML, for instance, is the file format used for creating web pages and is based upon the XML format. Starting from Microsoft Office 2007, Microsoft Office uses the XML-based file formats, such as `.docx`, `.xlsx`, `.pptx`, and so on.

Processing XML data using stream reader

In this section, we will learn how to process data taken from an XML file and extract it using the stream reader.

How to do it...

Let's create a simple program that reads and processes XML files by following these steps:

1. As usual, create a new **Qt Widgets Application** project at your desired location.

2. Next, open up any text editor and create an XML file that looks like the following, then save it as `scene.xml`:

```xml
<?xml version="1.0" encoding="UTF-8"?>
<scene>
  <object tag="building">
    <name>Library</name>
    <position>120.0,0.0,50.68</position>
    <rotation>0.0,0.0,0.0</rotation>
    <scale>1.0,1.0,1.0</scale>
  </object>
  <object tag="building">
    <name>Town Hall</name>
    <position>80.2,0.0,20.5</position>
    <rotation>0.0,0.0,0.0</rotation>
    <scale>1.0,1.0,1.0</scale>
  </object>
  <object tag="prop">
    <name>Tree</name>
    <position>10.46,-0.2,80.2</position>
    <rotation>0.0,0.0,0.0</rotation>
    <scale>1.0,1.0,1.0</scale>
  </object>
</scene>
```

3. Next, go back to Qt Creator and open up `mainwindow.h`. Add the following headers at the top of the script, right after `#include <QMainWindow>`:

```cpp
#include <QXmlStreamReader>
#include <QDebug>
#include <QFile>
#include <QFileDialog>
```

4. Then, open up `mainwindow.ui` and drag a **Push Button** from the widget box on the left-hand side to the UI editor. Change the object name of the button to `loadXmlButton` and its display text to **Load XML**:

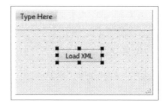

5. After that, right-click on the button and select **Go to slot....** A window will pop up with a list of signals available for selection.

6. Choose the default `clicked()` option and press the **OK** button. Qt will now insert a slot function in your header and source files called `on_loadXmlButton_clicked()`.

7. Now, add the following code to the `on_loadXmlButton_clicked()` function:

```cpp
void MainWindow::on_loadXmlButton_clicked()
{
    QXmlStreamReader xml;

    QString filename = QFileDialog::getOpenFileName(this, "Open Xml", ".", "Xml files (*.xml)");
    QFile file(filename);
    if (!file.open(QFile::ReadOnly | QFile::Text))
        qDebug() << "Error loading XML file.";
    xml.setDevice(&file);

    while (!xml.atEnd())
    {
        if (xml.isStartElement())
        {
            QString name = xml.name().toString();

            if (name == "object")
            {
                qDebug() << "[Object]=======================================";

                for (int i = 0; i < xml.attributes().size(); i++)
                {
                    qDebug() << xml.attributes().at(i).name() << xml.attributes().at(i).value();
                }
            }

            if (name == "name" || name == "position" || name == "rotation" || name == "scale")
            {
                QString text = xml.readElementText();
                qDebug() << name << text;
            }
        }

        if (xml.isEndElement())
        {
            QString name = xml.name().toString();

            if (name == "object")
            {
                qDebug() << "===========================================";
            }
        }

        xml.readNext();
    }

    if (xml.hasError())
    {
        qDebug() << "Error loading XML:" << xml.errorString();
    }
}
```

8. Build and run the project now and you see a window popping up that looks like the one you made in Step 4:

9. Click on the **Load XML** button and you should see the file selector window popping up on screen. Select the XML file you just created in Step 2 and press the **Select** button. After that, you should see the following debug text appear on the application output window in Qt Creator, which indicates the program has successfully loaded the data from the XML file you just selected:

```
[Object]==================================
"tag" "building"
"name" "Library"
"position" "120.0,0.0,50.68"
"rotation" "0.0,0.0,0.0"
"scale" "1.0,1.0,1.0"
==========================================
[Object]==================================
"tag" "building"
"name" "Town Hall"
"position" "80.2,0.0,20.5"
"rotation" "0.0,0.0,0.0"
"scale" "1.0,1.0,1.0"
==========================================
[Object]==================================
"tag" "prop"
"name" "Tree"
"position" "10.46,-0.2,80.2"
"rotation" "0.0,0.0,0.0"
"scale" "1.0,1.0,1.0"
==========================================
```

How it works...

What we're trying to do in this example is to extract and process data from an XML file using the QXmlStreamReader class. Imagine you're making a computer game and you're using XML files to store the attributes of all the objects in your game scene. In this case, the XML format plays an important role in storing the data in a structured way, which allows for easy extraction.

To begin with, we need to add the header of the class related to XML to our source file, which in this case is the QXmlStreamReader class. QXmlStreamReader is built into Qt's core library, so there is no need to include any additional modules with it, which also means that it's the recommended class to use for processing XML data in Qt.

Once we clicked on the **Load XML** button, the `on_loadXmlButton_clicked()` slot will be called; this is where we write the code for processing the XML data.

First, we use a file dialog for selecting the XML file we want to process. Then, send the selected file's filename, together with its path, to the `QFile` class to open and read the text data of the XML file. After that, the file's data is sent to the `QXmlStreamReader` class for processing.

We use a while-loop to read through the entire XML file and check every element processed by the stream reader. We determine whether the element is a start element or an end element. If it's a start element, we will then check the name of the element to determine whether the element should contain any data that we need.

Then, we will extract the data, either in the form of an attribute or text. An element may have more than one attribute, which is why we must loop through all the attributes and extract them one by one.

There's more...

Besides the web browser, many commercial game engines and interactive applications also use the XML format to store information for in-game scenes, meshes, and other forms of asset used in their product. This is because the XML format provides many benefits over other file formats, such as a compact file size, high flexibility and extendibility, easy file recovery, and a relational tree structure that allows it to be used for highly efficient and performance-critical applications such as search engines, intelligent data mining servers, scientific simulations, and so on.

Let's learn a little bit about the format of an XML file. We will use `scene.xml`, which we used in the previous example and looks like this:

```
<?xml version="1.0" encoding="UTF-8"?>
<scene>
  <object tag="building">
    <name>Library</name>
    <position>120.0,0.0,50.68</position>
    <rotation>0.0,0.0,0.0</rotation>
    <scale>1.0,1.0,1.0</scale>
  </object>
  <object tag="building">
    <name>Town Hall</name>
    <position>80.2,0.0,20.5</position>
    <rotation>0.0,0.0,0.0</rotation>
    <scale>1.0,1.0,1.0</scale>
  </object>
  <object tag="prop">
```

```
      <name>Tree</name>
      <position>10.46,-0.2,80.2</position>
      <rotation>0.0,0.0,0.0</rotation>
      <scale>1.0,1.0,1.0</scale>
   </object>
</scene>
```

In XML, a tag is a line of markup text that starts with a < symbol and ends with a > symbol. For example, `<scene>` is a tag called `scene`, `<object>` is a tag called `object` and so on. Tags come in three flavors:

▸ Start tag, for example `<scene>`

▸ End tag, for example `</scene>`

▸ Empty-element tag, for example `<scene />`

Whenever you write a start tag, it must end with an end tag, otherwise your XML data will be invalid. An empty-element tag, however, is a standalone tag and does not need an end tag behind it.

At the top of `scene.xml`, you will see a tag called `xml` which stores the version of the XML format and the encoding type, which in this case is XML version 1.0 and UTF-8 (8-bit Unicode) encoding. This line is called XML declaration and it must exist in any of your XML files to validate its format.

After that, you will see tags that have attributes stored in them, for example `<object tag="building">`. This means that the `object` tag contains an attribute called `tag`, which contains a value, `building`. You can put as many attributes as you like in a tag, for example `<object tag="building" color="red" name="LA Community Hospital" coordinate="34.0191757,-118.2567239">`. Each of these attributes stores distinctive data that can be retrieved easily using Qt.

Other than that, you can also store data between the start tag and the end tag, for example `<name>Town Hall</name>`. This method, however, is not relevant to the empty-element tag, since it is a standalone tag and isn't followed by a close tag. Therefore, you can only store attributes in an empty-element tag.

To learn more about the XML format, visit `http://www.w3schools.com/xml`.

Writing XML data using Stream Writer

Since we have learned how to process data obtained from an XML file in the previous recipe, we will move on to learning how to save data to an XML file. We will continue with the previous example and add to it.

How to do it...

We will learn how to save data into an XML file through the following steps:

1. First, add another button to `mainwindow.ui` and set its object name as `saveXmlButton` and its label as **Save XML**:

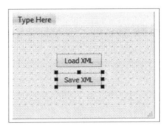

2. Next, right-click on the button and select **Go to slot...**. A window will pop up with a list of signals available for selection. Select the `clicked()` option and click **OK**. A signal function called `on_saveXmlButton_clicked()` will now be automatically added to both your `mainwindow.h` and `mainwindow.cpp` file by Qt:

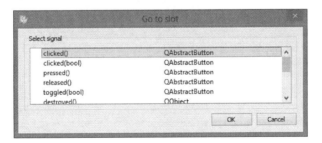

3. After that, add the following code to the `on_saveXmlButton_clicked()` function:

```
QXmlStreamWriter xml;

QString filename = QFileDialog::getSaveFileName(this, "Save
  Xml", ".", "Xml files (*.xml)");
QFile file(filename);
if (!file.open(QFile::WriteOnly | QFile::Text))
  qDebug() << "Error saving XML file.";
```

```
xml.setDevice(&file);

xml.setAutoFormatting(true);
xml.writeStartDocument();

xml.writeStartElement("contact");
xml.writeAttribute("category", "Friend");
xml.writeTextElement("name", "John Doe");
xml.writeTextElement("age", "32");
xml.writeTextElement("address", "114B, 2nd Floor, Sterling
    Apartment, Morrison Town");
xml.writeTextElement("phone", "0221743566");
xml.writeEndElement();

xml.writeStartElement("contact");
xml.writeAttribute("category", "Family");
xml.writeTextElement("name", "Jane Smith");
xml.writeTextElement("age", "24");
xml.writeTextElement("address", "13, Ave Park, Alexandria");
xml.writeTextElement("phone", "0025728396");
xml.writeEndElement();

xml.writeEndDocument();
```

4. Build and run the program and you should see an additional button on the program UI:

5. Click on the **Save XML** button and a save file dialog will appear on the screen. Type the filename you desire and click the **Save** button.

6. Open up the XML file you just saved with any text editor. The content of the file should look like this:

```xml
<?xml version="1.0" encoding="UTF-8"?>
<contact category="Friend">
  <name>John Doe</name>
  <age>32</age>
  <address>114B, 2nd Floor, Sterling Apartment, Morrison
    Town</address>
  <phone>0221743566</phone>
</contact>
<contact category="Family">
  <name>Jane Smith</name>
  <age>24</age>
  <address>13, Ave Park, Alexandria</address>
  <phone>0025728396</phone>
</contact>
```

How it works...

The saving process is more or less similar to loading an XML file in the previous example. The only difference is instead of using the `QXmlStreamReader` class, we switched to using the `QXmlStreamWriter` class instead.

We are still using the file dialog and the `QFile` class to save the XML file. This time, we have to change the open mode from `QFile::ReadOnly` to `QFile::WriteOnly` before passing the `QFile` class to the stream writer.

Before we start writing any data to the new XML file, we must set auto formatting to `true`, otherwise there will be no spacing; it also adds new lines and indentation to the XML file to make it look tidy and easier to read. However, if that is your intention (making it harder to read and edit by the user), then you can just ignore the `setAutoFormatting()` function.

Next, start writing the XML file by calling `writeStartDocument()`, followed by all the elements you want to save to the file, and at the end we call the `writeEndDocument()` function to stop writing.

Each element must have a start and end tag in order for the reading process to work properly. The attributes of an element will be stored in the start tag, while the text data will be stored between the start and end tags.

If we're writing an element that contains a group of child elements, then we must call `writeStartElement()` before writing the child elements. Then, call `writeEndElement()` after saving all its child elements to close the group with an end tag. The `writetextElement()` function, however, will automatically add the end tag for you so you don't have to worry about that one.

You can call the `writeAttribute()` function to add an attribute to an element. There is no limit on how many attributes you can add to a particular element.

Processing XML data using the QDomDocument class

Qt allows multiple ways to parse XML data, including the common method that we have covered in the previous examples. This time around, we're going to learn how to read data from an XML file using another class, called `QDomDocument`.

How to do it...

Processing XML data using the `QDomDocument` class is really simple:

1. First of all, we need to add the XML module to our project by opening the project (`.pro`) file and add the text `xml` at the back of `core` and `gui`, like so:

   ```
   QT += core gui xml
   ```

2. Then, just like what we did in the first example in this chapter, create a user interface that carries a button that says **Load XML**:

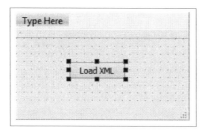

3. After that, right-click on the button, choose **Go to slot...**, and select the `clicked()` option. Press the **OK** button and Qt will add a slot function to your source code.

4. Go to `mainwindow.h` and add the following headers so that we can make use of these classes:

   ```
   #include <QDomDocument>
   #include <QDebug>
   #include <QFile>
   #include <QFileDialog>
   ```

5. Next, go to `mainwindow.cpp` and insert the following code to the button's `clicked()` slot function:

```cpp
void MainWindow::on_loadXmlButton_clicked()
{
    QDomDocument xml;

    QString filename = QFileDialog::getOpenFileName(this, "Open Xml", ".", "Xml files (*.xml)");
    QFile file(filename);
    if (!file.open(QFile::ReadOnly | QFile::Text))
        qDebug() << "Error loading XML file.";
    if (!xml.setContent(&file))
    {
        qDebug() << "Error setting content.";
        file.close();
        return;
    }
    file.close();

    QDomElement element = xml.documentElement();
    QDomNode node = element.firstChild();

    while (!node.isNull())
    {
        QDomElement nodeElement = node.toElement();
        if (!nodeElement.isNull())
        {
            if (nodeElement.tagName() == "object")
            {
                qDebug() << "[Object]=====================================";

                QDomNode childNode = nodeElement.firstChild();

                while (!childNode.isNull())
                {
                    QDomElement childNodeElement = childNode.toElement();

                    QString name = childNodeElement.tagName();
                    if (name == "name" || name == "position" || name == "rotation" || name == "scale")
                    {
                        QString text = childNodeElement.text();
                        qDebug() << name << text;
                    }

                    childNode = childNode.nextSibling();
                }
            }

            qDebug() << "=============================================================";
        }

        node = node.nextSibling();
    }
}
```

6. Compile and run the program now. Click on the **Load XML** button and select the XML file used in the first example. You should see the following output:

```
[Object]=====================================
"tag" "building"
"name" "Library"
"position" "120.0,0.0,50.68"
"rotation" "0.0,0.0,0.0"
"scale" "1.0,1.0,1.0"
=====================================
[Object]=====================================
"tag" "building"
"name" "Town Hall"
"position" "80.2,0.0,20.5"
"rotation" "0.0,0.0,0.0"
"scale" "1.0,1.0,1.0"
=====================================
[Object]=====================================
"tag" "prop"
"name" "Tree"
"position" "10.46,-0.2,80.2"
"rotation" "0.0,0.0,0.0"
"scale" "1.0,1.0,1.0"
=====================================
```

How it works...

Compared to `QXmlStreamReader`, the `QDomDocument` class is less straightforward when comes to loading or saving XML data. However, `QDomDocument` does it in a strict way by making sure each element is linked to its respective parent element recursively, like in a tree structure. Unlike `QXmlStreamReader`, `QDomDocument` allows us to save data to an element created earlier, in a later timeframe.

Since `QDomDocument` is not part of the Qt core library, we must add the XML module to our project manually. Otherwise, we will not be able to access `QDomDocument` and other classes related to it.

First, we load the XML file and extract its content to the `QDomDocument` class. Then, we get its document element, which acts as the root document, and obtain its direct children. We then convert each of the child nodes to `QDomElement` and obtain their tag names.

By checking tag names, we are able to determine the type of data we're expecting from each element. Since this is the first layer of elements with the tag name `object`, we don't expect any data from them; we repeat Step 3 again but this time around, we're going to do it on the element with the tag name `object` and obtain all its direct children, which means the grandchildren of the document element.

Again, by checking the tag name, we're able to know what data we're expecting from its children elements. If the tag name matches the ones we're expecting (in this case, name, position, rotation, scale) then we can obtain its data by calling QDomElement::text().

Writing XML data using the QDomDocument class

In this example, we will learn how to write data to an XML file using the QDomDocument class. We will continue from the previous example and just add stuff to it.

How to do it...

To learn how to save data into an XML file using the QDomDocument class, let's do the following:

1. First of all, add the second button to the UI, called **Save XML**:

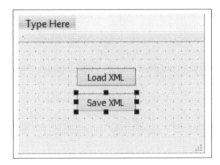

2. Right-click on the **Save XML** button and select **Go to slot...**. Then, pick the **clicked()** option and click **OK**. A new clicked() slot function will now be added to your source files.

3. After that, write the following code within the button's `clicked()` slot function:

```cpp
void MainWindow::on_saveXmlButton_clicked()
{
    QString filename = QFileDialog::getSaveFileName(this, "Save Xml", ".", "Xml files (*.xml)");
    QFile file(filename);
    if (!file.open(QFile::WriteOnly | QFile::Text))
    {
        qDebug() << "Error saving XML file.";
        file.close();
        return;
    }

    QDomDocument xml("contact");

    // John Doe
    QDomElement root = xml.createElement("contact");
    root.setAttribute("category", "Family");
    xml.appendChild(root);

    QDomElement tagName = xml.createElement("name");
    root.appendChild(tagName);
    QDomText textName = xml.createTextNode("John Doe");
    tagName.appendChild(textName);

    QDomElement tagAge = xml.createElement("age");
    root.appendChild(tagAge);
    QDomText textAge = xml.createTextNode("32");
    tagAge.appendChild(textAge);

    QDomElement tagAddress = xml.createElement("address");
    root.appendChild(tagAddress);
    QDomText textAddress = xml.createTextNode("114B, 2nd Floor, Sterling Apartment, Morrisontown");
    tagAddress.appendChild(textAddress);
```

```cpp
    QDomElement tagPhone = xml.createElement("phone");
    root.appendChild(tagPhone);
    QDomText textPhone = xml.createTextNode("0221743566");
    tagPhone.appendChild(textPhone);

    // Jane Smith
    QDomElement root2 = xml.createElement("contact");
    root2.setAttribute("category", "Friend");
    xml.appendChild(root2);

    QDomElement tagName2 = xml.createElement("name");
    root2.appendChild(tagName2);
    QDomText textName2 = xml.createTextNode("John Doe");
    tagName2.appendChild(textName2);

    QDomElement tagAge2 = xml.createElement("age");
    root2.appendChild(tagAge2);
    QDomText textAge2 = xml.createTextNode("24");
    tagAge2.appendChild(textAge2);

    QDomElement tagAddress2 = xml.createElement("address");
    root2.appendChild(tagAddress2);
    QDomText textAddress2 = xml.createTextNode("13, Ave Park, Alexandria");
    tagAddress2.appendChild(textAddress2);

    QDomElement tagPhone2 = xml.createElement("phone");
    root2.appendChild(tagPhone2);
    QDomText textPhone2 = xml.createTextNode("0025728396");
    tagPhone2.appendChild(textPhone2);

    // Save to file
    QTextStream output(&file);
    output << xml.toString();

    file.close();
}
```

4. Compile and run the program now and click on the **Save XML** button. Enter your desired filename in the save file dialog and click **Save**.

5. Open up the XML file you just saved in Step 4 with any text editor and you should see something like this:

```
<!DOCTYPE contact>
<contact category="Family">
  <name>John Doe</name>
  <age>32</age>
  <address>114B, 2nd Floor, Sterling Apartment,
    Morrisontown</address>
  <phone>0221743566</phone>
</contact>
<contact category="Friend">
  <name>John Doe</name>
  <age>32</age>
  <address>114B, 2nd Floor, Sterling Apartment,
    Morrisontown</address>
  <phone>0221743566</phone>
</contact>
```

How it works...

Similar to the previous example, we first initiate the file dialog and declare a QDomDocument object.

Then, we create the root element by calling QDomDocument::createElement(). Any element created from the QDomDocument will NOT automatically become its direct child unless we append the newly created element as its child.

To create the grandchildren of QDomDocument, simply append the newly created elements to the root element instead. By utilizing the append() function, we can easily arrange the XML data in a tree structure without wrapping our head around it. This, in my opinion, is the advantage of using QDomDocument instead of QXmlStreamReader.

We can then add attributes to an element by calling QDomElement::setAttribute(). We can also create a text node by calling QDomDocument::createTextNode() and appending it to any of the elements in the XML structure.

After we are done structuring the XML data, we can then output all the data in the form of text to the QTextStream class and allow it to save the data into a file.

Using Google's Geocoding API

In this example, we will learn how to obtain the full address of a specific location by using Google's Geocoding API.

How to do it...

Let's create a program that utilizes the Geocoding API by following these steps:

1. First, create a new **Qt Widgets Application** project.

2. Next, open up `mainwindow.ui` and add a couple of text labels, input fields, and a button to make your UI to look similar to this:

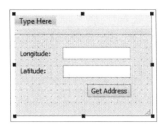

3. After that, open up your project (`.pro`) file and add the network module to your project. You can do that by simply adding the `network` text after `core` and `gui`, like so:

   ```
   QT += core gui network
   ```

4. Then, open up `mainwindow.h` and add the following headers to the source code, right after the line `#include <QMainWindow>`:

   ```
   #include <QDebug>
   #include <QtNetwork/QNetworkAccessManager>
   #include <QtNetwork/QNetworkReply>
   #include <QXmlStreamReader>
   ```

5. Next, declare a slot function manually and call it `getAddressFinished()`:

   ```
   private slots:
      void getAddressFinished(QNetworkReply* reply);
   ```

6. Right after that, declare a `private` variable called `addressRequest`:

   ```
   private:
      QNetworkAccessManager* addressRequest;
   ```

7. Once you are done with that, open up `mainwindow.ui` again, right-click on the **Get Address** button, and select **Go to slot....** Then choose the **clicked()** option and press **OK**. A slot function will now be added to both the `mainwindow.h` and `mainwindow.cpp` source files.

8. Now, open up `mainwindow.cpp` and add the following code to the class constructor:

```
MainWindow::MainWindow(QWidget *parent) :
  QMainWindow(parent),
  ui(new Ui::MainWindow)
{
  ui->setupUi(this);

  addressRequest = new QNetworkAccessManager();
  connect(addressRequest, SIGNAL(finished(QNetworkReply*)),
    SLOT(getAddressFinished(QNetworkReply*)));
}
```

9. Then, we will add the following code to the `getAddressFinished()` slot function we declared manually just now:

```
void MainWindow::getAddressFinished(QNetworkReply* reply)
{
  QByteArray bytes = reply->readAll();

  //qDebug() << QString::fromUtf8(bytes.data(),
    bytes.size());

  QXmlStreamReader xml;
  xml.addData(bytes);

  while(!xml.atEnd())
  {
    if (xml.isStartElement())
    {
      QString name = xml.name().toString();
      //qDebug() << name;

      if (name == "formatted_address")
      {
        QString text = xml.readElementText();
        qDebug() << "Address:" << text;
        return;
      }
    }
  }
```

```
        xml.readNext();
    }

    if (xml.hasError())
    {
        qDebug() << "Error loading XML:" <<
            xml.errorString();
        return;
    }

    qDebug() << "No result.";
}
```

10. Finally, add the following code to the `clicked()` slot function created by Qt:

```
void MainWindow::on_getAddressButton_clicked()
{
    QString latitude = ui->latitude->text();
    QString longitude = ui->longitude->text();

    QNetworkRequest request;
    request.setUrl(QUrl("http://maps.googleapis.com/
        maps/api/geocode/xml?latlng=" + latitude + "
        ," + longitude + "&sensor=false"));
    addressRequest->get(request);
}
```

11. Build and run the program now and you should be able to obtain the address by inserting the longitude and latitude values and clicking the **Get Address** button:

12. Let's try with longitude `-73.9780838` and latitude `40.6712957`. Click the **Get Address** button and you will see the following result in the application output window:

```
Address: "180-190 7th Ave, Brooklyn, NY 11215, USA"
```

How it works...

I won't be able to tell you exactly how Google obtains the address from its backend system, but I can teach you how to request the data from Google by using `QNetworkRequest`. Basically, all you need to do is to set the URL of the network request to the URL I used in the previous source code and append both the latitude and longitude information to the URL. After that, all we can do is wait for the response from the Google API server.

Do notice that we need to specify XML as the desired format when sending the request to Google; otherwise, it may return the results in JSON format instead. This can be done by adding the `xml` keyword within the network request URL, as highlighted here:

```
request.setUrl(QUrl("http://maps.googleapis.com/maps/
    api/geocode/xml?latlng=" + latitude + "," + longitude +
    "&sensor=false"));
```

When the program the received the response from Google, the `getAddressFinished()` slot function will be called and we will be able to obtain the data sent by Google through `QNetworkReply`.

Google usually replies with a long text in XML format, which contains a ton of data we don't need. We used `QXmlStreamReader` to parse the data because in this case we don't have to care about the parent-child relationship of the XML structure.

All we need is the text stored in the `formatted_address` element in the XML data. Since there is more than one element by the name of `formatted_address`, we just need to find the first one and ignore the rest.

You can also do the reverse by providing an address to Google and obtain the location's coordinate from its network response.

There's more...

Google's Geocoding API is part of the Google Maps APIs Web Services, which provides geographical data for your map applications. Besides the Geocoding API, you can also use their Location API, Geolocation API, Time Zone API, and so on to achieve your desired results.

For more information regarding the Google Maps APIs Web Services, visit this link: `https://developers.google.com/maps/web-services`

7
Conversion Library

In this chapter, we will cover the following recipes:

- ▸ Data conversion
- ▸ Image conversion
- ▸ Video conversion
- ▸ Currency conversion

Introduction

Data kept within our computer environment is encoded in a variety of ways. Sometimes it can be used directly for a certain purpose, other times it needs to be converted to another format in order to fit the context of the task. The process of converting the data from one format to another also varies, depending on the source format as well as the target format. Sometimes the process can be very complex, especially when dealing with data that is feature-rich and sensitive, such as image or video conversion. Even a small error during the conversion process may render the file unusable.

Data conversion

Qt provides a set of classes and functions for easily converting between different types of data. This makes Qt more than just a GUI library; it is a complete platform for software development. The `QVariant` class, which we will be using in the following example, makes Qt even more flexible and powerful compared to similar conversion functionalities provided by the C++ standard library.

How to do it...

Let's learn how to convert various data types in Qt by following these steps:

1. Open up Qt Creator and create a new **Qt Console Application** project by going to **File | New File or Project**:

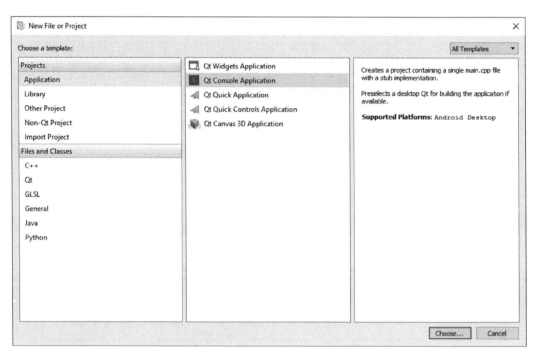

2. Next, open up `main.cpp` and add the following headers to it:

```cpp
#include <QCoreApplication>
#include <QDebug>
#include <QtMath>
#include <QDateTime>
#include <QTextCodec>
#include <iostream>
```

3. Then, in the `main()` function, add the following code to convert a string to a number:

```cpp
int numberA = 2;
QString numberB = "5";
qDebug() << "1) " << "2 + 5 =" << numberA + numberB.toInt();
```

4. After that, we'll convert a number back to a string:

```
float numberC = 10.25;
float numberD = 2;
QString result = QString::number(numberC * numberD);
qDebug() << "2) " << "10.25 * 2 =" << result;
```

5. We also learn how to round down a value by using `qFloor()`:

```
float numberE = 10.3;
float numberF = qFloor(numberE);
qDebug() << "3) " << "Floor of 10.3 is" << numberF;
```

6. Then, by using `qCeil()`, we are able to round a number to the smallest integral value not smaller than its initial value:

```
float numberG = 10.3;
float numberH = qCeil(numberG);
qDebug() << "4) " << "Ceil of 10.3 is" << numberH;
```

7. After that, we will create a date time variable by converting from a string:

```
QString dateTimeAString = "2016-05-04 12:24:00";
QDateTime dateTimeA =
    QDateTime::fromString(dateTimeAString, "yyyy-MM-dd hh:mm:ss");
qDebug() << "5) " << dateTimeA;
```

8. Subsequently, we can also convert the date time variable back to a string with our own custom format:

```
QDateTime dateTimeB = QDateTime::currentDateTime();
QString dateTimeBString = dateTimeB.toString("dd/MM/yy hh:mm");
qDebug() << "6) " << dateTimeBString;
```

9. We can call the `QString::toUpper()` function to convert a string variable to all capital letters:

```
QString hello1 = "hello world!";
qDebug() << "7) " << hello1.toUpper();
```

10. On the other hand, calling `QString::toLower()` will convert the string to all lowercase:

```
QString hello2 = "HELLO WORLD!";
qDebug() << "8) " << hello2.toLower();
```

11. The `QVariant` class provided by Qt is a very powerful data type that can be easily converted to other types without any effort by the programmer:

```
QVariant aNumber = QVariant(3.14159);
double aResult = 12.5 * aNumber.toDouble();
qDebug() << "9) 12.5 * 3.14159 =" << aResult;
```

12. This demonstrates how a single `QVariant` variable can be simultaneously converted to multiple data types without any effort by the programmer:

```
qDebug() << "10) ";
QVariant myData = QVariant(10);
qDebug() << myData;
myData = myData.toFloat() / 2.135;
qDebug() << myData;
myData = true;
qDebug() << myData;
myData = QDateTime::currentDateTime();
qDebug() << myData;
myData = "Good bye!";
qDebug() << myData;
```

The full source code in `main.cpp` will now look like this:

```cpp
#include <QCoreApplication>
#include <QDebug>
#include <QtMath>
#include <QDateTime>
#include <QTextCodec>
#include <iostream>

int main(int argc, char *argv[])
{
    QCoreApplication a(argc, argv);

    // String to number
    int numberA = 2;
    QString numberB = "5";
    qDebug() << "1) " << "2 + 5 =" << numberA + numberB.toInt();

    // Number to string
    float numberC = 10.25;
    float numberD = 2;
    QString result = QString::number(numberC * numberD);
    qDebug() << "2) " << "10.25 * 2 =" << result;

    // Floor
    float numberE = 10.3;
    float numberF = qFloor(numberE);
    qDebug() << "3) " << "Floor of 10.3 is" << numberF;

    // Ceil
    float numberG = 10.3;
    float numberH = qCeil(numberG);
    qDebug() << "4) " << "Ceil of 10.3 is" << numberH;

    // Date time from string
    QString dateTimeAString = "2016-05-04 12:24:00";
    QDateTime dateTimeA = QDateTime::fromString(dateTimeAString, "yyyy-MM-dd hh:mm:ss");
    qDebug() << "5) " << dateTimeA;
```

```cpp
    // Date time to string
    QDateTime dateTimeB = QDateTime::currentDateTime();
    QString dateTimeBString = dateTimeB.toString("dd/MM/yy hh:mm");
    qDebug() << "6) " << dateTimeBString;

    // String to all uppercase
    QString hello1 = "hello world!";
    qDebug() << "7) " << hello1.toUpper();

    // String to all lowercase
    QString hello2 = "HELLO WORLD!";
    qDebug() << "8) " << hello2.toLower();

    // QVariant to double
    QVariant aNumber = QVariant(3.14159);
    double aResult = 12.5 * aNumber.toDouble();
    qDebug() << "9) 12.5 * 3.14159 =" << aResult;

    // QVariant different types
    qDebug() << "10) ";
    QVariant myData = QVariant(10);
    qDebug() << myData;
    myData = myData.toFloat() / 2.135;
    qDebug() << myData;
    myData = true;
    qDebug() << myData;
    myData = QDateTime::currentDateTime();
    qDebug() << myData;
    myData = "Good bye!";
    qDebug() << myData;

    return a.exec();
}
```

13. Compile and run the project now and you should see something like this:

How it works...

All the data types provided by Qt, such as `QString`, `QDateTime`, `QVariant`, and so on, contain functions that make conversion to other types easy and straightforward.

Qt also provides its own object conversion function, `qobject_cast()`, which doesn't rely on the standard library. It is also more compatible with Qt and works well for converting between Qt's widget types and data types.

Qt also provides you with the `QtMath` class, which helps you to manipulate number variables, such as rounding up a floating point number or converting an angle from degrees to radians.

`QVariant` is a special class that can be used to store data of all kinds of type. It can automatically determine the data type by examining the value stored in the variable. You can also easily convert the data to any of the types supported by the `QVariant` class by just calling a single function, such as `toFloat()`, `toInt()`, `toBool()`, `toChar()`, `toString()`, and so on.

There's more...

Be aware that each of these conversions takes computing power to make it happen. Even though modern computers are extremely fast at handling operations such as these, you should be careful not to overdo it with a large quantity at the same time. If you're converting a large set of variables for complex calculations, it might slow down your computer significantly, so therefore try to convert variables only whenever it's deemed necessary.

Image conversion

In this section, we will learn how to build a simple image converter that converts an image from one format to another. Qt supports reading and writing different types of image formats, and this support comes in the form of external DLL files due to licensing issues. However, you don't have to worry about that because as long as you include those DLL files in your project, it will work seamlessly across different formats. There are certain formats that only support reading and not writing, and some that support both. You can check out the full details at `http://doc.qt.io/qt-5/qtimageformats-index.html`.

How to do it...

Qt's built-in image libraries make image conversion really simple:

1. First of all, open up Qt Creator and create a new **Qt Widgets Application** project.

2. Open up `mainwindow.ui` and add a line edit and push button to the canvas for selecting image files, a combo box for selecting the desired file format, and another push button for starting the conversion process:

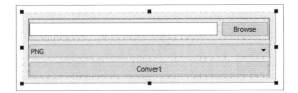

3. Next, double-click the combo box and a window will appear for editing the combo box. We will add three items to the combo box list by clicking the **+** button three times and renaming the items PNG, JPEG, and BMP:

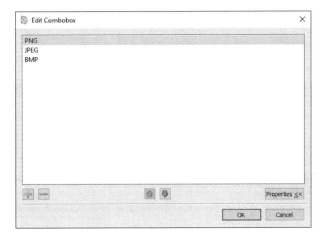

4. After that, right-click on one of the push buttons and select **Go to slot...**, then click the **OK** button. A slot function will then be automatically added to your source files. Then, repeat this step for the other push button as well:

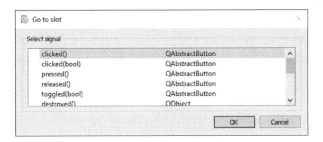

5. Once you are done with the UI, let's move over to the source code. Open up mainwindow.h and add in the following header:

```
#include <QMainWindow>
#include <QFileDialog>
#include <QMessageBox>
#include <QDebug>
```

6. Then, open up `mainwindow.cpp` and define what will happen when the **Browse** button is clicked, which in this case is opening the file dialog to select an image file:

```
void MainWindow::on_browseButton_clicked()
{
    QString fileName = QFileDialog::getOpenFileName(this,
        "Open Image", "", "Image Files (*.png *.jpg *.bmp)");
    ui->filePath->setText(fileName);
}
```

7. Finally, we also define what will happen when the **Convert** button is clicked:

```
void MainWindow::on_convertButton_clicked()
{
    QString fileName = ui->filePath->text();

    if (fileName != "")
    {
        QFileInfo fileInfo = QFile(fileName);
        QString newFileName = fileInfo.path() + "/" + fileInfo.completeBaseName();

        QImage image = QImage(ui->filePath->text());

        if (!image.isNull())
        {
            // 0 - PNG
            // 1 - JPG
            // 2 - BMP
            int format = ui->fileFormat->currentIndex();
            if (format == 0)
            {
                newFileName += ".png";
            }
            else if (format == 1)
            {
                newFileName += ".jpg";
            }
            else if (format == 2)
            {
                newFileName += ".bmp";
            }

            qDebug() << newFileName << format;

            if (image.save(newFileName, 0, -1))
            {
                QMessageBox::information(this, "Success", "Image successfully converted.");
            }
            else
            {
                QMessageBox::warning(this, "Failed", "Failed to convert image.");
            }
        }
        else
        {
            QMessageBox::warning(this, "Failed", "Failed to open image file.");
        }
    }
    else
    {
        QMessageBox::warning(this, "Failed", "No file is selected.");
    }
}
```

8. Build and run the program now and we should get a pretty simple image converter that looks like this:

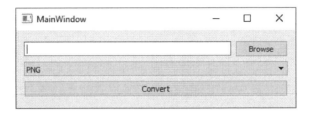

How it works...

The previous example uses the native `QImage` class from Qt, which contains functions that can access pixel data and manipulate it. It is also used to load an image file and extract its data through different decompression methods, depending on the format of the image. Once the data is extracted, you can then do anything you want with it, such as displaying the image on screen, manipulating its color information, resizing the image, or compressing it with another format and saving it as a file.

We used `QFileInfo` to separate the filename from the extension so that we can amend the extension name with the new format selected by the user from the combo box. This way we can save the newly converted image in the same folder as the original image and automatically give it the same file name as well, except in a different format.

As long as you're trying to convert the image to a format supported by Qt, all you need to do is to call `QImage::save()`. Internally, Qt will figure out the rest for you and output the image to the chosen format. In the `QImage::save()` function, there is a parameter that sets the image quality and another for setting the format. In this example, we just set both as the default values, which saves the image at the highest quality and lets Qt figure out the format by checking the extension stated in the output file name.

There's more...

Here are some tips. You can also convert an image to PDF by using the `QPdfWriter` class provided by Qt. Essentially, what you do is paint the selected image to the layout of a newly created PDF document and set its resolution accordingly. For more information about the `QPdfWriter` class, visit `http://doc.qt.io/qt-5/qpdfwriter.html`.

Video conversion

In this recipe, we will create a simple video converter using Qt and FFmpeg, a leading multimedia framework that is free and open source. Although Qt does support playing video files through its widget, it does not support video conversion at the moment. Fear not! You can actually still achieve the same goal by making your program cooperate with another standalone program through the `QProcess` class provided by Qt.

How to do it...

Let's make a simple video converter with the following steps:

1. Download FFmpeg (static package) from `http://ffmpeg.zeranoe.com/builds` and extract the contents to `C:/FFmpeg/`.

2. Then, open up Qt Creator and create a new **Qt Widgets Application** project by going to **File | New File or Project...**.

3. After that, open up `mainwindow.ui` and we're going to work on the program's user interface. Its UI is very similar to the previous example, except we add an extra text edit widget to the canvas, just below the combo box:

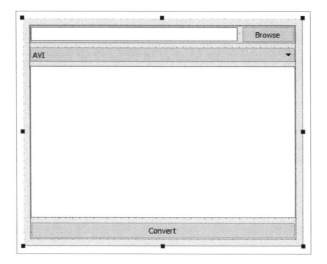

4. Double-click the combo box and a window will appear to edit the combo box. We will add three items to the combo box list by clicking the **+** button three times, and rename the items AVI, MP4, and MOV:

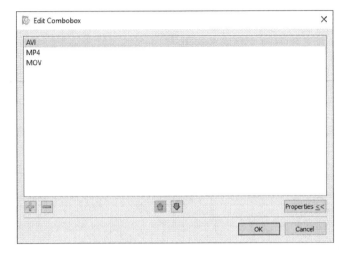

5. After that, right-click on one of the push buttons and select **Go to slot...**, then click the **OK** button. A slot function will then be automatically added to your source files. Then, repeat this step for the other push button as well.

6. After that, open up mainwindow.h and add the following headers to the top:

```
#include <QMainWindow>
#include <QFileDialog>
#include <QProcess>
#include <QMessageBox>
#include <QScrollBar>
#include <QDebug>
```

7. Then, add the following pointers under the public keyword:

```
public:
    explicit MainWindow(QWidget *parent = 0);
    ~MainWindow();

    QProcess* process;
    QString outputText;
    QString fileName;
    QString outputFileName;
```

8. Besides that, we also need to add three extra slot functions under the two functions that Qt created for us previously:

```
private slots:
  void on_browseButton_clicked();
  void on_convertButton_clicked();

  void processStarted();
  void readyReadStandardOutput();
  void processFinished();
```

9. Next, open up mainwindow.cpp and add the following code to the class constructor:

```
MainWindow::MainWindow(QWidget *parent) :
  QMainWindow(parent), ui(new Ui::MainWindow)
{
  ui->setupUi(this);

  process = new QProcess(this);
  connect(process, SIGNAL(started()), this,
    SLOT(processStarted()));
  connect(process,SIGNAL(readyReadStandardOutput()),
    this,SLOT(readyReadStandardOutput()));
  connect(process, SIGNAL(finished(int)), this,
    SLOT(processFinished()));
}
```

10. After that, we define what will happen when the **Browse** button is clicked, which in this case will open up the file dialog to choose the video file:

```
void MainWindow::on_browseButton_clicked()
{
  QString fileName = QFileDialog::getOpenFileName(this,
    "Open Video", "", "Video Files (*.avi *.mp4 *.mov)");
  ui->filePath->setText(fileName);
}
```

11. Then, we also define what will happen if the **Convert** button is clicked. What we are doing here is passing the filenames and arguments to FFmpeg and then the conversion process will be handled externally by FFmpeg:

```
void MainWindow::on_convertButton_clicked()
{
    QString ffmpeg = "C:/FFmpeg/bin/ffmpeg";
    QStringList arguments;

    fileName = ui->filePath->text();
    if (fileName != "")
    {
        QFileInfo fileInfo = QFile(fileName);
        outputFileName = fileInfo.path() + "/" + fileInfo.completeBaseName();

        if (QFile::exists(fileName))
        {
            // 0 - AVI
            // 1 - MP4
            // 2 - MOV
            int format = ui->fileFormat->currentIndex();
            if (format == 0)
            {
                outputFileName += ".avi";
            }
            else if (format == 1)
            {
                outputFileName += ".mp4";
            }
            else if (format == 2)
            {
                outputFileName += ".mov";
            }

            qDebug() << outputFileName << format;

            arguments << "-i" << fileName << outputFileName;

            qDebug() << arguments;

            process->setProcessChannelMode(QProcess::MergedChannels);
            process->start(ffmpeg, arguments);
        }
        else
        {
            QMessageBox::warning(this, "Failed", "Failed to open video file.");
        }
    }
    else
    {
        QMessageBox::warning(this, "Failed", "No file is selected.");
    }
}
```

12. Once we are done with that, we will then tell our program what to do when the conversion process has started:

```
void MainWindow::processStarted()
{
    qDebug() << "Process started.";

    ui->browseButton->setEnabled(false);
    ui->fileFormat->setEditable(false);
    ui->convertButton->setEnabled(false);
}
```

13. Next, we will write the slot function that gets called during the conversion process whenever FFmpeg returns an output to the program:

```
void MainWindow::readyReadStandardOutput()
{
   outputText += process->readAllStandardOutput();
   ui->outputDisplay->setText(outputText);

   ui->outputDisplay->verticalScrollBar()->setSliderPosition
      (ui->outputDisplay->verticalScrollBar()->maximum());
}
```

14. Lastly, we define the slot function that gets called when the entire conversion process has been completed:

```
void MainWindow::processFinished()
{
   qDebug() << "Process finished.";

   if (QFile::exists(outputFileName))
   {
      QMessageBox::information(this, "Success",
         "Video successfully converted.");
   }
   else
   {
      QMessageBox::information(this, "Failed",
         "Failed to convert video.");
   }

   ui->browseButton->setEnabled(true);
   ui->fileFormat->setEditable(true);
   ui->convertButton->setEnabled(true);
}
```

15. Build and run the project now and you should get a simple yet workable video converter:

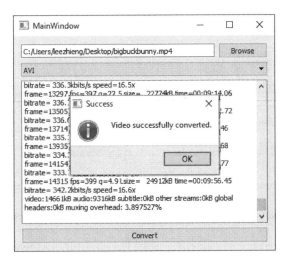

How it works...

The QProcess class provided by Qt is used to start external programs and communicate with them. In this case, we started ffmpeg.exe located in C:/FFmpeg/bin/ as a process and started communicating with it. We also sent it a set of arguments to tell it what to do when started. The arguments we used in this example are relatively basic; we only told FFmpeg the path to the source image and the output filename. For more information regarding the argument settings available in FFmpeg, check out https://www.ffmpeg.org/ffmpeg.html.

FFmpeg does more than just converting video files. You can also use it to convert audio files and even images. For more information regarding all the formats supported by FFmpeg, check out https://www.ffmpeg.org/general.html#File-Formats.

Other than that, you can also play a video or audio file by running ffplay.exe, located in C:/FFmpeg/bin, or print out the information of the video or audio file in human-readable fashion by running ffprobe.exe. Check out FFmpeg's full documentation at https://www.ffmpeg.org/about.html.

There's more...

There are lots of things you can do using this method. It means that you're not limited to what Qt provides and you can break out of such limitations by carefully selecting a third-party program that provides what you need. One such example is making your own anti-virus GUI by utilizing the command-line-only anti-virus scanners available on the market, such as Avira ScanCL, Panda Antivirus Command Line Scanner, SAV32CLI, ClamavNet, and so on. You can build your own GUI using Qt and essentially send commands to the anti-virus process to tell it what to do.

Currency conversion

In this example, we will learn how to create a simple currency converter using Qt, with the help of an external service provider called `Fixer.io`.

How to do it...

Make yourself a currency converter with these simple steps:

1. We start by opening Qt Creator and creating a new **Qt Widgets Application** project from **File | New File or Project**.

2. Next, open up the project file (`.pro`) and add the network module to our project:

   ```
   QT += core gui network
   ```

3. After that, open up `mainwindow.ui` and remove the menu bar, tool bar, and status bar from the UI.

4. Then, add three horizontal layouts, a horizontal line, and a push button to the canvas. Once they're all placed, left-click on the canvas and follow by clicking the **Lay Out Vertically** button above the canvas. Then, set the label of the push button as **Convert**. The UI should now look something like this:

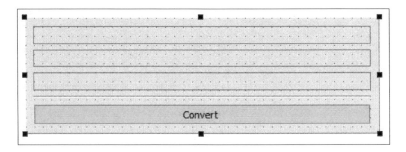

5. After that, add two labels to the top layout and set the text of the left one as **From:**, followed by the right one as **To:**. Right after that, add two line edit widgets to the second layout and set both their default values as `1`:

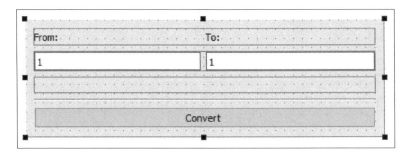

6. Before we proceed to add the last batch of widgets to the last layout, let's select the line edit on the right and enable the `readOnly` checkbox located in the property pane:

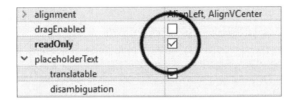

7. Other than that, we also must set its **cursor** property to **Forbidden** so that users know it's not editable when mousing over the widget:

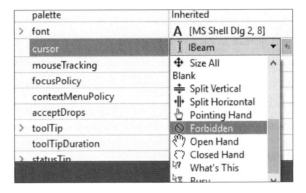

8. Once you're done with that, let's add two combo boxes to the third layout located at the bottom. We will just leave them empty for now:

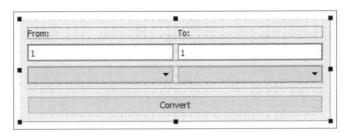

9. After that, right-click on the **Convert** button and select **Go to slot...**. A window will now pop up, asking you to select an appropriate signal. Let's keep the default `clicked()` signal as the selection and click **OK**. Qt Creator will now automatically add a slot function for you to both `mainwindow.h` and `mainwindow.cpp`.

10. Next, open up `mainwindow.h` and make sure the following headers are being added to the top of the source file:

```
#include <QMainWindow>
#include <QDoubleValidator>
#include <QNetworkAccessManager>
#include <QNetworkRequest>
#include <QNetworkReply>
#include <QJsonDocument>
#include <QJsonObject>
#include <QDebug>
#include <QMessageBox>
```

11. Then, we need to add another slot function called `finished()`:

```
private slots:
  void on_convertButton_clicked();
  void finished(QNetworkReply* reply);
```

12. Besides that, we also need to add two variables under the `private` label:

```
private:
  Ui::MainWindow *ui;
  QNetworkAccessManager* manager;
  QString targetCurrency;
```

13. Once you're done, let's open up `mainwindow.cpp` this time. We will add several currency shortcodes to both the combo boxes in the class constructor. We also set a validator to the line edit widget on the left so that it can only accept inputs that are numbers. Lastly, we also initialize the network access manager and connect its `finished()` signal to our `finished()` slot function:

```
MainWindow::MainWindow(QWidget *parent) :
  QMainWindow(parent), ui(new Ui::MainWindow)
{
  ui->setupUi(this);

  QStringList currencies;
  currencies.push_back("EUR");
  currencies.push_back("USD");
  currencies.push_back("CAD");
  currencies.push_back("MYR");
  currencies.push_back("GBP");

  ui->currencyFrom->insertItems(0, currencies);
  ui->currencyTo->insertItems(0, currencies);
```

```
QValidator *inputRange = new QDoubleValidator(this);
ui->amountFrom->setValidator(inputRange);

manager = new QNetworkAccessManager(this);
connect(manager, SIGNAL(finished(QNetworkReply*)),
    this, SLOT(finished(QNetworkReply*)));
}
```

14. After that, we define what will happen if the **Convert** button is being clicked by the user:

```
void MainWindow::on_convertButton_clicked()
{
    if (ui->amountFrom->text() != "")
    {
        ui->convertButton->setEnabled(false);
        QString from = ui->currencyFrom->currentText();
        QString to = ui->currencyTo->currentText();
        targetCurrency = to;
        QString url = "http://api.fixer.io/latest?base=" +
            from + "&symbols=" + to;
        QNetworkRequest request= QNetworkRequest(QUrl(url));
        manager->get(request);
    }
    else
    {
        QMessageBox::warning(this, "Error", "Please insert a value.");
    }
}
```

15. Lastly, define what will happen when the `finished()` signal is triggered:

```
void MainWindow::finished(QNetworkReply* reply)
{
    QByteArray response = reply->readAll();
    qDebug() << response;
    QJsonDocument jsonResponse = QJsonDocument::fromJson(response);
    QJsonObject jsonObj = jsonResponse.object();
    QJsonObject jsonObj2 = jsonObj.value("rates").toObject();
    double rate = jsonObj2.value(targetCurrency).toDouble();
    if (rate == 0)
        rate = 1;
    double amount = ui->amountFrom->text().toDouble();
    double result = amount * rate;
    ui->amountTo->setText(QString::number(result));
    ui->convertButton->setEnabled(true);
}
```

16. Compile and run the project now and you should be able to get a simple currency converter that looks like this:

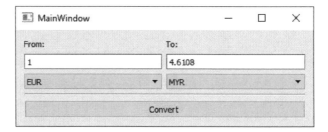

How it works...

Similar to the previous example we saw, which uses an external program to achieve a specific task, this time we use an external service provider who provided us with an open **Application Programming Interface** (**API**) that is free for all and easy to use.

This way, we don't have to think about the method to retrieve the latest currency rate. Instead, the service provider has already done the job for us and we just have to send a polite request and ask for it. Then, we just wait for the response from their server and process the data according to our intended purposes.

There are quite a few different service providers you can choose from besides `Fixer.io` (`http://fixer.io`). Some are free but without any advanced features; some provide you with additional functionalities, although they come at a premium price. Some of these alternatives are Open Exchange Rate (`https://openexchangerates.org`), Currencylayer (`https://currencylayer.com`), Currency API (`https://currency-api.appspot.com`), XE Currency Data API (`http://www.xe.com/xecurrencydata`), and Jsonrates (`http://jsonrates.com`).

There's more...

Besides currency exchange rates, you can also use this method to do other more advanced tasks that are perhaps too complicated to do by yourself, or are simply impossible to access unless you use the services provided by specialists, for example, programmable **Short Message Service** (**SMS**) and voice services, web analytics and statistic generation, online payment gateways, and the list goes on. Most of these services are not free, but you can easily achieve those functions in minutes without even setting up the server infrastructure, backend system, and whatnot; it's definitely the cheapest and fastest way to get your product up and running without much hassle.

8

Accessing Databases

In this chapter, we will cover the following recipes:

- ▶ Setting up SQL Driver for Qt
- ▶ Connecting to a database
- ▶ Writing basic SQL queries
- ▶ Creating a login screen with Qt
- ▶ Displaying information from a database on a model view
- ▶ Advanced SQL queries

Introduction

SQL stands for **Structured Query Language**, a special programming language used to manage data held in a relational database management system. A SQL server is a database system designed to use one of the many types of SQL programming language to manage its data.

 If you want to learn more about SQL, visit this link: `http://www.w3schools.com/sql/sql_intro.asp`.

Qt supports several different types of SQL driver in the form of plugins/add-ons. However, it's very easy to integrate these drivers to your Qt project. We will learn how to do it in the following example.

How to do it...

Let's set up our SQL server before we dive into Qt:

1. Before setting up Qt for SQL, we need to install and set up a MySQL server. There are many ways you can install it. The first method is to download MySQL from the official website at `http://dev.mysql.com/downloads/mysql/` and install it. After that, you also need to install the MySQL Workbench from `http://dev.mysql.com/downloads/workbench/` to administrate your databases.

2. An alternative method is to install a third-party package that comes with MySQL and other useful applications, such as Apache web server, phpMyAdmin, and so on, all in a unified installer. Examples of such packages are XAMPP, `https://sourceforge.net/projects/xampp/`, and AppServ, `https://www.appservnetwork.com/en/download/`.

3. In this example, we will install XAMPP. Open up your web browser, download the XAMPP installer from `https://sourceforge.net/projects/xampp/`, and proceed to install it on your computer.

4. Once you have installed XAMPP, open up XAMPP Control Panel and you should see something like this:

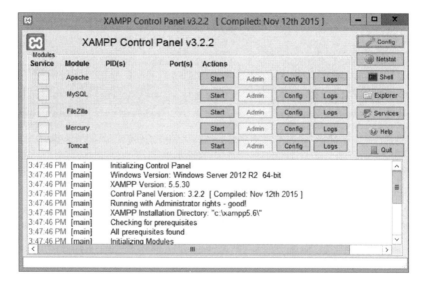

5. What we need is the Apache web server and the MySQL database server. Click the **Start** buttons next to the **Apache** and **MySQL** options on the control panel.

6. Once the servers have been started, open up your web browser and visit `http://localhost/phpmyadmin/`. You will see a web interface by the name of **PhpMyAdmin** that looks like this:

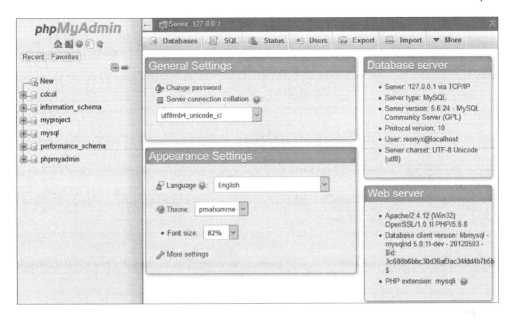

7. phpMyAdmin is a web-based utility that help you manage your MySQL databases, much like the official MySQL Workbench. In my opinion, phpMyAdmin is a lot simpler and better suited for beginners, which is why I recommend using it instead of MySQL Workbench.

8. By default, phpMyAdmin automatically logs in to MySQL using the default user account `root`, which is saved in its configuration file. We don't want to use that for security reasons. So the next thing we need to do is to create an account for ourselves. Go to the **Users** tab located at the top and once you're on that page, click **Add user** located at the bottom. Key in your desired username and password in the fields in the login information pane. Choose **Local** for the **Host** option for now. At the bottom, you will see options related to **Global privileges**; check the **Check All** option and click **Go**:

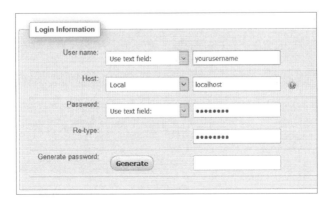

9. Now that you have created your user account, go to XAMPP Control Panel and click **Stop** for both Apache and MySQL. Then, click the **Config** button on the **Apache** column and select the **phpMyAdmin (config.inc.php)** option. After that, the `config.inc.php` file will be opened with your choice of text editor.

10. Search for the following line in `config.inc.php` and change the word `config` to `cookie`:

```
$cfg['Servers'][$i]['auth_type'] = 'config';
$cfg['Servers'][$i]['auth_type'] = 'cookie';
```

11. After that, start Apache and MySQL again by clicking the **Start** buttons. This way, we force phpMyAdmin to reload its configurations and apply the changes. Go to phpmyAdmin again from your web browser, and this time around, a login screen should appear on the screen:

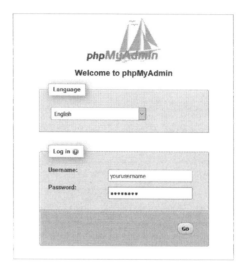

12. Log in to phpMyAdmin, then click on the **New** link located on the side bar:

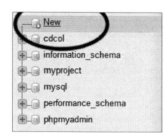

13. Key in your desired database name and press the **Create** button. Once it's been created, the database name will appear on the side bar. Click on the database name and it will bring you to another page, which displays a message, **No tables found in database**. Under the message, you can create your first data table by filling in your desired table name and the number of columns for the table:

14. After you click the **Go** button, you will be brought to another page where you will set up the new table you're going to create. In this example, we created an `employee` table that consists of five columns of data: `id`, `name`, `age`, `gender`, and `married`:

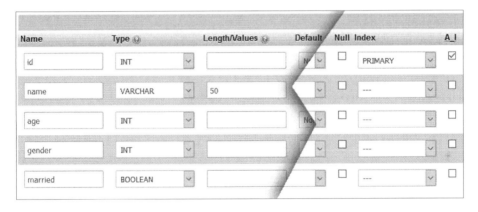

15. Once you are done with that, click **Save** and now you will be able to see the `employee` table name appear on the side bar. We have successfully installed MySQL and set up our first database and data table.

16. After that, we need to insert data into the database from phpMyAdmin so that we will be able to retrieve it in the next example. Click on the **Insert** tab while you're still in the `employee` table; you will then be brought to another page for inserting new data into the `employee` table:

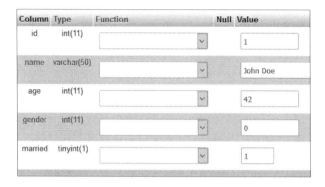

Column	Type	Function	Null	Value
id	int(11)			1
name	varchar(50)			John Doe
age	int(11)			42
gender	int(11)			0
married	tinyint(1)			1

17. Next, we will proceed to set up the SQL driver for our Qt project. Basically, all you need to do is to go to your Qt installation folder and look for the `sqldrivers` folder. For example, mine is located at `C:\Qt\5.5\mingw492_32\plugins\sqldrivers`.

18. Copy the entire `sqldrivers` folder to your project's build directory. You can remove the DLL files that are not relevant to the SQL server you're running. In our case, since we're using a MySQL server, we can delete everything except `qsqlmysql.dll` and `qsqlmysqld.dll`. The DLL file with the letter d at the back is for debug builds only, while the other one is for release builds. Put those DLL files in their respective build directories, for example, `builds/debug/sqldrivers/qsqlmysqld.dll` for debug builds and `builds/release/sqldrivers/qsqlmysql.dll` for release builds.

19. The DLL files mentioned in the previous step are the drivers that enable Qt to communicate with different types of SQL architecture. You may also need the DLL file of the SQL client library in order for the driver to work. In our case, we need `libmysql.dll` to be located in the same directory as our program's executable. You can either get it from the installation directory of MySQL or download the Connector/C++ package from the official website, `https://dev.mysql.com/downloads/connector/cpp/`.

How it works...

Qt provides us with SQL drivers so that we can easily connect to different types of SQL servers without implementing them ourselves.

Currently, Qt officially supports SQLite, MySQL, ODBC, and PostgreSQL. SQL architectures that are forks from one of the supported architectures, such as MariaDB (a fork of MySQL), may still compatible with Qt without much problem.

If you are using an architecture that isn't supported by Qt, you can still interact with your SQL database indirectly by sending an HTTP request using QNetworkAccessManager to your backend script (such as PHP, ASP, JSP, and so on), which can then communicate with the database.

If you only need a simple file-based database and don't plan to use a server-based database, SQLite is a good choice for you.

Connecting to a database

In this recipe, we will learn how to connect to our SQL database using Qt's SQL module.

How to do it...

Connecting to SQL server in Qt is really simple:

1. First of all, open up Qt Creator and create a new **Qt Widgets Application** project.

2. Open up your project file (.pro) and add the SQL module to your project, like so:

   ```
   QT += core gui sql
   ```

3. Next, open up mainwindow.ui and drag seven label widgets, a combo box, and a checkbox to the canvas. Set the text properties of four of the labels to Name:, Age:, Gender:, and Married:. Then, set the objectName properties of the rest to name, age, gender, and married. There is no need to set the object name for the previous four labels because they're for display purposes only:

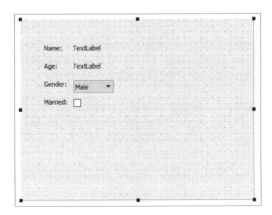

4. After that, open up `mainwindow.h` and add the following headers below the `QMainWindow` header:

```
#include <QMainWindow>
#include <QtSql>
#include <QSqlDatabase>
#include <QSqlQuery>
#include <QDebug>
```

5. Then, open up `mainwindow.cpp` and insert the following code to the class constructor:

```
MainWindow::MainWindow(QWidget *parent) :
  QMainWindow(parent), ui(new Ui::MainWindow)
{
  ui->setupUi(this);

  QSqlDatabase db = QSqlDatabase::addDatabase("QMYSQL");
  db.setHostName("127.0.0.1");
  db.setUserName("yourusername");
  db.setPassword("yourpassword");
  db.setDatabaseName("databasename");

  if (db.open())
  {
    QSqlQuery query;
    if (query.exec("SELECT name, age, gender, married FROM
employee"))
    {
      while (query.next())
      {
        qDebug() << query.value(0) << query.value(1) <<
          query.value(2) << query.value(3);

        ui->name->setText(query.value(0).toString());
        ui->age->setText(query.value(1).toString());
        ui->gender->setCurrentIndex(query.value(2).toInt());
        ui->married->setChecked(query.value(3).toBool());
      }
    }
    else
    {
      qDebug() << query.lastError().text();
    }
```

```
        db.close();
    }
    else
    {
        qDebug() << "Failed to connect to database.";
    }
}
```

6. Compile and run your project now and you should get something like the following:

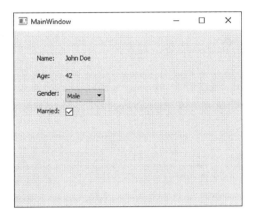

How it works...

The previous example shows you how to connect to your SQL database using the `QSqlDatabase` class derived from the SQL module. You won't be able to access any of the classes related to SQL without adding the module to your Qt project.

We must tell Qt which SQL architecture we are running by mentioning it when calling the `addDatabase()` function. Options supported by Qt are QSQLITE, QMYSQL, QMYSQL3, QODBC, QODBC3, QPSQL, and QPSQL7

If you encounter an error message that says, **QSqlDatabase: QMYSQL driver not loaded**, then you should again check whether the DLL files are placed in the correct directory.

We can send our SQL statements to the database through the `QSqlQuery` class, and wait for it to return the results, which usually are either the data you requested or error messages due to invalid statements.

If there is any data coming from the database server, it will all be stored in the `QSqlQuery` class. All you need to do to retrieve this data is to do a `while` loop on the `QSqlQuery` class to check for all existing records, and retrieve them by calling the `value()` function.

Writing basic SQL queries

In the previous example, we wrote our very first SQL query, which involves the SELECT statement. This time, we will learn how to use some other SQL statements, such as INSERT, UPDATE, and DELETE.

How to do it...

Let's create a simple program that demonstrates basic SQL query commands by following these steps:

1. We can use our previous project files, but there are couples of things we need to change. First, open up `mainwindow.ui` and replace the labels for name and age with line edit widgets. Then, add three buttons to the canvas and call them **Update**, **Insert**, and **Delete**:

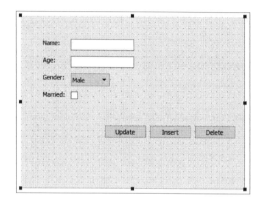

2. After that, open up `mainwindow.h` and add the following variables under private inheritance:

```
private:
   Ui::MainWindow *ui;
   QSqlDatabase db;
   bool connected;
   int currentID;
```

3. Next, open up `mainwindow.cpp` and go to the class constructor. It is still pretty much the same as the previous example, except we store the database connection status in a Boolean variable called `connected` and we also obtain the ID of the data from the database and store it to an integer variable called `currentID`:

```
MainWindow::MainWindow(QWidget *parent) :
   QMainWindow(parent), ui(new Ui::MainWindow)
{
```

```
    ui->setupUi(this);

    db = QSqlDatabase::addDatabase("QMYSQL");
    db.setHostName("127.0.0.1");
    db.setUserName("yourusername");
    db.setPassword("yourpassword");
    db.setDatabaseName("databasename");

    connected = db.open();

    if (connected)
    {
      QSqlQuery query;
        if (query.exec("SELECT id, name, age, gender, married FROM
employee"))
        {
          while (query.next())
          {
            currentID = query.value(0).toInt();
            ui->name->setText(query.value(1).toString());
            ui->age->setText(query.value(2).toString());
            ui->gender->setCurrentIndex(query.value(3).toInt());
            ui->married->setChecked(query.value(4).toBool());
          }
        }
        else
        {
          qDebug() << query.lastError().text();
        }
    }
    else
    {
      qDebug() << "Failed to connect to database.";
    }
}
```

4. Then, go to `mainwindow.ui` and right-click on one of the buttons we added to the canvas in step 1. Select **Go to slot...** and click **OK**. Repeat these steps on the other button, and now you should see three slot functions being added to both your `mainwindow.h` and `mainwindow.cpp`:

```
private slots:
  void on_updateButton_clicked();
  void on_insertButton_clicked();
  void on_deleteButton_clicked();
```

5. After that, open up `mainwindow.cpp` and we will declare what the program will do when we click on the **Update** button:

```cpp
void MainWindow::on_updateButton_clicked()
{
  if (connected)
  {
    if (currentID == 0)
    {
      qDebug() << "Nothing to update.";
    }
    else
    {
      QString id = QString::number(currentID);
      QString name = ui->name->text();
      QString age = ui->age->text();
      QString gender = QString::number
        (ui->gender->currentIndex());
      QString married = QString::number(ui->married->isChecked());

      qDebug() << "UPDATE employee SET name = '" + name + "',
        age = '" + age + "', gender = " + gender + ",
        married = " + married + " WHERE id = " + id;

      QSqlQuery query;
      if (query.exec("UPDATE employee SET name = '" + name + "',
        age = '" + age + "', gender = " + gender + ",
        married = " + married + " WHERE id = " + id))
      {
        qDebug() << "Update success.";
      }
      else
      {
        qDebug() << query.lastError().text();
      }
    }
  }
  else
  {
    qDebug() << "Failed to connect to database.";
  }
}
```

6. Once you have done that, we will proceed to declare what will happen when the **Insert** button is clicked:

```cpp
void MainWindow::on_insertButton_clicked()
{
  if (connected)
  {
    QString name = ui->name->text();
    QString age = ui->age->text();
    QString gender = QString::number(ui->gender->currentIndex());
    QString married = QString::number(ui->married->isChecked());

    qDebug() << "INSERT INTO employee (name, age, gender,
      married) VALUES ('" + name + "','" + age + "',
      " + gender + "," + married + ")";

    QSqlQuery query;
    if (query.exec("INSERT INTO employee (name, age, gender,
      married) VALUES ('" + name + "','" + age + "',
      " + gender + "," + married + ")"))
    {
      currentID = query.lastInsertId().toInt();
      qDebug() << "Insert success.";
    }
    else
    {
      qDebug() << query.lastError().text();
    }
  }
  else
  {
    qDebug() << "Failed to connect to database.";
  }
}
```

7. After that, we also declare what will happen when the **Delete** button is clicked:

```cpp
void MainWindow::on_deleteButton_clicked()
{
  if (connected)
  {
    if (currentID == 0)
    {
      qDebug() << "Nothing to delete.";
    }
```

```
        else
        {
            QString id = QString::number(currentID);
            qDebug() << "DELETE FROM employee WHERE id = " + id;
            QSqlQuery query;
            if (query.exec("DELETE FROM employee WHERE id = " + id))
            {
                currentID = 0;
                qDebug() << "Delete success.";
            }
            else
            {
                qDebug() << query.lastError().text();
            }
        }
    }
    else
    {
        qDebug() << "Failed to connect to database.";
    }
}
```

8. Lastly, call `QSqlDatabase::close()` at the class destructor to properly terminate the SQL connection before exiting the program:

```
MainWindow::~MainWindow()
{
    db.close();
    delete ui;
}
```

9. Compile and run the program now and you should be able to select the default data from the database; then you can choose to update it or delete it from the database. You can also insert new data into the database by clicking the **Insert** button. You can use phpMyAdmin to check whether the data is being altered correctly or not:

How it works...

It's very important to check whether or not the database is connected in the first place before we proceed to send a SQL query to the database. Therefore, we keep that status in a variable and use it to check before sending out any queries. This, however, is not recommended for complex programs that are kept open for long periods of time, as the database might get disconnected during these periods, and a fixed variable may not be accurate. In that case, it's better to check the actual status by calling `QSqlDatabase::isOpen()`.

The `currentID` variable is used to save the ID of the current data you obtained from the database. When you want to update the data or delete it from the database, this variable is crucial for letting the database know which data you're trying to update or delete. If you set your database table correctly, MySQL will treat each item of data as a unique entry, so you can be sure that no repeated ID will be produced in the database when new data is being saved.

After inserting new data into the database, we call `QSqlQuery::lastInsertId()` to obtain the ID of the new data and save it as a `currentID` variable, so that it becomes the current data that we can update or delete from the database.

It is a good habit to test your SQL queries on phpMyAdmin first before using them in Qt. You can instantly find out whether your SQL statements are correct or incorrect, instead of waiting for your project to get built, then try it out, then rebuild again. As a programmer, we must work in the most efficient way. Work hard, and work smart.

Creating a login screen with Qt

In this recipe, we will learn how put our knowledge to use and create a functional login screen using Qt and MySQL.

How to do it...

Create your first functional login screen by following these steps:

1. First, open up a web browser and go to phpMyAdmin. We will create a new data table called `user`, which looks like this:

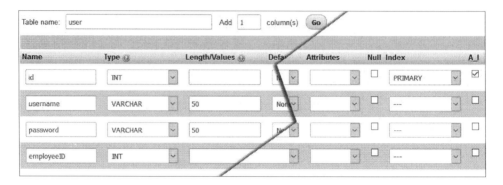

2. Next, insert our first item of data into the newly created table and set the `employeeID` to the ID of an existing employee's data. This way, the user account we created will be linked to the data of one of the employees:

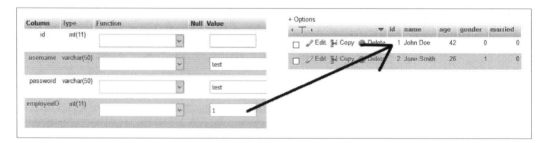

3. After that, open up Qt Creator and create a new **Qt Widgets Application** project. We will start off with `mainwindow.ui`. First, place a stacked widget on the canvas and make sure it contains two pages. Then, set up the two pages in the stacked widget like this:

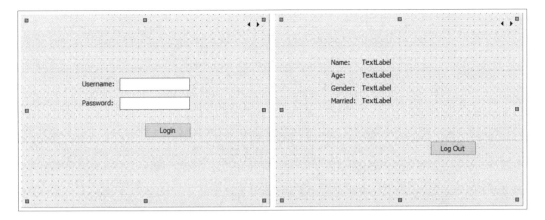

4. Then, on the first page of the stacked widget, click the **Edit Tab Order** button on top of the widget so that we can adjust the order of the widgets in our program:

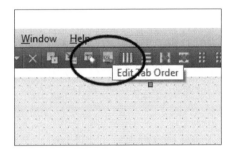

5. Once you click the **Edit Tab Order** button, you will see some numbers appear on top of each widget in the canvas. Make sure the numbers look like this. Otherwise, click on the numbers to change their order. We only do this for the first page of the stacked widget; it's okay to keep the second page as it is:

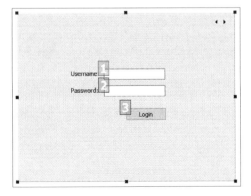

6. Next, right-click on the **Login** button and select **Go to slot...**. Then, make sure the **clicked()** option is selected and press **OK**. Qt will then create a slot function for you in your project source files. Repeat this step for the **Log Out** button as well.

7. Then, open up `mainwindow.h` and add the following headers after the line `#include <QMainWindow>`:

```
#include <QMainWindow>
#include <QtSql>
#include <QSqlDatabase>
#include <QSqlQuery>
#include <QMessageBox>
#include <QDebug>
```

8. After that, add the following variable to `mainwindow.h`:

```
private:
    Ui::MainWindow *ui;
    QSqlDatabase db;
```

9. Once we're done with that, let's open up `mainwindow.cpp` and put this code in the class constructor:

```
MainWindow::MainWindow(QWidget *parent) :
    QMainWindow(parent),
    ui(new Ui::MainWindow)
{
    ui->setupUi(this);
    ui->stackedWidget->setCurrentIndex(0);
    db = QSqlDatabase::addDatabase("QMYSQL");
    db.setHostName("127.0.0.1");
    db.setUserName("yourusername");
    db.setPassword("yourpassword");
    db.setDatabaseName("databasename");

    if (!db.open())
    {
        qDebug() << "Failed to connect to database.";
    }
}
```

10. After that, we will define what will happen if the **Login** button is clicked:

```
void MainWindow::on_loginButton_clicked()
{
    QString username = ui->username->text();
    QString password = ui->password->text();
```

```cpp
QSqlQuery query;
if (query.exec("SELECT employeeID from user WHERE
  username = '" + username + "' AND password = '" +
  password + "'"))
{
  if (query.size() > 0)
  {
    while (query.next())
    {
      QString employeeID = query.value(0).toString();
      QSqlQuery query2;
      if (query2.exec("SELECT name, age, gender,
        married FROM employee WHERE id = " + employeeID))
      {
        while (query2.next())
        {
          QString name = query2.value(0).toString();
          QString age = query2.value(1).toString();
          int gender = query2.value(2).toInt();
          bool married = query2.value(3).toBool();
          ui->name->setText(name);
          ui->age->setText(age);

          if (gender == 0)
            ui->gender->setText("Male");
          else
            ui->gender->setText("Female");

          if (married)
            ui->married->setText("Yes");
          else
            ui->married->setText("No");

          ui->stackedWidget->setCurrentIndex(1);
        }
      }
    }
  }
  else
  {
    QMessageBox::warning(this, "Login failed",
      "Invalid username or password.");
  }
```

```
      }
      else
      {
         qDebug() << query.lastError().text();
      }
   }
```

11. Then, we also define what will happen if the **Log Out** button is clicked:

```
void MainWindow::on_logoutButton_clicked()
{
   ui->stackedWidget->setCurrentIndex(0);
}
```

12. Lastly, close the database when the main window is closed:

```
MainWindow::~MainWindow()
{
   db.close();

   delete ui;
}
```

13. Compile and run the program now and you should be able to log in with the dummy account. After you have logged in, you should be able to see the dummy employee information linked to the user account. You can also log out by clicking on the **Log Out** button:

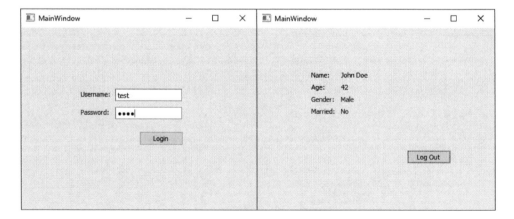

How it works...

In this example, we select data from the user table that matches the username and password that we have inserted into the text fields. If nothing is found, it means we have provided an invalid username or password. Otherwise, obtain the employeeID data from the user account and do another SQL query to look for information from the employee table that matches the employeeID variable. Then, display the data accordingly to the UI of our program.

We must set the widget order in the **Edit Tab Order** mode so that when the program has started, the first widget that gets focused on is the username line edit widget. If the user presses on the **TAB** button on the keyboard, the focus should switch to the second widget, which is the password line edit. Incorrect widget order will totally ruin the user experience and drive away your potential users.

Do make sure that the **echoMode** option of the password line edit is set to Password. That setting will hide the actual password inserted into the line edit and replace it with dot symbols for security purposes.

Displaying information from a database on a model view

In this recipe, we will learn how to display multiple sets of data obtained from our SQL database on a model view in our program.

How to do it...

Follow these steps to display information from a database on a model view widget:

1. We will be using the database table called employee, which we used in the previous example. This time, we need a lot more data in the employee table. Open up your web browser and log in to your phpMyAdmin control panel. Add data for a few more employees so that we can display it later in our program:

2. After that, open up Qt Creator, create a new **Qt Widgets Application** project, and then add the SQL module to your project.

3. Next, open up `mainwindow.ui` and add a table widget (not table view) from **Item Widget (Item-Based)** under the **Widget** box pane. Select the main window on the canvas and click on either the **Layout Vertically** or **Layout Horizontally** button to make the table widget stick to the size of the main window, even when it's resized:

4. After that, double-click on the table widget and a window will then appear. Under the **Columns** tab, add five items by clicking on the **+** button at the top-left corner. Name the items ID, Name, Age, Gender, and Married. Click **OK** when you're done:

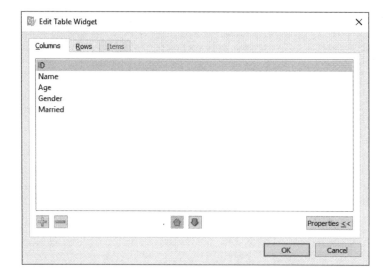

5. Then, right-click on the table widget and select **Go to slot...** in the pop-up menu. Scroll all the way down, select the **itemChanged(QTableWidgetItem*)** option in the pop-up window, and press **OK**. A slot function will be created in both your source files.

6. Open up `mainwindow.h` and add these private variables to our `MainWindow` class:

```
private:
    Ui::MainWindow *ui;
    bool hasInit;
    QSqlDatabase db;
```

7. We also add the following class headers to `mainwindow.h`:

```
#include <QtSql>
#include <QSqlDatabase>
#include <QSqlQuery>
#include <QMessageBox>
#include <QDebug>
#include <QTableWidgetItem>
```

8. Once you're done with that, open up `mainwindow.cpp` and we're going to write tons of code there. First, we need to declare what will happen when the program is started. Add the following code to the constructor of the `MainWindow` class:

```
MainWindow::MainWindow(QWidget *parent) :
  QMainWindow(parent),
  ui(new Ui::MainWindow)
{
  hasInit = false;

  ui->setupUi(this);

  db = QSqlDatabase::addDatabase("QMYSQL");
  db.setHostName("127.0.0.1");
  db.setUserName("yourusername");
  db.setPassword("yourpassword");
  db.setDatabaseName("databasename");

  ui->tableWidget->setColumnHidden(0, true);

  if (db.open())
  {
    QSqlQuery query;
    if (query.exec("SELECT id, name, age, gender,
      married FROM employee"))
    {
      while (query.next())
      {
        qDebug() << query.value(0) << query.value(1) <<
          query.value(2) << query.value(3) << query.value(4);

        QString id = query.value(0).toString();
        QString name = query.value(1).toString();
        QString age = query.value(2).toString();
        int gender = query.value(3).toInt();
        bool married = query.value(4).toBool();
```

```cpp
      ui->tableWidget->setRowCount(ui->tableWidget->rowCount()
        + 1);

      QTableWidgetItem* idItem = new QTableWidgetItem(id);
      QTableWidgetItem* nameItem = new QTableWidgetItem(name);
      QTableWidgetItem* ageItem = new QTableWidgetItem(age);
      QTableWidgetItem* genderItem = new QTableWidgetItem();

      if (gender == 0)
        genderItem->setData(0, "Male");
      else
        genderItem->setData(0, "Female");

      QTableWidgetItem* marriedItem = new QTableWidgetItem();

      if (married)
        marriedItem->setData(0, "Yes");
      else
        marriedItem->setData(0, "No");

      ui->tableWidget->setItem(ui->tableWidget->rowCount() -
        1, 0, idItem);
      ui->tableWidget->setItem(ui->tableWidget->rowCount() -
        1, 1, nameItem);
      ui->tableWidget->setItem(ui->tableWidget->rowCount() -
        1, 2, ageItem);
      ui->tableWidget->setItem(ui->tableWidget->rowCount() -
        1, 3, genderItem);
      ui->tableWidget->setItem(ui->tableWidget->rowCount() -
        1, 4, marriedItem);
    }

    hasInit = true;
  }
  else
  {
    qDebug() << query.lastError().text();
  }
}
else
{
  qDebug() << "Failed to connect to database.";
}
}
```

9. After that, declare what will happen when an item of the table widget has been edited. Add the following code to the slot function called `on_tableWidget_itemChanged()`:

```cpp
void MainWindow::on_tableWidget_itemChanged(QTableWidgetItem
  *item)
{
  if (hasInit)
  {
    QString id = ui->tableWidget->item(item->row(),
      0)->data(0).toString();
    QString name = ui->tableWidget->item(item->row(),
      1)->data(0).toString();
    QString age = QString::number(ui->tableWidget->
      item(item->row(), 2)->data(0).toInt());
    ui->tableWidget->item(item->row(), 2)->setData(0, age);

    QString gender;
    if (ui->tableWidget->item(item->row(), 3)->
      data(0).toString() == "Male")
    {
      gender = "0";
    }
    else
    {
      ui->tableWidget->item(item->row(), 3)->setData(0, "Female");
      gender = "1";
    }

    QString married;
    if (ui->tableWidget->item(item->row(),
      4)->data(0).toString() == "No")
    {
      married = "0";
    }
    else
    {
      ui->tableWidget->item(item->row(), 4)->setData(0, "Yes");
      married = "1";
    }

    qDebug() << id << name << age << gender << married;
    QSqlQuery query;
```

```
      if (query.exec("UPDATE employee SET name = '" + name + "',
        age = '" + age + "', gender = '" + gender + "',
        married = '" + married + "' WHERE id = " + id))
      {
        QMessageBox::information(this, "Update Success", "Data
          updated to database.");
      }
      else
      {
        qDebug() << query.lastError().text();
      }
    }
  }
}
```

10. Lastly, close the database at the class destructor:

```
MainWindow::~MainWindow()
{
  db.close();
  delete ui;
}
```

11. Compile and run the example now and you should be getting something like this:

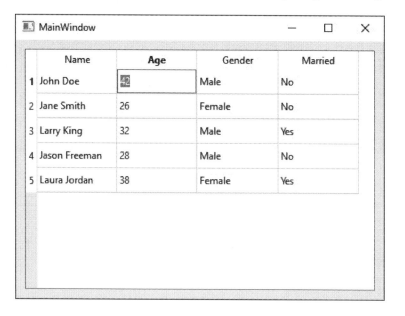

How it works...

A table widget is similar to the one you see in spreadsheet applications such as Microsoft Excel and Open Office Calc. In contrast with other types of model viewers such as list view or tree view, table view (or table widget) is a two-dimensional model viewer, which displays data in the form of rows and columns.

The main difference between a table view and table widget in Qt is that a table widget is built on top of a table view class, which means a table widget is easier to use and more suitable for beginners. However, a table widget is less flexible and tends to be less scalable than a table view, which is not the best choice if you want to customize your table.

After retrieving data from MySQL, we created a `QTableWidgetItem` item for each of the data items and set which column and row should be added to the table widget. Before adding an item to the table widget, we must increase the row count of the table by calling `QTableWidget::setRowCount()`. We can also get the current row count of the table widget by simply calling `QTableWidget::rowCount()`.

The first column from the left is hidden from view because we only use it to save the ID of the data so that we can use it to update the database when one of the data items in its row has changed.

The slot function `on_tableWidget_itemChanged()` will be called when the data in one of the cells has changed. It will not only get called when you edit the data in the cell, but also when the data is first added to the table after being retrieved from the database. To ensure that this function is only triggered when we edit the data, we used a Boolean variable called `hasInit` to check whether we have done the initialization process (adding the first batch of data to the table) or not. If `hasInit` is `false`, ignore the function call.

To prevent users from entering a totally irrelevant type of data, such as inserting alphabets into a supposedly numerical-only data cell, we checked manually whether the data is anything close to what we'd expected when it's being edited. Revert it to a default value if it doesn't come close to anything considered as valid. This is of course a simple hack, which does the job but is not the most professional method. Alternatively, you can try to create a new class that inherits the `QItemDelegate` class and define how your model view should behave. Then, call `QTableWidget::setItemDelegate()` to apply the class to your table widget.

Advanced SQL queries

By following this recipe, we will learn how to use advanced SQL statements such as `INNER JOIN`, `COUNT`, `LIKE`, `DISTINCT`, and so on.

How to do it...

You can do a lot more than just perform simple queries of SQL database:

1. First of all, we need to add a few tables to our database before we can dive into the programming part. Open up your web browser and access your phpMyAdmin. We need several tables for this example to work:

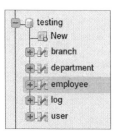

2. I will show you the structure of each of the tables required for this project and the dummy data inserted to the tables for testing. The first table is called `branch`, which is used to store the IDs and names of different branches of the dummy company:

3. Secondly, we have the `department` table, which stores the IDs and names of different departments of the dummy company, which is also linked to the branch data by the branch IDs:

4. Next, we also have an `employee` table, which stores the information of all the employees in the dummy company. This table is similar to the one we used in the previous examples, except it has two more extra columns, namely `birthday` and `departmentID`:

	id	name	age	birthday	gender	married	departmentID
Edit Copy Delete	1	John Doe	42	1974-03-15	0	0	1
Edit Copy Delete	2	Jane Smith	26	1990-08-06	1	0	1
Edit Copy Delete	3	Larry King	32	1984-01-28	0	1	2
Edit Copy Delete	4	Jason Freeman	28	1988-11-21	0	0	4
Edit Copy Delete	5	Laura Jordan	38	1978-08-02	1	1	3

5. Other than that, we also have a table called `log`, which contains dummy records of the login time for each employee. The `loginTime` column can be a `timestamp` or `date time` variable type:

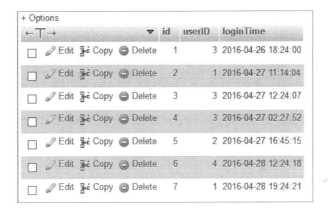

	id	userID	loginTime
Edit Copy Delete	1	3	2016-04-26 18:24:00
Edit Copy Delete	2	1	2016-04-27 11:14:04
Edit Copy Delete	3	3	2016-04-27 12:24:07
Edit Copy Delete	4	3	2016-04-27 02:27:52
Edit Copy Delete	5	2	2016-04-27 16:45:15
Edit Copy Delete	6	4	2016-04-28 12:24:18
Edit Copy Delete	7	1	2016-04-28 19:24:21

6. Lastly, we have the `user` table that we also used in the previous examples:

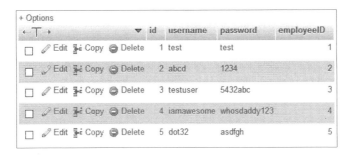

	id	username	password	employeeID
Edit Copy Delete	1	test	test	1
Edit Copy Delete	2	abcd	1234	2
Edit Copy Delete	3	testuser	5432abc	3
Edit Copy Delete	4	iamawesome	whosdaddy123	4
Edit Copy Delete	5	dot32	asdfgh	5

7. We are done with the database; let's move on to Qt. Open up Qt Creators, and this time, instead of choosing **Qt Widgets Application**, we create **Qt Console Application**:

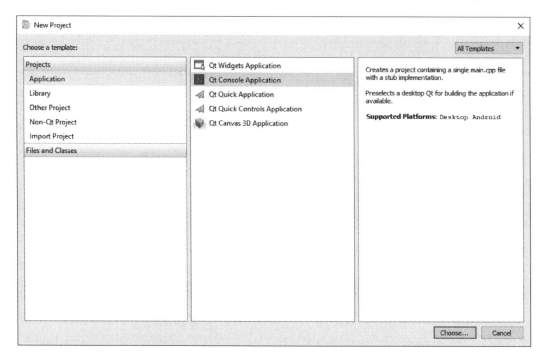

8. After you have done creating your console project, open up your project file (.pro) and add the SQL module to your project:

    ```
    QT += core sql
    QT -= gui
    ```

9. Next, open up main.cpp and add the following header files to the top of the source file:

    ```
    #include <QSqlDatabase>
    #include <QSqlQuery>
    #include <QSqlError>
    #include <QDate>
    #include <QDebug>
    ```

10. Then, add the following function to display employees who are above 30 years old:

    ```
    void filterAge()
    {
      qDebug() << "== Employees above 30 year old =============";
      QSqlQuery query;
      if (query.exec("SELECT name, age FROM employee WHERE age > 30"))
    ```

```
  {
    while (query.next())
    {
      qDebug() << query.value(0).toString() <<
        query.value(1).toString();
    }
  }
  else
  {
    qDebug() << query.lastError().text();
  }

  qDebug() << "\n";
}
```

11. After that, add this function for displaying the department and branch information of each employee:

```
void getDepartmentAndBranch()
{
  qDebug() << "== Get employees' department and branch
    =============";

  QSqlQuery query;
  if (query.exec("SELECT myEmployee.name, department.name,
    branch.name FROM (SELECT name, departmentID FROM employee)
    AS myEmployee INNER JOIN department ON
    department.id = myEmployee.departmentID
    INNER JOIN branch ON branch.id = department.branchID"))
  {
    while (query.next())
    {
      qDebug() << query.value(0).toString() <<
      query.value(1).toString() << query.value(2).toString();
    }
  }
  else
  {
    qDebug() << query.lastError().text();
  }

  qDebug() << "\n";
}
```

12. Next, add this function, which displays employees who are working in the `New York` branch and are below 30 years old:

```
void filterBranchAndAge()
{
    qDebug() << "== Employees from New York and age below 30
        =============";

    QSqlQuery query;
    if (query.exec("SELECT myEmployee.name, myEmployee.age,
        department.name, branch.name
        FROM (SELECT name, age, departmentID FROM employee) AS
        myEmployee INNER JOIN department ON
        department.id = myEmployee.departmentID INNER JOIN branch ON
          branch.id = department.branchID
        WHERE branch.name = 'New York' AND age < 30"))
    {
        while (query.next())
        {
            qDebug() << query.value(0).toString() <<
                query.value(1).toString() <<
                query.value(2).toString() << query.value(3).toString();
        }
    }
    else
    {
        qDebug() << query.lastError().text();
    }

    qDebug() << "\n";
}
```

13. Then, add this function which counts the total number of female employees in the dummy company:

```
void countFemale()
{
    qDebug() << "== Count female employees =============";

    QSqlQuery query;
    if (query.exec("SELECT COUNT(gender) FROM employee WHERE
        gender = 1"))
    {
        while (query.next())
        {
            qDebug() << query.value(0).toString();
        }
```

```
    }
    else
    {
      qDebug() << query.lastError().text();
    }

    qDebug() << "\n";
}
```

14. Once you're done with that, we will add another function, which filters the employee list and only displays those who have name that starts with `Ja`:

```
void filterName()
{
    qDebug() << "== Employees name start with 'Ja' =============";

    QSqlQuery query;
    if (query.exec("SELECT name FROM employee WHERE name
      LIKE '%Ja%'"))
    {
      while (query.next())
      {
        qDebug() << query.value(0).toString();
      }
    }
    else
    {
      qDebug() << query.lastError().text();
    }

    qDebug() << "\n";
}
```

15. Next, we also add another function, which displays employees who have their birthdays in `August`:

```
void filterBirthday()
{
    qDebug() << "== Employees birthday in August =============";

    QSqlQuery query;
    if (query.exec("SELECT name, birthday FROM employee WHERE
      MONTH(birthday) = 8"))
    {
      while (query.next())
      {
```

```
          qDebug() << query.value(0).toString() <<
            query.value(1).toDate().toString("d-MMMM-yyyy");
      }
   }
   else
   {
      qDebug() << query.lastError().text();
   }

   qDebug() << "\n";
}
```

16. Then, we add the last function, which checks who logged in to the dummy system on 27 April 2016 and displays their names on the terminal:

```
void checkLog()
{
   qDebug() << "== Employees who logged in on 27 April 2016
      =============";

   QSqlQuery query;
   if (query.exec("SELECT DISTINCT myEmployee.name, FROM
      (SELECT id, name FROM employee) AS myEmployee INNER JOIN
      user ON user.employeeID = myEmployee.id INNER JOIN log ON
      log.userID = user.id WHERE DATE(log.loginTime) =
      '2016-04-27'"))
   {
      while (query.next())
      {
         qDebug() << query.value(0).toString();
      }
   }
   else
   {
      qDebug() << query.lastError().text();
   }

   qDebug() << "\n";
}
```

17. Lastly, in our `main()` function, connect our program to the MySQL database and call all the functions that we have defined in the previous steps. After that, close the database connection and we're done:

```cpp
int main(int argc, char *argv[])
{
    QCoreApplication a(argc, argv);

    QSqlDatabase db = QSqlDatabase::addDatabase("QMYSQL");
    db.setHostName("127.0.0.1");
    db.setUserName("reonyx");
    db.setPassword("reonyx");
    db.setDatabaseName("testing");

    if (db.open())
    {
        filterAge();
        getDepartmentAndBranch();
        filterBranchAndAge();
        countFemale();
        filterName();
        filterBirthday();
        checkLog();

        db.close();
    }
    else
    {
        qDebug() << "Failed to connect to database.";
    }

    return a.exec();
}
```

18. Compile and run the project now and you should see a terminal window, which displays the filtered results from the database as defined earlier:

How it works...

A console application does not have any GUI at all and only shows you a text display in a terminal window. This is usually used in a backend system, as it uses fewer resources compared to a widget application. We use it in this example because it's faster to display the result without the need to place any widgets in the program, which we don't need in this case.

We separated the SQL queries into different functions so that it's easier to maintain the code and it doesn't become too messy. Do note that in C++, the functions have to be located before the `main()` function, or they will not be able to be called by `main()`.

There's more...

The INNER JOIN statement used in the preceding example joins two tables together and selects all rows from both tables, as long as there is a match between the columns in both tables. There are many other types of JOIN statement that you can use in MySQL (and some other types of SQL architecture), such as LEFT JOIN, RIGHT JOIN, FULL OUTER JOIN, and so on. The following diagram shows the different types of JOIN statements and their effects:

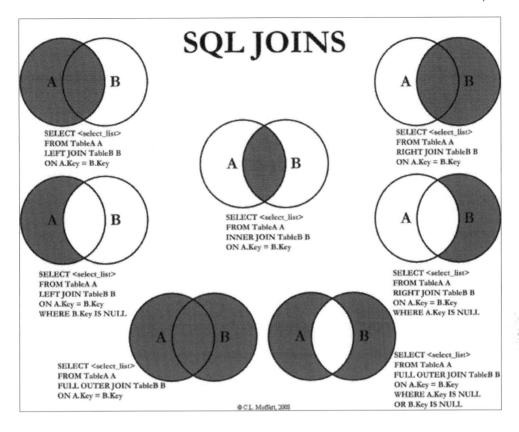

1. The `LIKE` statement is normally used to search for a string variable in the database without the full word. Notice that there are two `%` symbols, located before and after the search keyword.

2. The `DISTINCT` statement used in the previous example filters out results that have the exact same variable. For example, without the `DISTINCT` statement, you will see two versions of Larry King appear in the terminal because there are two records of him logging in to the system on the same day. By adding the `DISTINCT` statement, MySQL will eliminate one of the repeating results and ensure every result is unique.

3. You may be wondering what `d-MMMM-yyyy` stands for and why we used it in the preceding example. That is actually an expression supplied to the `QDateTime` class in Qt to display the date time result using a given format. In this case, it will change the date time data that we get from MySQL, `2016-08-06`, to the format that we specified, resulting in `6-August-2016`. For more information, check out Qt's documentation at `http://doc.qt.io/qt-5/qdatetime.html#toString`, which has the full list of expressions that can be used to determine the format of the date and time string.

9
Developing a Web Application Using Qt Web Engine

In this chapter, we will cover the following recipes:

- ▶ Introduction to Qt WebEngine
- ▶ WebView and web settings
- ▶ Embedding Google Maps in your project
- ▶ Calling C++ functions from JavaScript
- ▶ Calling JavaScript functions from C++

Introduction

Qt includes a module called **Qt WebEngine** that allows us to embed a web browser widget into our program and use it to display web pages or local HTML contents. Prior to version 5.6, Qt used another similar module called **Qt WebKit**, which is now deprecated and has since been replaced by the Chromium-based **web engine** module. Qt also allows communication between JavaScript and C++ code through the "web channel", which enables us to make use of this module in a much more effective fashion.

Introduction to Qt WebEngine

In this example project, we will explore the basic features of the web engine module in Qt and try building a simple working web browser. Since Qt 5.6, Qt's WebKit module has been deprecated and replaced by the WebEngine module, which is based on Google's Chromium engine. Note that when this chapter was written, WebEngine was still heavily under development and may be subject to changes in the near future.

How to do it...

First, let's set up our web engine project:

1. First, you are required to download and install Microsoft Visual Studio if you do not have it installed on your computer. This is because at the moment, Qt's WebEngine module only works with the Visual C++ compiler and not others, such as MinGW or Clang. This might change in the future, but it all depends on whether Google wants to make their Chromium engine support other compilers or not. Meanwhile, you can download the latest Visual Studio from here: `https://www.visualstudio.com`.

2. At the same time, you may also need to make sure that the Qt you installed on your computer supports the Visual C++ compiler. You can add the **mvc2015** component to your Qt installation using Qt's maintenance tool. Also, make sure that you have installed the **Qt WebEngine** component in your Qt as well:

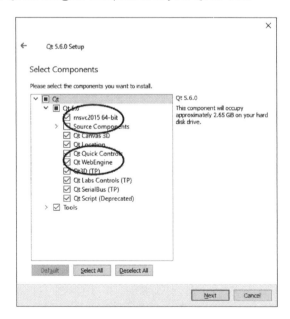

3. Once you are done with that, open up Qt Creator and create a new **Qt Widgets Application** project. This time, you must select a kit that uses the Visual C++ compiler:

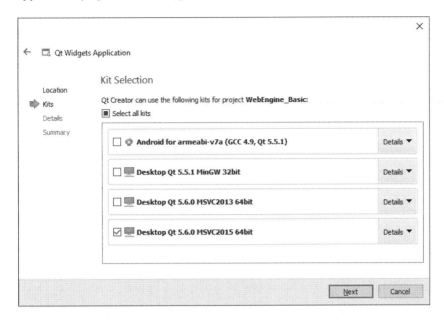

4. After that, open up your project file (`.pro`) and add the following modules to your project:

```
QT += core gui webengine webenginewidgets
```

5. Open up `mainwindow.ui` and remove the `menuBar`, `mainToolBar`, and `statusBar` objects, as we don't need those in this project:

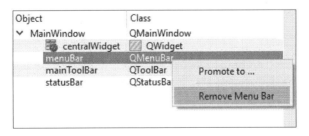

6. Place two horizontal layouts on the canvas, then place a line edit widget and a push button for the layout at the top:

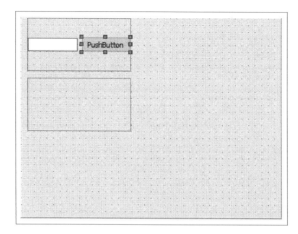

7. After that, select the canvas and click on the **Lay Out Vertically** button located at the top of the editor:

8. Once you have clicked on the **Lay Out Vertically** button, the layouts will expand and follow the size of the main window. The line edit will also expand horizontally based on the width of the horizontal layout:

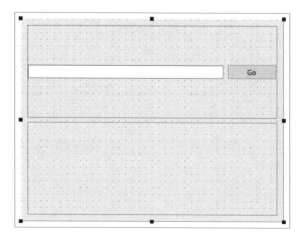

9. Next, add two buttons to the left side of the line edit. We'll use these two buttons to move back and forward between page histories. Then, add a Progress bar widget at the bottom of the main window so that we can find out whether the page has finished loading, or loading is still in progress. We don't have to worry about the horizontal layout in the middle at this point, as we'll be adding the web view to it later using C++ code, and the space will then be occupied:

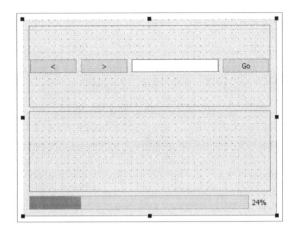

10. Right-click on one of the buttons and select **Go to slot...**, then select **clicked()** and click **OK**. A slot function will be automatically created for you in mainwindow.h and mainwindow.cpp. Repeat this step for all the other buttons as well.

11. After that, right-click on the line edit and select **Go to slot...**, then select **returnPressed()** and click **OK**. Another slot function will now be automatically created for you in mainwindow.h and mainwindow.cpp.

12. Now that we are done with our UI design, let's hop over to mainwindow.h. The first thing we need to do is to add the following header to mainwindow.h:

```
#include <QtWebEngineWidgets/QtWebEngineWidgets>
```

13. Then, declare loadUrl() function under the class destructor:

```
public:
    explicit MainWindow(QWidget *parent = 0);
    ~MainWindow();

    void loadUrl();
```

14. After that, add a custom slot function called loading() to mainwindow.h as we'll be using it pretty soon:

```
private slots:
    void on_goButton_clicked();
```

```
    void on_address_returnPressed();
    void on_backButton_clicked();
    void on_forwardButton_clicked();
    void loading(int progress);
```

15. Lastly, declare a QWebEngineView object and call it webview:

```
private:
    Ui::MainWindow *ui;
    QWebEngineView* webview;
```

16. Once you're done with that, open up mainwindow.cpp and initiate the web engine view. Then, add it to the second horizontal layout and connect its loadProgress() signal to the loading() slot function we just added to mainwindow.h:

```
MainWindow::MainWindow(QWidget *parent) :
    QMainWindow(parent),
    ui(new Ui::MainWindow)
{
    ui->setupUi(this);

    webview = new QWebEngineView;
    ui->horizontalLayout_2->addWidget(webview);

    connect(webview, SIGNAL(loadProgress(int)),
        SLOT(loading(int)));
}
```

17. After that, we declare what will happen when the loadUrl() function is called:

```
void MainWindow::loadUrl()
{
    QUrl url = QUrl(ui->address->text());
    url.setScheme("http");
    webview->page()->load(url);
}
```

18. Next, call the loadUrl() function when the **Go** button is clicked or when the Return/Enter key is clicked:

```
void MainWindow::on_goButton_clicked()
{
    loadUrl();
}

void MainWindow::on_address_returnPressed()
{
    loadUrl();
}
```

19. As for the other two buttons, we'll ask the web view to load the previous page or the next page if it is available in the history stack:

```cpp
void MainWindow::on_backButton_clicked()
{
    webview->back();
}

void MainWindow::on_forwardButton_clicked()
{
    webview->forward();
}
```

20. Lastly, change the value of the `progressBar` when the web page is being loaded:

```cpp
void MainWindow::loading(int progress)
{
    ui->progressBar->setValue(progress);
}
```

21. Build and run the program now and you will get a very basic but functional web browser!

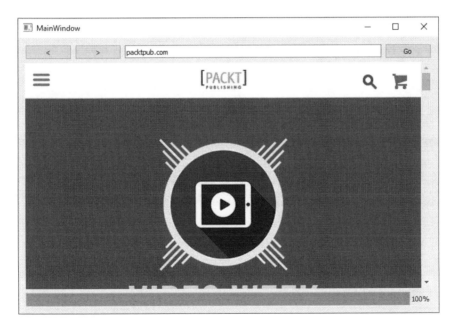

How it works...

The old web view system was based on Apple's WebKit engine and only available in Qt 5.5 and its predecessor. Since 5.6, WebKit has been completely abandoned by Qt and replaced with Google's Chromium engine. The API has been completely changed and therefore all the code related to Qt WebKit will not work correctly once migrated to 5.6. If you're new to Qt, it's recommended to skip WebKit and learn the WebEngine API since it is becoming the new standard in Qt. If you have used Qt's WebKit in the past, this web page teaches you how to port your old code over to WebEngine, `https://wiki.qt.io/Porting_from_QtWebKit_to_QtWebEngine`.

In Step 16, we connected the `loadProgress()` signal that belongs to the web view widget to the `loading()` slot function. The signal will be called automatically when the web view is loading the web page you requested by calling `QWebEnginePage::load()` in Step 17. You can also connect the `loadStarted()` and `loadFinished()` signals as well if you need to.

In Step 17, we used the `QUrl` class to convert the text obtained from the line edit to URL format. By default, the address we inserted will lead to the local path if we do not specify the URL scheme (`http`, `https`, `ftp`, and so on). We may not be able to load the page if, say, we gave it `packtpub.com` instead of `http://packtpub.com`. Therefore, we manually specify a URL scheme for it by calling `QUrl::setScheme()`. This will ensure the address is properly formatted before passing it to the web view.

There's more...

If you're running Qt 5.6 or above and for some reason you need the WebKit module for your project (usually for maintaining an old project), you can obtain the module code from GitHub and build it by yourself:

`https://github.com/qt/qtwebkit`

WebView and web settings

In this section, we will dive deeper into the features available in Qt's WebEngine and explore the settings that we can use to customize our WebView. We will use the source files from the previous example and add more code to it.

How to do it...

Let's explore some of the basic features of the Qt WebEngine:

1. First of all, open up `mainwindow.ui` and add a vertical layout under the progress bar. Then, add a **Plain Text Edit** widget (under the input widget category) and a Push button to the vertical layout. Change the display of the Push button to **Load HTML** and set the `plaintext` property of the plain text edit widget to the following:

```
<Img src="https://www.google.com/images/
  branding/googlelogo/1x/googlelogo_color_272x92dp.png">
  </img>
<h1>Hello World!</h1>
<h3>This is our custom HTML page.</h3>

<script>alert("Hello!");</script>
```

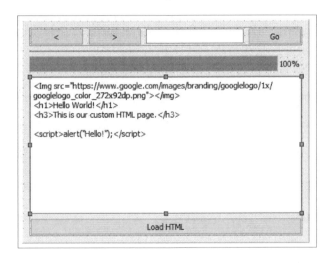

2. Next, go to **File** | **New File or Project**. A window will then pop up and ask you to choose a file template. Select **Qt Resource File** under the **Qt** category and click on the **Choose...** button. Type in your desired filename and click **Next** followed by **Finish**.

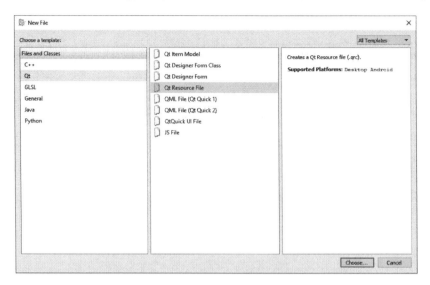

3. After that, open up the resource file we just created by right-clicking on it in the **Projects** pane and selecting the **Open in Editor** option. Once the file is opened by the editor, click on the **Add** button, followed by **Add Prefix**. Then, set the prefix as / and click **Add**, followed by **Add Files**. This time, the file browser window will appear and we will select the **tux.png** image file and click **Open**. We have now added the image file to our project, where it will be embedded into the executable file (.exe) once it's compiled:

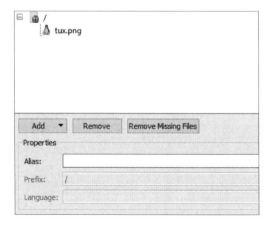

4. Next, open up `mainwindow.h` and add the following headers to it:

```
#include <QMainWindow>
#include <QtWebEngineWidgets/QtWebEngineWidgets>
#include <QDebug>
#include <QFile>
```

5. Then, make sure the following functions and pointers have been declared in `mainwindow.h`:

```
public:
    explicit MainWindow(QWidget *parent = 0);
    ~MainWindow();
    void loadUrl();

private slots:
    void on_goButton_clicked();
    void on_address_returnPressed();
    void on_backButton_clicked();
    void on_forwardButton_clicked();

    void startLoading();
    void loading(int progress);
    void loaded(bool ok);

    void on_loadHtml_clicked();
private:
    Ui::MainWindow *ui;
    QWebEngineView* webview;
```

6. Once you're done with that, open up `mainwindow.cpp` and add the following code to the class constructor:

```
MainWindow::MainWindow(QWidget *parent) :
    QMainWindow(parent),
    ui(new Ui::MainWindow)
{
    ui->setupUi(this);

    webview = new QWebEngineView;
    ui->horizontalLayout_2->addWidget(webview);

    //webview->page()->settings()>
        setAttribute(QWebEngineSettings::JavascriptEnabled, false);
    //webview->page()->settings()
        ->setAttribute(QWebEngineSettings::AutoLoadImages, false);
```

```
//QString fontFamily = webview->page()->settings()
  ->fontFamily(QWebEngineSettings::SerifFont);
QString fontFamily = webview->page()->settings()
  ->fontFamily(QWebEngineSettings::SansSerifFont);
int fontSize = webview->page()->settings()
  ->fontSize(QWebEngineSettings::MinimumFontSize);
QFont myFont = QFont(fontFamily, fontSize);
webview->page()->settings()->setFontFamily
  (QWebEngineSettings::StandardFont, myFont.family());

QFile file(":://tux.png");
if (file.open(QFile::ReadOnly))
{
  QByteArray data = file.readAll();
  webview->page()->setContent(data, "image/png");
}
else
{
  qDebug() << "File cannot be opened.";
}

connect(webview, SIGNAL(loadStarted()),
  SLOT(startLoading()));
connect(webview, SIGNAL(loadProgress(int)),
  SLOT(loading(int)));
connect(webview, SIGNAL(loadFinished(bool)),
  SLOT(loaded(bool)));
}
```

7. The `MainWindow::loadUrl()` function still remains the same as the previous example, which sets the URL scheme to `http` before loading the page:

```
void MainWindow::loadUrl()
{
  QUrl url = QUrl(ui->address->text());
  url.setScheme("http");
  webview->page()->load(url);
}
```

8. The same goes for the following functions, which also remain the same:

```
void MainWindow::on_goButton_clicked()
{
  loadUrl();
}
```

```
void MainWindow::on_address_returnPressed()
{
  loadUrl();
}

void MainWindow::on_backButton_clicked()
{
  webview->back();
}

void MainWindow::on_forwardButton_clicked()
{
  webview->forward();
}
```

9. In the previous example, we only had `MainWindow::loading()`, which sets the value of the progress bar when the web page is being loaded. This time, we also added both the `MainWindow::startLoading()` and `MainWindow::loaded()` slot functions, which will be called by the `loadStarted()` and `loadFinished()` signals. What these two functions do is basically show the progress bar when a page is starting to load, and hide the progress bar when the page has finished loading:

```
void MainWindow::startLoading()
{
  ui->progressBar->show();
}

void MainWindow::loading(int progress)
{
  ui->progressBar->setValue(progress);
}

void MainWindow::loaded(bool ok)
{
  ui->progressBar->hide();
}
```

10. Lastly, we call `webview->loadHtml()` to convert the plain text to HTML content when the **Load HTML** button is clicked:

```
void MainWindow::on_loadHtml_clicked()
{
  webview->setHtml(ui->source->toPlainText());
}
```

11. Build and run the program now and you should see something like this:

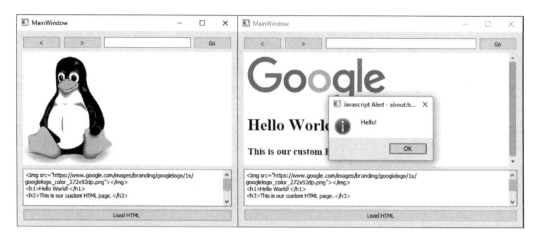

How it works...

In this example, we used C++ to load an image file and set it as the WebView's default content (instead of a blank page). We could achieve the same result by loading a default HTML file with an image at startup.

Some of the code in the class constructor has been commented out. You can remove the double slashes // and see the difference it makes—the JavaScript alert will no longer appear (since JavaScript is being disabled) and any images will no longer appear in your web view.

Another thing you can try is to change the font family from QWebEngineSettings::SansS erifFont to QWebEngineSettings::SerifFont. You will notice a slight difference in the font as it appears in the web view:

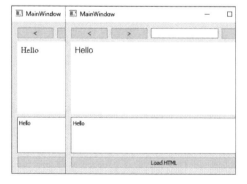

By clicking the **Load HTML** button, we ask the WebView to treat the content of the plain text edit widget as HTML code and load it as an HTML page. You can use this to make a simple HTML editor powered by Qt!

Embedding Google Maps in your project

In this example, we will learn how to embed Google Maps in our project through Qt's WebEngine module. This example doesn't focus much on Qt and C++, but rather on the Google Maps API in HTML code.

How to do it...

Let's create a program that displays Google Maps by following these steps:

1. First, create a new **Qt Widgets Application** project and remove the status bar, menu bar, and tool bar.

2. Then, open up your project file (.pro) and add the following modules to your project:

    QT += core gui **webengine webenginewidgets**

3. Next, open up `mainwindow.ui` and add a vertical layout to the canvas. Then, select the canvas and click the **Lay Out Vertically** button on top of the canvas. You will get something like this:

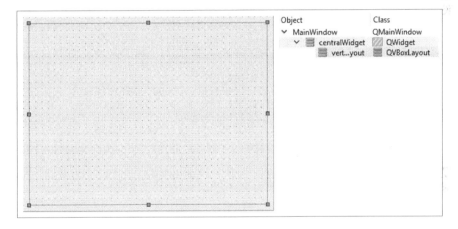

4. Then, open up `mainwindow.cpp` and add the following headers to the top of the source code:

    ```
    #include <QtWebEngineWidgets/QWebEngineView>
    #include <QtWebEngineWidgets/QWebEnginePage>
    #include <QtWebEngineWidgets/QWebEngineSettings>
    ```

5. After that, add the following code to the `MainWindow` constructor:

```
MainWindow::MainWindow(QWidget *parent) :
  QMainWindow(parent),
  ui(new Ui::MainWindow)
{
  ui->setupUi(this);
  QWebEngineView* webview = new QWebEngineView;
  QUrl url = QUrl("qrc:/map.html");
  webview->page()->load(url);
  ui->verticalLayout->addWidget(webview);
}
```

6. Then, go to **File | New File or Project** and create a Qt resource file (`.qrc`). We will add an HTML file to our project called `map.html`:

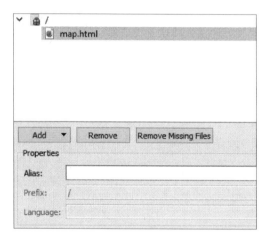

7. Once you're done with that, open up `map.html` with your favorite text editor. It's not recommended to open an HTML file using Qt Creator, as it does not provide any color coding for HTML syntax.

8. After that, we will start writing the HTML code by declaring the important tags, such as `<html>`, `<head>`, and `<body>`, like so:

```
<!DOCTYPE html>
<html>
  <head>
  </head>
  <body ondragstart="return false">
  </body>
</html>
```

9. Then, add a `<div>` tag to the body and set its ID as `map-canvas`:

```
<body ondragstart="return false">
  <div id="map-canvas" />
</body>
```

10. After that, add the following code to the head of the HTML document:

```
<meta name="viewport" content="initial-scale=1.0,
  user-scalable=no" />
<style type="text/css">
  html { height: 100% }
  body { height: 100%; margin: 0; padding: 0 }
  #map-canvas { height: 100% }
</style>
<script type="text/javascript"
  src="https://maps.googleapis.com/maps/api/js?
  key=YOUR_KEY_HERE&libraries=drawing"></script>
```

11. Then, add the following code, also to the head of the HTML document, right at the bottom of the code we inserted in the previous step:

```
<script type="text/javascript">
  var map;
  function initialize()
  {
    // Add map
    var mapOptions =
    {
      center: new google.maps.LatLng
        (40.705311, -74.2581939),
        zoom: 6
    };

    map = new google.maps.Map
      (document.getElementById
      ("map-canvas"),mapOptions);

    // Add event listener
    google.maps.event.addListener(map,
      'zoom_changed', function()
    {
      //alert(map.getZoom());
    });
```

```
// Add marker
var marker = new google.maps.Marker(
{
  position: new google.maps.LatLng
    (40.705311, -74.2581939),
    map: map,
    title: "Marker A",
});
google.maps.event.addListener
  (marker, 'click', function()
{
  map.panTo(marker.getPosition());
});
marker.setMap(map);

// Add polyline
var points = [ new google.maps.LatLng
  (39.8543, -73.2183), new google.maps.
  LatLng(41.705311, -75.2581939), new
  google.maps.LatLng(40.62388, -75.5483) ];
var polyOptions =
{
  path: points,
  strokeColor: '#FF0000',
  strokeOpacity: 1.0,
  strokeWeight: 2
};
historyPolyline = new
  google.maps.Polyline(polyOptions);
historyPolyline.setMap(map);

// Add polygon
var points = [ new google.maps.LatLng
  (37.314166, -75.432),
  new google.maps.LatLng(40.2653, -74.4325),
  new google.maps.LatLng(38.8288, -76.5483) ];
  var polygon = new google.maps.Polygon(
{
  paths: points,
  fillColor:  '#000000',
  fillOpacity: 0.2,
  strokeWeight: 3,
  strokeColor: '#fff000',
});
polygon.setMap(map);
```

```
      // Setup drawing manager
      var drawingManager =
        new google.maps.drawing.DrawingManager();
      drawingManager.setMap(map);
    }

    google.maps.event.addDomListener
      (window, 'load', initialize);

  </script>
```

12. Once you're done with that, compile and run the project. You should see something similar to this:

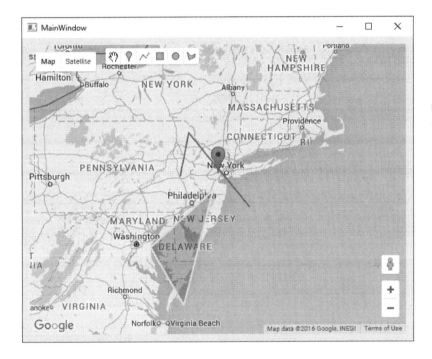

How it works...

Google allows you to embed Google Maps in a web page by using their JavaScript library called the Google Maps API. Through Qt's WebEngine module, we can embed Google Maps in our C++ project by loading a HTML file to our web view widget, which uses the Google Maps API. The only downside of this method is that we cannot load the map when there is no Internet connection.

Google allows your website to call any Google API, many thousands of times per day. If you plan for heavier traffic, you should get a free API key from Google. Go to `https://console.developers.google.com` to get a free key and replace the word `YOUR_KEY_HERE` in the JavaScript source path with the API key you obtained from Google.

We must define a `<div>` object, which serves as a container for the map. Then, when we initialize the map, we specify the ID of the `<div>` object so that the Google Maps API knows which HTML element to look for when embedding the map.

By default, we set the center of the map to the coordinates of New York and set the default zoom level to 6. Then, we added an event listener that gets triggered when the zoom level of the map changes. Remove the double slashes `//` from the code to see it in action.

After that, we also added a marker to the map through JavaScript. The marker also has an event listener attached to it, which will trigger the `panTo()` function when the marker is clicked. What it does is basically pan the map view to the marker that has been clicked.

Although we have added the drawing manager to the map (the icon buttons beside the **Map** and **Satellite** buttons), which allows users to draw any type of shape on top of the map, it's also possible to add the shapes manually using JavaScript, similar to how we added the marker in the previous step.

Lastly, you may have noticed that the headers are added to `mainwindow.cpp` instead of `mainwindow.h`. This is totally fine unless you are declaring class pointers in `mainwindow.h`; then you have to include those headers in it.

Calling C++ functions from JavaScript

In this recipe, we will learn how put our knowledge to use and create a functional login screen using Qt and MySQL.

How to do it...

Learn how to call C++ functions from JavaScript through the following steps:

1. First, create a **Qt Widgets Application** project and, once you're done, open up the project file (`.pro`) and add the following modules to the project:

   ```
   QT += core gui webengine webenginewidgets
   ```

2. Then, open up `mainwindow.ui` and delete the tool bar, menu bar, and status bar, as we don't need any of these in this example program.

3. After that, add a vertical layout to the canvas, and then select the canvas and click on the **Lay Out Vertically** button on top of the canvas. Then, add a text label to the top of the vertical layout and set its text to **Hello!**. Also, make its font bigger by setting its `stylesheet` property:

```
font: 75 26pt "MS Shell Dlg 2";
```

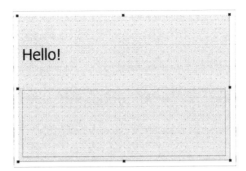

4. Next, go to **File | New File or Project** and create a resource file. Then, add an empty HTML file and all the JavaScript files, CSS files, font files, and so on belonging to jQuery, Boostrap, and Font Awesome to your project resources:

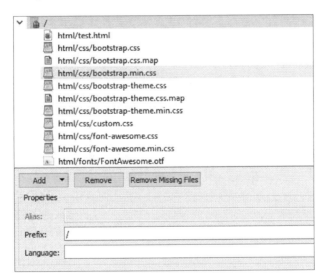

5. After that, open up your HTML file, which in this case is called `test.html`. First, link all the necessary JavaScript and CSS files to the HTML source code, between the `<head>` tags:

```
<!DOCTYPE html>
<html>
  <head>
    <script src="qrc:///qtwebchannel/qwebchannel.js"></script>

    <script src="js/jquery.min.js"></script>
    <script src="js/bootstrap.js"></script>

    <link rel="stylesheet" type="text/css"
      href="css/bootstrap.css">
    <link rel="stylesheet" type="text/css" href="css/font-
      awesome.css">
  </head>
  <body>
  </body>
</html>
```

6. Then, add the following JavaScript to the `<head>` element, wrapped between the `<script>` tags:

```
<script>
  $(document).ready(function()
  {
    new QWebChannel(qt.webChannelTransport,
      function(channel)
      {
        mainWindow = channel.objects.mainWindow;
      });

    $("#login").click(function(e)
    {
      e.preventDefault();

      var user = $("#username").val();
      var pass = $("#password").val();
      mainWindow.showLoginInfo(user, pass);
    });

    $("#changeText").click(function(e)
    {
      e.preventDefault();
```

```
            mainWindow.changeQtText("Good bye!");
        });
    });
</script>
```

7. Then, add the following code to the `<body>` element:

```
<div class="container-fluid">
    <form id="example-form" action="#" class=
        "container-fluid">
        <div class="form-group">
            <div class="col-md-12"><h3>Call C++ Function
                from Javascript</h3></div>

            <div class="col-md-12"><div class="alert
                alert-info" role="alert">
            <i class="fa fa-info-circle"></i>
            <span id="infotext">Click "Login" to send
                username and password variables to C++.
                Click "Change Cpp Text" to change the text
                label on Qt GUI.</span></div></div>

            <div class="col-md-12">
                <label>Username:</label>
                <input id="username" type="text"><p />
            </div>

            <div class="col-md-12">
                <label>Password:</label> <input id=
                    "password" type="password"><p />
            </div>

            <div class="col-md-12">
                <button id="login" class="btn btn-success"
                    type="button"><i class="fa fa-check"></i>
                    Login</button> <button id="changeText"
                    class="btn btn-primary" type="button">
                <i class="fa fa-pencil"></i>
                    Change Cpp Text</button>
            </div>
        </div>
    </form>
</div>
```

8. Once you are done with that, let's open up `mainwindow.h` and add the following public functions to the `MainWindow` class:

    ```
    public:
      explicit MainWindow(QWidget *parent = 0);
      ~MainWindow();

      Q_INVOKABLE void changeQtText(QString newText);
      Q_INVOKABLE void showLoginInfo(QString user,
        QString pass);
    ```

9. After that, open up `mainwindow.cpp` and add the following headers to the top of the source code:

    ```
    #include <QtWebEngineWidgets/QWebEngineView>
    #include <QtWebChannel/QWebChannel>
    #include <QMessageBox>
    ```

10. Then, add the following code to the `MainWindow` constructor:

    ```
    MainWindow::MainWindow(QWidget *parent) :
      QMainWindow(parent),
      ui(new Ui::MainWindow)
    {
      qputenv("QTWEBENGINE_REMOTE_DEBUGGING", "1234");

      ui->setupUi(this);

      QWebEngineView* webview = new QWebEngineView();
      ui->verticalLayout->addWidget(webview);

      QWebChannel* webChannel = new QWebChannel();
      webChannel->registerObject("mainWindow", this);
      webview->page()->setWebChannel(webChannel);

      webview->page()->load(QUrl("qrc:///html/test.html"));
    }
    ```

11. After that, we will declare what happens when `changeQtText()` and `showLoginInfo()` are called:

    ```
    void MainWindow::changeQtText(QString newText)
    {
      ui->label->setText(newText);
    }
    ```

```
void MainWindow::showLoginInfo(QString user, QString pass)
{
    QMessageBox::information(this, "Login info", "Username
        is " + user + " and password is " + pass);
}
```

12. Let's compile and run the program now; you should see something similar to the following screenshot. If you click on the **Change Cpp Text** button, the word **Hello!** at the top will change to **Goodbye!** If you click on the **Login** button, a message box will appear and show you exactly what you typed in the **Username** and **Password** input fields:

How it works...

In this example, we used two JavaScript libraries, jQuery and Boostrap. We also used an iconic font package called **Font Awesome**. These third-party add-ons were used to make the HTML user interface more interesting and responsive to different screen resolutions. We also used jQuery to detect the document's ready status, as well as to obtain the values of the input fields. You can download jQuery from `https://jquery.com/download`, Bootstrap from `http://getbootstrap.com/getting-started/#download`, and Font Awesome from `http://fontawesome.io`.

Qt's WebEngine uses a mechanism called **Web Channel** that enables peer-to-peer communication between the C++ program and the HTML page. The WebEngine module provides a JavaScript library that makes the integration a lot easier. The JavaScript is embedded in your project's resource by default, so you don't need to import it into your project manually. You just have to include it in your HTML page by calling the following:

```
<script src="qrc:///qtwebchannel/qwebchannel.js"></script>
```

Once you have included `qwebchannel.js`, you can initialize the `QWebChannel` class and assign the Qt object we registered earlier in C++ to a JavaScript variable.

In C++, it as follows:

```
QWebChannel* webChannel = new QWebChannel();
webChannel->registerObject("mainWindow", this);
webview->page()->setWebChannel(webChannel);
```

Then in JavaScript, it is as follows:

```
new QWebChannel(qt.webChannelTransport, function(channel)
{
  mainWindow = channel.objects.mainWindow;
});
```

You may be wondering what this line means:

```
qputenv("QTWEBENGINE_REMOTE_DEBUGGING", "1234");
```

Qt's web engine uses the remote debugging method to check for JavaScript errors and other problems. The number `1234` defines the port number you want to use for remote debugging. Once you have enabled remote debugging, you can access the debugging page by opening up a Chromium-based web browser, such as Google Chrome (this will not work in Firefox and other browsers) and typing in `http://127.0.0.1:1234`. You will then see a page that look like this:

The first page will display all the HTML pages that are currently running in your program, which in this case is `test.html`. Click on the page link and it will take you to another page for inspection. You can use this to check for CSS errors, JavaScript errors, missing files, and so on. Note that you should disable remote debugging once your program is bug-free and ready for deployment. This is because remote debugging takes time to initiate and it will increase your program's startup time.

If you want to call a C++ function from JavaScript, you must place the `Q_INVOKABLE` macro in front the function's declaration; otherwise, it will not work:

```
Q_INVOKABLE void changeQtText(QString newText);
```

Calling JavaScript functions from C++

In the previous example, we have learned how to call C++ functions from JavaScript through Qt's Web Channel system. In this example, we will try to do the reverse: call JavaScript functions from C++ code.

How to do it...

We can call JavaScript functions from C++ through the following steps:

1. As usual, create a new **Qt Widgets Application** project and add the `webengine` and `webenginewidgets` modules to your project.

2. Then, open up `mainwindow.ui` and remove the tool bar, menu bar, and status bar.

3. After that, add a vertical layout and a horizontal layout to the canvas. Then, select the canvas and click **Lay Out Vertically**. Make sure the horizontal layout is located at the bottom of the vertical layout.

4. Add two push buttons to the horizontal layout; one is called **Change HTML Text** and the other one is called **Play UI Animation**. Right-click on one of the buttons and click **Go to slot...**. A window will now pop up and ask you to pick a signal. Select the **clicked()** option and click **OK**. Qt will automatically add a slot function to your source code. Repeat this step for the other button as well:

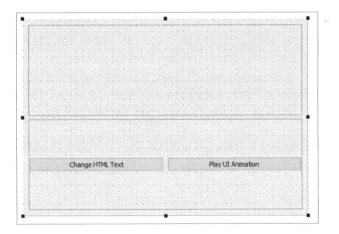

5. Now, open up `mainwindow.h` and add the following headers to it:

```
#include <QtWebEngineWidgets/QWebEngineView>
#include <QtWebChannel/QWebChannel>
#include <QMessageBox>
```

6. Then, declare the class pointer of a `QWebEngineView` object called `webview`:

```
public:
    explicit MainWindow(QWidget *parent = 0);
    ~MainWindow();

    QWebEngineView* webview;
```

7. After that, open up `mainwindow.cpp` and add the following code to the `MainWindow` constructor:

```
MainWindow::MainWindow(QWidget *parent) :
    QMainWindow(parent),
    ui(new Ui::MainWindow)
{
    //qputenv("QTWEBENGINE_REMOTE_DEBUGGING", "1234");

    ui->setupUi(this);

    webview = new QWebEngineView();
    ui->verticalLayout->addWidget(webview);

    QWebChannel* webChannel = new QWebChannel();
    webChannel->registerObject("mainWindow", this);
    webview->page()->setWebChannel(webChannel);

    webview->page()->load(QUrl("qrc:///html/test.html"));
}
```

8. Then, define what will happen when the `changeHtmlText` button and the `playUIAnimation` button are clicked:

```
void MainWindow::on_changeHtmlTextButton_clicked()
{
    webview->page()->runJavaScript("changeHtmlText('Text
        has been replaced by C++!');");
}

void MainWindow::on_playUIAnimationButton_clicked()
{
    webview->page()->runJavaScript("startAnim();");
}
```

9. Once you're done with that, let's create a resource file for our project by going to **File | New File or Project**. Then, select **Qt Resource File** under the **Qt** category and click **Choose**. Then, insert your desired file name and click **Next**, followed by **Finish**.

10. Then, add an empty HTML file and all the required add-ons (jQuery, Bootstrap, and Font Awesome) to our project resources. Also, add the `tux.png` image file to the resources file as well, as we'll be using it in a short while.

11. After that, open up the HTML file we just created and add it to the project resources, in our case, it's called `test.html`. Then, add the following HTML code to the file:

```html
<!DOCTYPE html>
<html>
  <head>
    <script src="qrc:///qtwebchannel/qwebchannel.js">
      </script>

    <script src="js/jquery.min.js"></script>
    <script src="js/bootstrap.js"></script>

    <link rel="stylesheet" type="text/css"
      href="css/bootstrap.css">
    <link rel="stylesheet" type="text/css" href="css/
      font-awesome.css">
  </head>
  <body>
  </body>
</html>
```

12. Add the following JavaScript code, which is wrapped within the `<script>` tags, to the `<head>` element of our HTML file:

```html
<script>
  $(document).ready(function()
  {
    $("#tux").css({ opacity:0, width:"0%",
    height:"0%" });
    $("#listgroup").hide();
    $("#listgroup2").hide();

    new QWebChannel(qt.webChannelTransport,
    function(channel)
    {
      mainWindow = channel.objects.mainWindow;
    });
  });
```

```
function changeHtmlText(newText)
{
  $("#infotext").html(newText);
}

function startAnim()
{
  // Reset
  $("#tux").css({ opacity:0, width:"0%",
    height:"0%" });
  $("#listgroup").hide();
  $("#listgroup2").hide();

  $("#tux").animate({ opacity:1.0, width:"100%",
    height:"100%" }, 1000, function()
  {
    // tux animation complete
    $("#listgroup").slideDown(1000,
      function()
    {
      // listgroup animation complete
      $("#listgroup2").fadeIn(1500);
    });
  });
}
</script>
```

13. Lastly, add the following code to the `<body>` element of our HTML file:

```
<div class="container-fluid">
  <form id="example-form" action="#" class="container-
    fluid">
    <div class="form-group">
      <div class="col-md-12"><h3>Call Javascript Function
        from C++</h3></div>

      <div class="col-md-12"><div class="alert alert-
        info" role="alert"><i class="fa
        fa-info-circle"></i> <span id="infotext">
        Change this text using C++.</span></div></div>

      <div class="col-md-2">
        <img id="tux" src="tux.png"></img>
      </div>
```

```
<div class="col-md-5">
  <ul id="listgroup" class="list-group">
    <li class="list-group-item">Cras justo
      odio</li>
    <li class="list-group-item">Dapibus ac
      facilisis in</li>
    <li class="list-group-item">Morbi leo
      risus</li>
    <li class="list-group-item">Porta ac
      consectetur ac</li>
    <li class="list-group-item">Vestibulum at
      eros</li>
  </ul>
</div>

<div id="listgroup2" class="col-md-5">
  <a href="#" class="list-group-item active">
    <h4 class="list-group-item-heading">
      Item heading</h4>
    <p class="list-group-item-text">
      Cras justo odio</p>
  </a>
  <a href="#" class="list-group-item">
    <h4 class="list-group-item-heading">
      Item heading</h4>
    <p class="list-group-item-text">
      Dapibus ac facilisis in</p>
  </a>
  <a href="#" class="list-group-item">
    <h4 class="list-group-item-heading">
      Item heading</h4>
    <p class="list-group-item-text">
      Morbi leo risus</p>
  </a>
</div>

      </div>
    </form>
</div>
```

14. Build and run the program now; you should get a similar result to that shown in the following screenshot. When you click on the **Change HTML Text** button, the information text is located within the top panel. If you click on the **Play UI Animation** button, the penguin image alongside the two sets of widgets will appear one after the other, with different animations:

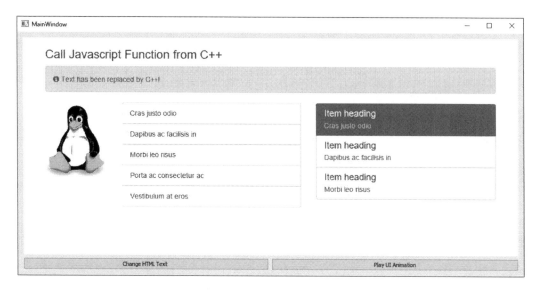

How it works...

This example is similar to the previous one. Once we have included the Web Channel JavaScript library and initiated the QWebChannel class, we can call any of the JavaScript functions from C++ by calling webview->page()->runJavascript("jsFunctionNameHere();"). Don't forget to apply the web channel created in C++ to the WebView's page as well; otherwise, it will not be able to communicate with the QWebChannel class in your HTML file.

By default, we change the CSS properties of the penguin image and set its opacity to 0, width to 0%, and height to 0%. We also hide the two list groups by calling the jQuery function hide(). When the **Play UI Animation** button is clicked, we repeat the same steps again just in case the animations have been played before (the same button has been clicked before), then we hide them again in order for the animations to be replayed.

One powerful feature of jQuery is that you can define what happens after an animation is done, which allows us to play the animations in sequence. In this example, we started with the penguin image and interpolated its CSS properties to a targeted setting within a second (`1000` milliseconds). Once that's done, we start another animation, which makes the first list group slide from top to bottom in 1 second. After that, we run the third animation, which makes the second list group fade in from nowhere within 1.5 seconds.

To replace the information text located in the top panel, we created a JavaScript function called `changeHtmlText()` and within the function itself, we got the HTML element by referring to its ID and calling `html()` to change its contents.

Index

N

nested animation group
creating 47-49

O

object
moving, with keyboard control 122-125
Open Exchange Rate
reference link 206
Open Graphics Library (OpenGL)
filtering effects, applying 118-122
lighting effects, applying 118-122
setting up, in Qt 100-103
texture filter, applying 118-122
texturing 114-117

P

parameters, curves
amplitude 43
overshoot 43
period 43
PhpMyAdmin
reference link 208
Plain Text Edit widget 253
property animation, Qt
controlling, with easing curves 42-44
using 39-42
property animations, QML
anchor animation 57
color animation 57
number animation 57
parent animation 57
path animation 57
property animation 57
rotation animation 57
vector3d animation 57
pseudo states
reference link 27
Push Button 168

Q

QDomDocument class
used, for processing XML data 176-178
used, for writing XML data 179-181

QML
2D canvas, rendering 94-98
animation 149-155
animations 53-56
integrating, with C++ 160-165
sprite animation, using 59-63
states 53-56
styling 27-36
transitions 53-56
used, for designing basic user
interface 138-142
used, for rendering 3D images 125-130
QML elements
canvas 36
imports window 35
library window 35
navigator window 35
properties pane 36
resources window 35
state pane 36
QML object pointer
exposing, to C++ 36-38
QPdfWriter class
reference link 195
QPropertyAnimation class 40
Qt
about 1
documentation, reference link 243
OpenGL, setting up 100-103
property animation, using 39-41
QParallelAnimationGroup class 47
QSequentialAnimationGroup class 47
setting up, for mobile application 132-137
state machine, using 50-52
used, for creating login screen 221-227
Qt Designer
style sheets, using with 1-5
Qt Designer interface
Action Editor and Signals & Slots Editor 5
build shortcuts 4
form editor 5
form toolbar 5
menu bar 4
mode selector 4
object inspector 5
output panes 5

W

Web Channel 269
web engine module 245
web settings 252-258
WebView 252-258
widget properties
    animating, with animators 57-59

X

XAMPP
    download link 208
    reference link 208
XML
    about 167
    format, reference link 172
XML data
    processing, with QDomDocument
        class 176-178
    processing, with stream reader 167-172
    writing, with QDomDocument class 179-181
    writing, with Stream Writer 173-175

Made in the USA
Lexington, KY
05 January 2017